OFF-THE-SHELF
IT SOLUTIONS

BCS, THE CHARTERED INSTITUTE FOR IT

BCS, The Chartered Institute for IT champions the global IT profession and the interests of individuals engaged in that profession for the benefit of all. We promote wider social and economic progress through the advancement of information technology science and practice. We bring together industry, academics, practitioners and government to share knowledge, promote new thinking, inform the design of new curricula, shape public policy and inform the public.

Our vision is to be a world-class organisation for IT. Our 70,000 strong membership includes practitioners, businesses, academics and students in the UK and internationally. We deliver a range of professional development tools for practitioners and employees. A leading IT qualification body, we offer a range of widely recognised qualifications.

Further Information
BCS, The Chartered Institute for IT,
First Floor, Block D,
North Star House, North Star Avenue,
Swindon, SN2 1FA, United Kingdom.
T +44 (0) 1793 417 424
F +44 (0) 1793 417 444
www.bcs.org/contact

http://shop.bcs.org/

OFF-THE-SHELF IT SOLUTIONS

A practitioner's guide to selection and procurement

Martin Tate

Permission to reproduce extracts from British Standards is granted by BSI. British Standards can be obtained in PDF or hard copy formats from the BSI online shop: www.bsigroup.com/Shop or by contacting BSI Customer Services for hardcopies only: Tel: +44 (0)20 8996 9001, Email: cservices@bsigroup.com.

Published by BCS Learning & Development Ltd, a wholly owned subsidiary of BCS The Chartered Institute for IT, First Floor, Block D, North Star House, North Star Avenue, Swindon, SN2 1FA, UK.
www.bcs.org

Paperback ISBN: 978-1-78017-258-3
PDF ISBN: 978-1-78017-259-0
ePUB ISBN: 978-1-78017-260-6
Kindle ISBN: 978-1-78017-261-3

British Cataloguing in Publication Data.
A CIP catalogue record for this book is available at the British Library.

Disclaimer:
The views expressed in this book are of the author(s) and do not necessarily reflect the views of the Institute or BCS Learning & Development Ltd except where explicitly stated as such. Although every care has been taken by the authors and BCS Learning & Development Ltd in the preparation of the publication, no warranty is given by the authors or BCS Learning & Development Ltd as publisher as to the accuracy or completeness of the information contained within it and neither the authors nor BCS Learning & Development Ltd shall be responsible or liable for any loss or damage whatsoever arising by virtue of such information or any instructions or advice contained within this publication or by any of the aforementioned.

BCS books are available at special quantity discounts to use as premiums and sale promotions, or for use in corporate training programs. Please visit our Contact us page at www.bcs.org/contact

Typeset by Lapiz Digital Services, Chennai, India.

Printed at Berforts information Press, Eynsham, UK.

CONTENTS

List of figures and tables   x
List of executive perspectives   xii
Authors   xiii
Foreword   xiv
Acknowledgements   xviii
Abbreviations and glossary   xix

INTRODUCTION: PURPOSE AND PRINCIPLES   1
I.1 Overall purpose of this book   1
I.2 Why you should read this book   3
I.3 How to get the best from this book   4
I.4 Major guiding principles of the method   10
I.5 Nature and characteristics of the selection process   11
I.6 Chapter summary   13
I.7 References   14
I.8 Further reading   14

1.   **INTRODUCTION TO OFF-THE-SHELF SOLUTIONS**   16
     1.1 What you can learn from this chapter   16
     1.2 Introduction to off-the-shelf solutions   16
     1.3 Interaction of strategy and software   17
     1.4 Impetus – the project pre-conditions   18
     1.5 Why buy an off-the-shelf solution?   20
     1.6 Avoiding common pitfalls when procuring off-the-shelf software   22
     1.7 IT consultancy for IT selections   24
     1.8 Chapter summary   25
     1.9 References   25
     1.10 Further reading   26

2.   **TALENT MANAGEMENT: SUPPLIER PSYCHOLOGY (with Cathy
     Humphreys)**   27
     2.1 What you can learn from this chapter   27
     2.2 Overview   27
     2.3 Candidate supplier constraints   29
     2.4 Attitudes and relationships   30
     2.5 The sales process at the software suppliers   31
     2.6 Power, partnerships, fairness and good losers   34
     2.7. Chapter summary   37

	2.8. References	37
	2.9. Further reading	38
3.	**INITIATION: SHAPING AND AUTHORISING THE PROJECT**	**39**
	3.1 What you can learn from this chapter	39
	3.2 Overview	39
	3.3 Determining scope	40
	3.4 Scoping workshops	41
	3.5 Studying costs and feasibility	47
	3.6 Establishing project phases	51
	3.7 The executive sponsor	51
	3.8 Project initiation or terms of reference	52
	3.9 Launch events	53
	3.10 Chapter summary	54
	3.11 References	54
	3.12 Further reading	55
4.	**REQUIREMENTS ANALYSIS: CAPTURING THE ORGANISATIONAL NEEDS**	**56**
	4.1 What you can learn from this chapter	56
	4.2 Overview	56
	4.3 Some cautionary notes on requirements capture	58
	4.4 Studying best practice	58
	4.5 Capturing requirements	59
	4.6 Selecting interviewees and organising interviews	62
	4.7 Preparing attendees for interviews or workshops	64
	4.8 Preview of later use of requirements	65
	4.9 Chapter summary	66
	4.10 References	67
	4.11 Further reading	67
5.	**REQUIREMENTS DOCUMENT: DOCUMENTING AND AGREEING REQUIREMENTS**	**68**
	5.1 What you can learn from this chapter	68
	5.2 Overview	68
	5.3 Organising requirements (cataloguing)	69
	5.4 Requirement formats	70
	5.5 Guidelines for articulating requirements	72
	5.6 Validate, agree and refine requirements	77
	5.7 The weighting workshop	78
	5.8 Chapter summary	84
	5.9 References	84
	5.10 Further reading	85
6.	**TRAWLING THE MARKETPLACE: ESTABLISHING THE LONGLIST**	**86**
	6.1 What you can learn from this chapter	86
	6.2 Overview	86
	6.3 Creating the longlist	87
	6.4 Risks when engaging with the marketplace	91
	6.5 Longlist length and when to include candidates	91

	6.6 The incumbent solution as a candidate	93
	6.7 Chapter summary	94
	6.8 References	94
	6.9 Further reading	94

7.	**ASSESSING LONGLIST CANDIDATES: SELECTING THE SHORTLIST USING THE RFI**	**96**
	7.1 What you can learn from this chapter	96
	7.2 Overview	96
	7.3 Approach to evaluation at RFI stage	97
	7.4 Prior planning	98
	7.5 Formulating effective questions	99
	7.6 Preparing the RFI	104
	7.7 Technology used for RFI questions and responses	106
	7.8 Marking scheme	107
	7.9 Preparing ideal answers	108
	7.10 Distributing the RFI	108
	7.11 Who – roles on the assessment team	109
	7.12 Assessing the RFI responses	109
	7.13. How – the main RFI assessment meeting	110
	7.14 Summarising the assessment outcome	113
	7.15 Presentation to the project board	114
	7.16 Chapter summary	117
	7.17 References	119
	7.18 Further reading	119

8.	**DETAILED EVALUATION: ASSESSING THE SHORTLISTED CANDIDATES**	**120**
	8.1 What you can learn from this chapter	120
	8.2 Overview	120
	8.3 Who – the roles, teams and skills	121
	8.4 Where and when – the meeting administration	124
	8.5 How – the evaluation process and mindset	126
	8.6 Defence mechanisms in the evaluation	130
	8.7 Note-taking by the evaluation team	131
	8.8 Chapter summary	133
	8.9 References	133
	8.10 Further reading	134

9.	**SCORING: ESTABLISHING DEGREE OF FIT AND RANKING**	**135**
	9.1 What you can learn from this chapter	135
	9.2 Overview	135
	9.3 Crucial role of scoring	135
	9.4 Stage outputs – scoring matrix	137
	9.5 Definitions document with language ladders	140
	9.6 Who – the scoring team	146
	9.7 Where and when – the meeting administration	146
	9.8 How – the scoring meeting process and mindset	147
	9.9 Time management during the meeting	149
	9.10 Steps to complete the scoring	151

9.11 Verifying scores with suppliers   152
9.12 Thresholds, error and defences   154
9.13 Selecting demonstration candidates   157
9.14 Addressing significant gaps in capability   158
9.15 Presenting to your project board   160
9.16 Chapter summary   161
9.17 References   162
9.18 Further reading   162

10.   **DEMONSTRATIONS: PROVING THE FIT**   **163**
10.1 What you can learn from this chapter   163
10.2 Overview   163
10.3 Objectives and risks of demonstrations   165
10.4 Who – the people who make the difference at demonstrations   167
10.5 Where and when – setting up the meetings   169
10.6 Further preparations   170
10.7 How – conducting the demonstration   176
10.8 Analysis after the demonstrations   178
10.9 Decision-making after demonstrations   179
10.10 Chapter summary   180
10.11 References   181
10.12 Further reading   181

11.   **REFERENCE SITES: REAL CUSTOMER FEEDBACK**   **182**
11.1 What you can learn from this chapter   182
11.2 Overview   182
11.3 Why – objectives of references   183
11.4 Who – reference sites attendees   184
11.5 Where and when – meeting location and format   185
11.6 How – example questions   186
11.7 The 'anti-reference site'   188
11.8 Building relationships   189
11.9 Chapter summary   190
11.10 References   191
11.11 Further reading   191

12.   **CONTRACTS: NEGOTIATION AND AGREEMENTS**   **192**
12.1 What you can learn from this chapter   192
12.2 Overview   192
12.3 Why – objectives of a successful negotiation   193
12.4 What – decisions and preparation before the negotiation meetings   194
12.5 The scope of supply   196
12.6 Who – negotiation team members   200
12.7 Preparing to negotiate   202
12.8 Negotiation agenda with relevant terms   204
12.9 Free modifications   207
12.10 The supplier version of the agenda   210
12.11 Where and how – the negotiation process and mindset   210
12.12 After your negotiation   213

	12.13 Chapter summary	215
	12.14 References	216
	12.15 Further reading	216
13.	**IMPLEMENTATION: PREPARING THE GROUND**	**217**
	13.1 What you can learn from this chapter	217
	13.2 Overview	217
	13.3 Change of power positions	219
	13.4 Supplier responsibilities during implementation	219
	13.5 Customer responsibilities	220
	13.6 Your implementation plan	224
	13.7 Chapter summary	228
	13.8 References	229
	13.9 Further reading	230
14.	**VIEWPOINTS BY THEME**	**231**
	14.1 What you can learn from this chapter	231
	14.2 Overview	231
	14.3 Communications	231
	14.4 Defined responsibility with consultation	233
	14.5 Other sections of the book	235
	14.6 Chapter summary	236
	14.7 References	236
	14.8 Further reading	236
15.	**CONCLUDING - RECOMMENDATIONS AND RESOURCES**	**237**
	15.1 Summary	237
	15.2 References	240
	15.3 Further reading	241
	APPENDIX 1 SIZING QUESTIONNAIRE: TO SCOPE A SELECTION PROJECT	**242**
	APPENDIX 2 COMPARATIVE METRICS: EXAMPLE PROJECT PROFILES	**245**
	APPENDIX 3 CHECKLIST: DETAILED METHOD STEPS	**247**
	Index	258

LIST OF FIGURES AND TABLES

Figure I.1	Overview of approach with mapping to chapters	7
Figure I.2	Interlock and flow of main deliverables	9
Figure 3.1	Types of entries for scope decisions	42
Figure 3.2	Conceptual diagram of process to establish scope boundary	45
Figure 3.3	Spreadsheet for scoping workshop with drop-down triage values	46
Figure 5.1	Format of detailed requirements document	71
Figure 5.2	Format of requirements as scenarios	72
Figure 5.3	Examples of volumes in requirements	76
Figure 5.4	Weight voting spreadsheet	83
Figure 6.1	Spreadsheet for collating the longlist	88
Figure 7.1	Candidate response with drop-down values	106
Figure 7.2	Fragment of RFI assessment results	114
Figure 7.3	RFI assessment summary	115
Figure 7.4	Bubble chart for strongest candidates - RFI points, cost and price-performance	116
Figure 8.1	Timed agenda slots and attendance plan on spreadsheet	127
Figure 9.1	Simplified example of scoring matrix	138
Figure 9.2	Illustration of fit at category level – top two versus perfect	140
Figure 9.3	Sections of a definitions sheet	141
Figure 9.4	Default language ladder entries for 0 and 3	143
Figure 9.5	One completed definitions sheet as output by scoring	143
Figure 9.6	Matrix configured for scoring meeting	148
Figure 10.1	Page of demonstration outline	172
Figure 10.2	Demonstration feedback form	175
Figure 10.3	Spreadsheet to analyse feedback forms	178
Figure 11.1	Questions for reference site	187
Figure 12.1	Format to prepare for negotiation	205
Figure 12.2	Shared negotiation agenda revealing only some columns	211
Figure 13.1	Module interlock during a hypothetical implementation	225
Figure 14.1	Responsibilities and consultation as GDPM Responsibility Chart	234
Figure A.1.1	Metrics to assess size and risk of selection project	243
Figure A.2.1	Summary metrics for projects using this method	246
Table 5.1	Values used during weighting workshop	82
Table 7.1	Strong RFI questions	102

Table 7.2	Standard RFI marking scheme	110
Table 7.3	Extended RFI marking scheme	111
Table 9.1	Conceptual values for fit during scoring	142
Table 14.1	How the approach helps communications	232
Table A.3.1	Method checklist	247

LIST OF EXECUTIVE PERSPECTIVES

A division head experiences surprising reactions   3

An IT manager's experience of make versus buy   20

A senior sales executive's experience as candidate supplier   29

A financial IT specialist's experience of formal scoping   40

A director's experience of early, formal consultation   47

A project manager's experience of formal requirements capture   57

An IT support provider's experience of weighted requirements   79

An architectural partner's experience of premature shortlisting   87

A director's experience of formally measuring fit   118

A director's experience of delegated evaluation process   124

A financial representative on evaluation team's experience   130

A public sector training manager's experience of sponsoring the selection   136

A US general manager's analysis of the experience   179

An entrepreneur's experience of improving research during selection   184

A director's experience of negotiations based on scored fit   193

An implementation manager's experience of contractual safeguards   215

An evaluation team member's experience of transferring to implementation   218

A director's experience of two implementations using the same approach   228

An implementation consultant's experience of ownership and culture   235

A supplier's experience of contrasting approaches on the same project   239

A director's experience of rigorous evaluation that dodged substantial waste   239

AUTHORS

Martin Tate is founder and principal consultant at Decision Evaluation Ltd, an IT consultancy that has specialised in selecting off-the-shelf solutions for over 20 years. A former programmer, analyst and project leader, he was trained to sell software while working for an IT provider, and is now a 'poacher turned gamekeeper'.

He has personally executed over 50 projects using this method to select off-the-shelf solutions, interviewed over 700 users to capture requirements and appraised over 1,000 solutions on selections investing nearly £13 million in total. On two projects the winner was provably a better fit, but less than one-tenth the cost of the runner-up (i.e. 90 per cent cheaper). His most jealously guarded statistic is zero – never once has an IT selection gone through his process and procured software that proved unfit for purpose.

BCS awarded him Chartered Fellow status in 2007 for eminence in the field of IT selection.

Cathy Humphreys (co-author of Chapter 2) has more than 20 years' experience as both a customer and a supplier of off-the-shelf solutions. Starting her career as a logistics graduate for Spillers pet foods, she implemented off-the-shelf manufacturing scheduling solutions before joining Numetrix, a supply chain software development company, and later Baan enterprise solutions as a consultant.

She has the unique distinction of experiencing this method as both a prospective customer and then as a candidate supplier. In 2001, her supply chain experience placed her as the project manager for selecting an e-spares sales system for Adtranz (now Bombardier Transportation) where she was first introduced to this method. In 2011, she represented Infor, the enterprise solutions supplier, as account manager for supply chain management.

FOREWORD

'Everything should be made as simple as possible, but not simpler.'

Albert Einstein (1879–1955)

Enterprise software technology cannot make a company great, but a smart software selection is the key enabler for business and, when well implemented and supported, will allow good companies to concentrate on their core business and become great. This means that the strategic decision as to which commercial off-the-shelf solution to select is crucial as it will determine how well the business can function, communicate, make decisions and grow for the life of the software.

Few organisations carry the arcane knowledge and expertise for strategic enterprise software selection. While this might seem surprising, given its importance, it is the very nature of the problem that makes it difficult to identify readily the right skills and mindset within the organisation. The high-level elements of the problem are the complexity and the requirement for objectivity, where complexity refers to the business requirements and the matching complexity of potential solutions. Within the scope of that complexity, the selection team will deal with a number of distinct specialisms:

- Technical issues including requirements engineering, systems architecture, solution engineering and software process evaluation.

- Commercial management, including an understanding of the vendor perspective, contract law related to enterprise software procurement and supplier relationship management.

- The human aspects including business change management, socio-technical impact and team management.

- Due diligence and professional business administration, underpinning all of the above and ensuring visibility and auditability as the organisation navigates one of its most complex strategic projects.

The compelling aspect of the methodological framework presented in this book is that there is nothing new in terms of techniques and knowledge. Instead, it neatly combines and sequences a diverse taxonomy of knowledge allowing the user to focus on particular knowledge areas if required, but more importantly providing a defined route map from start to finish.

It might help at this point to provide some context based on my experience of the methodology. In the early 2000s, I was awarded the task of reviewing the enterprise software in use at a multinational, multi-company design engineering and construction group. My role was reward for delivering some highly technical and commercially challenging system development and integration projects over a period of some 10 years, and offered the opportunity to utilise key strengths on the most strategically important project the business faced at the time. Those strengths were highly relevant and included requirements engineering, system development, project management, operational management and commercial acumen. This skill set was coupled with extensive knowledge of the business, spanning the client base, the functional areas and key decision-makers and influencers within the business.

Perhaps the most helpful thing for you as reader is if I point out my three greatest mistakes when I set out on the enterprise system selection process, together with an explanation of the mitigating measures intrinsic to the methodology.

FAILURE TO ENGAGE ALL STAKEHOLDERS ADEQUATELY

My belief that my knowledge of the business, and particularly of key influencers and decision-makers, would ensure that my recommendations would be understood and accepted proved inaccurate. Large and strategically important projects quickly unearth the worst of company politics as people deal with feelings of being ignored or supplanted.

The methodology ensures that all stakeholders are informed of the process and a representative cross section of the key business experts are engaged in the requirements elicitation. A similar cross section of key business experts form the evaluation team, filtering and weighting the requirements and then later attending the evaluations and making recommendation to the project board.

The benefit is that nobody can claim that they were not consulted or given opportunity to engage as, from site-based operative to main board executive, all are involved in the process.

ATTEMPTING TO USE STANDARD LARGE ORGANISATION PROCUREMENT METHODS

My experience working with blue chip utility companies and their tier one consultants meant that my knowledge of procurement methods was biased towards standard forms of contract and the regulatory requirements of high-value procurement. Typically, the purchaser issues a comprehensive specification of the requirements and invites the vendors to submit a sealed fixed-cost bid. This works for large-scale engineering contracts, although it has intrinsic problems that are usually resolved during project delivery.

Given the vast complexity of the business requirements and solution options, this does not work in enterprise software selection, where the emphasis has to be the selection of a solution that best fits the requirements of the business. The weakness of this approach was proved by our early phase engagement with suppliers, where the credible vendors were cautious, either declining to bid or submitting proposals that were heavily qualified and extremely expensive. Much of the information provided was generic in nature and caveated to the effect that detailed requirements analysis would follow contract award. Specific feedback from vendors revealed their concerns on interpreting the requirements correctly, and the one-sided and punitive nature of the procurement process.

The methodology obviates these issues because it is structured for incremental effort on the part of purchaser and bidders. It effectively incorporates the vendor perspective throughout the process, allowing them to provide summary information as they enter the process, and only asking them to input greater effort at each stage gate that they successfully pass. The benefit is that you, as purchaser, only have to deal with the essential information to pass the best candidates at each stage and they have a clear view of their risk so that they can decide the effort they will invest.

The final innovation at the procurement stage is the invitation to the evaluated candidates to review and validate the evaluation records and scores, thereby capturing the knowledge garnered during the procurement lifecycle for use in contract negotiation and agreement.

USING THE COMPANY'S STANDARD PROJECT MANAGEMENT FRAMEWORK

Even though enterprise software selection is among the most important of strategic projects, and the key enabler for all other strategic decisions, companies still tend to treat it as normal business. This is manifested in the approach to project review and decision-making, which all too often are managed as the final 30 minutes of normal business review. This results in lack of focus, failure to understand risk and poor decisions taken on vague or incomplete information. It also allows political operators with nefarious objectives to circumvent or undermine the process.

This methodology is structured around a dedicated review process that enforces executive engagement at each project decision gate. The information required and the responsibilities are clearly defined and the project cannot proceed without effective engagement and timely decisions.

Once you have experienced the methodology, you may define its strengths differently based on your experience and background. However, the final point I make is that it offers a formal structured methodology that has been used successfully in many business sectors, and with verifiable and consistently positive results. No matter what role you have in selecting off-the-shelf solutions, using this methodology will allow you to focus on the project, rather than continuously trying to justify the method.

USING THE BOOK

My suggestion for using the book is that you can go directly to a particular subject area and pick out leading edge best practice guidance and business process to fulfil a particular need. My caution would be that by doing so you may miss the greatest value of the framework, so please take the opportunity to stand back and understand the benefit of the whole lifecycle approach.

You will see that, although you will be dealing with enormous complexity and multiple parties and stakeholders, the methodology ensures that you and your team are focused on the information required for the current stage and for planning the subsequent stage.

The methodology presented in this book ensures that complexity is minimised without damaging integrity, it simplifies without impairing clarity.

Peter Ogden

ACKNOWLEDGEMENTS

Many thanks to the following for providing expertise, opinion, tools, copy, comments, professionalism, support and kindness.

Mike Berners-Lee, Clare Briegal, Peter Churchill, John Clark, Matthew Flynn, Stuart Gale, Lee Gillam, Liz Gooster, Karen Greening, Mary Hobbins, David Hollinghurst, Cathy Humphreys, Sue Kelly, Florence Leroy, Jutta Mackwell, Steve Magraw, Paul Matthews, Peter Ogden, Dave Paton, Mike Provost, John Ray, David Redmond-Pyle, Andy Spooner, Phil Stunell, Lindsey Tate, Maria Tate, Kevin Tock, Katie Walsh, Andrew Webb, Mark Woodward and Matti Zadok.

ABBREVIATIONS AND GLOSSARY

For a glossary of over 1,000 IT management terms, see the AXELOS Common Glossary: www.axelos.com/glossaries-of-terms.aspx

Also see the ISACA interactive glossary: www.isaca.org/Pages/Glossary.aspx

Agreement	Preferred word for contract
AHP	Analytic hierarchy process
Approach	See **method**
Attribute	The list of requirements, criteria or 'attributes' are the yardstick to measure **candidates** on the **weighted attribute matrix**
Basis of decision	The set of criteria applied to select the most appropriate **candidate**
BATNA	Best Alternative To a Negotiated Agreement
BCC	Blind carbon copy
BI	Business intelligence
CAD	Computer aided design
Candidate	The combination of one solution (software product) put forward by one prospective supplier. Therefore, two candidates might be the same reseller putting forward two products, or the same product from two different resellers
Categories	A grouping of requirements used to structure the documentation and therefore help plan project effort
Category	When used in requirements documentation or on the weighted attribute matrix, a group or type of requirement, such as Finance
CMS	Customer management system
COBIT	Control Objectives for Information and related Technology
COTS	Commercial off-the-shelf
CRM	Customer relationship management
CSCW	Computer support for collaborative working

Definitions document	Format used during the **scoring meeting** to clarify the **basis of decision** (in the **issues** section) and record the levels of fit required for given level of score (in the **language ladder**)
Demonstration outline	Minimum steps the software demonstrators should show, usually expressed in **scenario** format
DNR	Did not respond
DRM	Digital rights management
DSDM	Dynamic systems development method
EDI	Electronic data interchange
ERP	Enterprise resource planning. Also see **MRP**
Evaluation meeting	A meeting (with multiple sessions) where one **response team** goes through **requirements** and explains the fit of their software and services to the **evaluation team**
Evaluation team	Your group, representing the customer during a selection
Executive sponsor	See **sponsor**
FMEA	Failure mode effects analysis
FMR	Failed mandatory requirements
FYE	Financial year end
GAAP	Generally accepted accounting principles
GDPM	Goal directed project management
Golden features	Software features that might impress but merely add cost without adding real value to the customer
GOTS	Government off-the-shelf
GSA	US General Services Administration
HR(M)	Human resources (management), i.e. Personnel
ID	Identity
Implementation	Process to exploit software, involving plans, solution designs, installation, configuration, data loading, consultancy and training
Infrastructure	Underpinning IT equipment, including hardware and software
Issues	Section of **definitions document** that clarifies the basis of scoring
ITIL	Information Technology Infrastructure Library
ITT	Invitation to tender
KPI	Key performance indicator
Language ladder	Section of **definitions document** that clarifies each level of capability necessary for the points awarded for fit

LCMS	Learning content management system
LMS	Learning management system
Longlist	Not a list of 'serious contenders', but simply the list of **candidates** you need to put through the RFI process to establish their suitability for the **shortlist**
Method	Systematic approach that interlocks techniques and deliverables to encapsulate good practice
MoSCoW	Must, Should, Could, Won't
MRP	Manufacturing resource planning. Also see **ERP**
MSP	Managing Successful Programmes
OJEU	Official Journal of the European Union
OTS	Off-the-shelf
OTSIS	Off-the-shelf IT solutions
PB	See **Project board**
PDM	Product data management
PID	Project initiation document – term from PRINCE2 for the project's terms of reference
Platform	See **infrastructure**
PLM	Product lifecycle management
PPI	Price performance index *aka* 'bang for buck'
PQQ	Pre-qualifying questionnaire. See **RFI**
PRINCE	PRojects IN a Controlled Environment
Project board	Formal project decision-making group or steering committee. Might be a specially set up group constituted to represent the business areas affected by the project. On large projects that cut across organisational boundaries, the project board will be the main board or senior management team
RACI	Responsible, Accountable, Consulted and Informed
RAM	Responsibility assignment matrix
RE	Requirements engineering
Reference site	Existing user of the solution and supplier, who will comment on their experiences
Requirement	Statement of business need for IT processing, software or services
Requirement categories	See **categories**

Requirements catalogue	Intermediate stage between 'raw' **requirements** and the finished **SoUR**, when fragmentary requirements are analysed, organised, classified and reflected upon
Response ladder	See **language ladder**
Response meeting	See **evaluation meeting**
Response team	Group from one candidate supplier during an **evaluation meeting**
RFI	Request for information – the preliminary shortlisting questionnaire
RFI response	One **RFI** questionnaire when it is completed and returned by a **candidate**
RFI response assessment	Process of assessing or 'marking' **RFI responses** once returned. Can be shortened to RFI assessing
RFQ	Request for quotation
SaaS	Software as a service
Scenario	A type of **use case** – the scenario shows the steps to achieve a goal as interactions between 'actor' and 'system'
SCM	Supply chain management
Scope	The coverage of a project – its extent, latitude or range, with associated boundaries. Scope establishes what can be changed by a project – or at least investigated with a view to change
Score for fit	During a **scoring meeting**, specific term for the match or fit that expresses how thoroughly the **evaluation team** believe the **candidate** met the **requirement**
Score verification	Process after **scoring meeting** of 'playing back' to **candidates** their respective **scores for fit**, to allow them to confirm or challenge them
Scores	See **score for fit**
Scoring blind	Means the **evaluation team**, when awarding the **score for fit**, are not aware of the **weight for importance** of the **requirement**
Scoring issues	See **issues**
Scoring matrix	See **weighted attribute matrix**
Scoring meeting	The meeting (after all the **evaluation meetings**) when the **evaluation team** (without any suppliers present) consider all **candidates** and award each a **score for fit** for each **requirement**

Seat belt requirement	Term to label a requirement you do not need to explicitly state, because the regulatory or competitive environment means that all candidates meet it (e.g. you do not stipulate your new car must be fitted with seat belts.) (By permission of Phil Stunell)
Shortlist	A much-reduced list of strong candidates, with unsuitable **candidates** eliminated from the **longlist**
SLA	Service level agreement
SMT	Senior management team
SoR	Statement of requirement. See **requirement**
SoUR	Statement of user requirement(s). See **requirement**
Sponsor	The main driving force behind a programme or project, usually a senior manager, who will ensure that resources are allocated and who monitors outcomes
SRO	Senior responsible owner. Also see **sponsor**
Supplier meeting	See **evaluation meeting**
ToR	Terms of reference
Use case	A software and engineering term that describes how someone uses a system to accomplish a particular goal
VPN	Virtual private network
WAM	See **weighted attribute matrix**
WBS	Work breakdown structure – a decomposition of a project into a hierarchy of smaller components. Normally uses technical numbering to reflect levels, such as parent task 1 with children 1.1 and 1.2
Weight	See **weight for importance**
Weight for importance	This term from the scoring approach specifically represents the number on the **weighted attribute matrix** that encapsulates how significant or important that requirement is to your organisation
Weighted attribute matrix	The scoring matrix created during **scoring meeting** that combines **attributes** with their **weight for importance** and the **score for fit** to calculate **candidate** rank order

INTRODUCTION: PURPOSE AND PRINCIPLES

'"Would you tell me, please, which way I ought to go from here?"
"That depends a good deal on where you want to get to," said the Cat.'

Lewis Carroll (1832–1898)

I.1 OVERALL PURPOSE OF THIS BOOK

- Recognise both the purpose and structure of the book, so that you can immediately exploit specific parts if necessary.

- Grasp the main characteristics and benefits of the method as introduced here, especially some themes that run through every chapter.

- Understand that collaborative behaviour is a success factor on IT software selections.

I wrote this book to steer the reader towards good practice and clear of the common pitfalls when evaluating, selecting and procuring an off-the-shelf solution. This may be a software product installed on machines in-house (often termed a package), a hosted solution or a cloud-based monthly subscription covering hardware, software and services.

Despite the benefits and sophistication of modern software products (or partly **because** of the sophistication of the products), organisations often cannot choose which one to adopt or they buy a product or subscription and then wish they had not. However, many of the problems that emerge with new solutions are predictable and avoidable with solid early processes.

I.1.1 Pre-conditions

This book assumes that you have decided to buy software, or at least investigate the viability of buying new software, and your preference is for an off-the-shelf solution ('software product') created by a specialist external supplier (rather than developing bespoke or tailor-made software).

The method of selecting a solution that is described here addresses those software implementations where the following conditions apply:

- Off-the-shelf solutions are available for the process where you want improved work automation.
- Pragmatically, you expect to adopt one solution, for reasons of technical feasibility, economic affordability, IT capacity or organisational culture.
- You have a choice of different solutions because there are multiple software authors, resellers and products (but no directive to adopt a specific solution).

I.1.2 Position of selection method

The method described in this book has been used successfully by commercial and public sector organisations. Although the approach here concentrates on commercial use, there is a companion article explaining adaptations for public sector procurement, such as under *Official Journal of the European Union (OJEU)* or *US General Services Administration (GSA)* (see www.bcs.org/offtheshelfextras).

The method is not a strategic IT planning method in the sense that it does not identify which parts of the organisation **should** be automated. Instead, it picks up when an area has been targeted and you have tricky choices about which product to adopt.

The method is an IT selection process rather than a wider business change approach. It is a major part of the procurement process, but fits with other approaches. It cannot cover such standalone disciplines as requirements engineering, interviewing, shortlisting, option evaluation, negotiation, contracting or meetings management. However, it can act as a central jigsaw piece linking these approaches. It concentrates on the processes and decision-making information that are unique to buying an off-the-shelf solution. Also see the article on the relationship to organisational change at www.bcs.org/offtheshelfextras.

If you have a mature IT organisation, there will be other methods or approaches in use. For example:

- **PRINCE2**, for project approval and project management, possibly with **MSP** for programme management.
- **COBIT**, for IT governance and alignment.
- **ITIL**, for best practices in operational management.
- **Agile** or **DSDM**, for the development of bespoke interfaces from existing in-house software to your new off-the-shelf solution.
- **ISO 11000** for collaboration with external IT providers.

Integration of methods and techniques (like the integration of multiple software solutions) involves working out boundaries and agreeing where it is appropriate to use each approach. Some of the requirements you capture will relate to your internal standards, such as the software accepting automated license management as part of your operational standards.

The companion BCS page has an article on the interaction of this and other approaches (see www.bcs.org/offtheshelfextras).

I.2 WHY YOU SHOULD READ THIS BOOK

This book leads you from the initial decision to buy an off-the-shelf solution through to a signed contract to buy the new software product and its associated services.

The book delivers the following advantages to the reader:

- Benefit from a method for selecting off-the-shelf IT software that is proven (see Appendix 2).
- Understand that the organisation is not simply buying technology, but beginning substantial change. This change both reflects and makes concrete your organisational strategy.
- Appreciate the importance of internal stakeholder engagement and external supplier talent management.
- Understand the crucial nature of the requirements definition in reducing mistakes, and therefore costs. This means that your requirements are central in driving the candidate shortlisting, detailed evaluation, demonstrations and negotiation.
- Recognise the risks and pitfalls in system selection exercises. These are often severely underestimated in terms of nature, complexity and risk.
- Avoid the common mistakes, such as buying the high-profile brand, finding the cheapest (but unsuitable) solution or choosing for social reasons (such as the professionalism of the sales executive).
- Help to balance unequal skills. Those selling software are trained to sell, but those buying are rarely specifically trained to buy.
- Make sure senior management attention to your project is efficient and effective. The process ensures that they are not bogged down in detail, but inspect and approve at suitable times, with highly specific aims and input information.

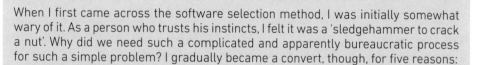

EXECUTIVE PERSPECTIVE: A DIVISION HEAD EXPERIENCES SURPRISING REACTIONS

When I first came across the software selection method, I was initially somewhat wary of it. As a person who trusts his instincts, I felt it was a 'sledgehammer to crack a nut'. Why did we need such a complicated and apparently bureaucratic process for such a simple problem? I gradually became a convert, though, for five reasons:

- The method is rigorous, thorough and robust, with enough flexibility to capture all software, training and documentation needs but enough structure to make sure everything is covered.
- We found the process easier and more enjoyable than we expected and everyone saw both the logic of the approach and how important it was to participate. Those who were not on the initial software selection working party started demanding to be let in as the project gained momentum.

- As more people used it, they saw how well it helped them articulate and record their thoughts on what they wanted, so everyone got the necessary sense of ownership of their bit of the process, which helped them stay focused and on track.

- Potential vendors, when they saw the number and calibre of questions that emerged from the process about their offerings, immediately stopped trying to blind everyone with marketing 'flannel' and started treating us as intelligent customers. They soon realised that they faced instant rejection if they did not quickly raise their game and wheel out their experts for us to talk to.

- At the end, we had something that stood up to the scrutiny of the decision-makers and answered all their questions, giving everyone confidence that we had the correct result that could not be overturned during the purchasing approval process without very good reason. We could all sleep at night, knowing that we had got it right!

I.3 HOW TO GET THE BEST FROM THIS BOOK

The book is set out to be read in different ways by different readerships:

- If you are a senior-level reader or someone who wants to understand the benefits of the method without delving into the step guidance, you can concentrate on the Executive Viewpoint panels. These summarise the experiences other senior managers have had with using the method, and how they have benefitted from it.

- If you are a hands-on practitioner who needs to 'turn the handle' of the evaluation and selection process, you will find all the information you need in the method step guidance in Chapters 3 to 13. The format illustrations help to explain the principle, and you can download the matching blank templates.

- If you want to explore some of the underlying issues, you can turn to the References and especially the Further Reading sections for each chapter.

For simplicity's sake, this book addresses you as though you are leading the evaluation project. You may be the formal leader, such as an appointed project or programme manager. You may be an informal opinion leader, for instance where a project for which you lobbied has been agreed and you are expected to advance it.

Therefore, when using such terms as 'your evaluation team', this can mean the organisation's evaluation team, or the team you literally lead.

I.3.1 The importance of adapting the approach

One major warning note about using this method – this is not a rulebook to be slavishly followed. You should adapt the process described in this book to your level of project risk, to the capital cost, to the degree of disruption in the technology and to your experience (organisational or personal) with IT selections. This section suggests some ways to mould the method to your project.

Scale the method to match your project profile

One adaptation is to adjust the scale of your project to match the gravity of the evaluation and implementation.

- Aim for an executive sponsor whose seniority is appropriate to the scope. Ideally, the sponsor should be senior enough to span all the organisational silos affected. The method ensures that the sponsor contributes at predictable times, chiefly at the decision-making gates. Their workload is defined and timetabled, so you have a better chance of securing a high-ranking sponsor.

- Aim for a project board where the number and seniority of members reflects the number of organisational silos that your new solution will affect. As with the sponsor, the same benefits apply for the project board – they are presented with predictable workload. Most enterprise-class software projects need to report to the full board in a commercial company or the senior management team in a public sector organisation. Rather than find slots for separate project steering meetings, it may be easier to schedule if your project becomes a standing agenda item for some months, and you ask for decisions at the next available meeting.

- Agree the number of interviewees that is appropriate to the coverage (breadth) and risk of your project. A wide, risky project needs safety in numbers. A small project within one department can possibly concentrate on a few critical representatives to articulate requirements.

- Document requirements, such that the volume of requirements also reflects your project profile. You need more requirements to accommodate increased coverage, more organisational units and more stakeholder groups, and when adopting more than one type of software in a single evaluation project.

- Determine the appropriate number of candidates. In practice this means setting the length of the various lists – longlist, shortlist, number of reference sites, demonstrations and number of negotiation candidates. These numbers need to be higher for large, enterprise-wide, risky projects than for small, safer projects that fit in one silo.

Determine the applicable stages

Readers may come across this book at different project stages. Ideally, you will read the full book before you start your project. However, if you discover the book partway through your project, it is possible to jump in. The book is comprehensively indexed, and the table of contents will allow you to find the most relevant sections. The icons label different content.

If you need an emergency fast track because your project is in trouble or in a hurry, the following imperatives and chapters are the most fundamental ones.

- **Engage the stakeholders.** Identify those people who influence your project. Ensure they are informed and consulted. Find out what is needed from your project to enlist their support (Eskerod and Jepsen, 2013). See Chapter 3 for project initiation and Chapter 4 for requirements capture.

- **Drive the evaluation by requirements.** Your organisation's requirements for the software **product**, with its associated IT **services** such as support, must form the basis of decision. If your project does not capture requirements, it has little chance of succeeding. Without requirements, you have neither understood nor managed expectations. See Chapter 5 for requirements documentation and Chapter 7 for using them to assess the longlist.
- **Measure consistently.** Make sure that you apply your criteria fairly and consistently to all candidates. Most of all, do not compare systems with each other, but rather measure them against the same yardstick – your requirements (see Section I.4). See Chapter 7 for assessing the longlist, Chapter 9 for scoring the shortlist, Chapter 10 for the demonstrations, Chapter 11 for reference sites and Chapter 12 for negotiation.

The diagram at Figure I.1 is a standard graphic of the evaluation, selection and procurement process. The ovals contain the related chapter numbers. You can see the three major phases in the outer boxes. Each major phase produces a concrete deliverable or product.

- The **Requirements Definition** phase outputs an agreed statement of requirements.
- The **Evaluation and Selection** phase outputs one or two preferred candidates for negotiation.
- The **Negotiation and Contract** phase outputs a signed contract with your chosen supplier.

You can also see the inner dashed box that encloses those steps where the project 'comes in for inspection' at project board reviews. This is where senior groups assess readiness to move to the next stage.

You will see at Figure I.1 that certain boxes have 'by-pass arrows' meaning you can skip round them. However, this usually means greater project risk of bias or failure, so you should reflect your specific context. For example:

- Project initiation may have already been completed to your organisational standards using a generic project approval process. This means that the project has been previously authorised and you do not need to determine scope (already set), study feasibility (assumed or already calculated) or establish phasing (single phase evaluation or phases already agreed). You only need to challenge the project boundaries if you believe that the generic authorisation was inappropriate and needs more project-specific detail, such as identifying critical IT requirements. See Chapter 3.
- You might choose not to weight requirements. You may not need weighting if you have a low number of requirements and you have deliberately concentrated on those requirements that are the most important, such that all recorded requirements are roughly equal in importance. However, remember that the weighting meeting is an extremely effective process to clarify requirements and to approve your requirements document. If you skip the formal weighting

Figure I.1 Overview of approach with mapping to chapters

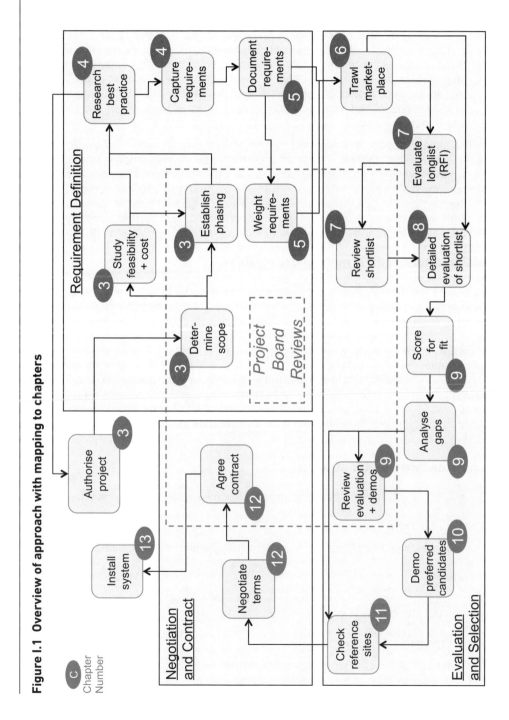

meeting, you will need to replace these two benefits with another, presumably smaller, process. See Chapter 5.

- You might jump straight to the shortlist, skipping the long list and request for information (RFI) process. This would apply if you were confident that there are only a small number of contenders in the marketplace. A manageable number on your shortlist for detailed evaluation is three or four. If there are only two or three credible contenders, you may start your detailed evaluation soon after contacting the marketplace. On one project, the IT manager declared that there were only two credible commercial off-the-shelf solutions in this 'software space' and that the project only had to tell him which one to buy. See Chapters 6 and 7.

- You might skip the demonstrations. They may be meaningless if the software has low visual content – such as one that implements complex algorithms while drawing on and feeding other software (rather than screens). Another reason would be a front-runner with such a significant gap that comparative demonstrations are farcical. You may be better gaining similar reassurance with more reference site work on a single candidate – perhaps stepping up your effort to organise site visits with a larger group. See Chapters 10 and 11.

I.3.2 Interlock of main method deliverables

As well as the method diagram, or roadmap, at Figure I.1 (which looks at the process) another way to look at the method is to see how the major products, documents or deliverables interlock.

At Figure I.2, the most important document on your project will be (G) the scoring matrix (see Chapter 9), which receives (B) requirements and (C) weights for importance (see Chapter 5). The weights help select (D) the RFI criteria (see Chapter 7). The RFI feeds back (E) the shortlist for evaluation (see Chapter 8), after which (F) scoring creates the scores for fit and (H) the definitions of each score (see Chapter 9). The requirements, scores and definitions (B, G, H) are crucial attachments as a contractual safeguard (see Chapter 12).

I.3.3 Standard chapter structure

The main method chapters have a standard structure, with the following sections.

What you can learn from this chapter

This explains what this chapter aims to deliver and what you will gain from reading it.

Overview

This section raises the main themes covered in the chapter. There may be notes to position the chapter, such as relating it to other chapters.

Body of chapter

The main part of the chapter explains the method with its goals, mindsets, techniques and formats. It is often organised with a sub-structure:

- **why** – the goals;
- **who** – does it;
- **what** – to do;
- **when** – timing and scheduling;
- **how** – technique points.

Chapter summary

The chapter summary always contains two parts.

- **Take-away points** are the most important aspects of the chapter content, usually stated without evidence. Read these first if you are skimming or speed-reading.
- **Link between current and next chapter** sets the context for the next chapter.

References

These are specific citations from the chapter text.

Figure I.2 Interlock and flow of main deliverables

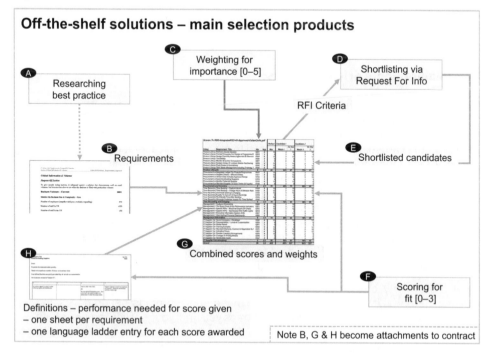

Off-the-shelf solutions – main selection products

Further reading

These are other books, journal articles or web pages with useful background information, not specifically cited in the chapter. Some chapters touch on huge bodies of knowledge – indeed entire IT disciplines, such as requirements engineering (RE). This book is neither a primer nor a survey of the literature. However, it can at least act as a pointer to useful supporting material if you want to explore. In addition, there are electronic templates available from the BCS website at www.bcs.org/offtheshelfextras.

I.4 MAJOR GUIDING PRINCIPLES OF THE METHOD

I.4.1 Team working allows participants to specialise

Put simply, the evaluation process allows people to do what they are best at, exploiting the division of labour (Smith, 1776). The customer or prospective user of the solution understands the organisational need. Suppliers understand their own off-the-shelf solution. During the evaluation, the approach does not need the customer to understand fully multiple complex software products – nor the candidate suppliers to understand fully their prospective customer's processes.

Moreover, the specialisation is not merely a bi-polar split between two parties – customer and supplier. The process brings together teams from both customer and supplier, such that individuals can apply their specialist knowledge within a framework that brings together multiple sets of understanding and gives it traction in your decision-making. Hence, this method assumes that there will be an evaluation team – its size depends on the nature of your project.

I.4.2 Requirements drive decisions

The process starts with needs and is guided by them throughout. At every stage, organisational requirements provide the 'basis of decision'. Requirements allow you to measure candidates against the full scope of supply – both software and services. They form the yardstick or benchmark, used to measure all candidates. As well as being a crucial foundation for your actual selection, this approach can also feed into other possible outcomes of your evaluation.

- While the approach assumes that a suitable off-the-shelf solution exists, it is conceivable (although improbable in many fields) that your selection filters yield a 'shortlist of zero' (there are no candidates left). You would deal with this later in the method and by exception. If you have to abandon the selection, your requirements work then feeds the start of bespoke development (building software).

- A more likely outcome is that the overall best solution has weaknesses. Your gap analysis will reveal whether these shortcomings need addressing (see Chapter 9, Section 9.14). Whatever gaps you find, your earlier requirements work is never wasted. It will find the strongest candidates, it will find the gaps and it will help decisions about closing these gaps. At the highest level, requirements will help you decide whether to continue with the selection.

I.4.3 Evaluate the 'shipping' version without customisation

You should always evaluate the current standard 'production' or 'shipping' version of the software. This is sometimes called processing available 'out of the box'. You should not evaluate future software versions.

This principle is the one that is probably neglected the most often, causing the project to hit difficulty. All software is malleable; with enough will and resource, it could be made perfect. If you evaluate solutions in their hypothetical perfected state, they become indistinguishable.

You should always assume 'configuration' rather than 'customisation'. This means that you will not commission modifications to the base code that are specific to your organisation. You will fully exploit settings and set-up facilities. Naturally, you will add specific data, some of which will trigger extra processing, such as setting flags on perishable items to trigger stock rotation.

If you have highly sophisticated needs that eclipse generic software products, you may adopt specialist-supporting software for targeted areas, such as supply chain or warehouse management. See Chapter 9.

Moreover, adopting standard software can go deeper. My experience in the most recent five years is that organisations adopting off-the-shelf software are increasingly inclined to also adopt the processes that are built into the software. During implementation, there will be a process redesign operation. Many organisations use the standard processes in the off-the-shelf software as the start point for their new processes. This is partly for reasons of compliance, but mostly it reflects the fact that one of the many things you are buying is encapsulated knowledge and experience.

I.5 NATURE AND CHARACTERISTICS OF THE SELECTION PROCESS

This section maps out the essential characteristics of the process so that you can bear them in mind when digesting the detailed method (see Chapters 3 to 13).

I.5.1 Decisions are staged and evidence-based

Many processes within this method clearly exhibit evidence-based decision-making. While the evaluation team are not the decision-makers, the decision will be made based on the large body of evidence they collect, organise and present.

The process exhibits the classic characteristics of progressive shortlisting. As your evaluation advances, you invest in fewer candidates but in more detail.

The decision-making is staged. The understanding and evidence that you marshal is adequate, but not excessive. At each gate, it only matters that the margin of assessment error is smaller than the gap between the two outcome groups: those candidates that go through and those candidates that are held or parked.

Staged decision-making also makes sure that the process is subjected to repeated reviews and acceptance by your sponsor and your project board. They can ensure that the project continues to move in the agreed direction and continues to support the organisational strategy.

I.5.2 The Cost of Change Curve is respected

A recognised effect with IT projects, applicable to exploiting off-the-shelf solutions, is the Cost of Change Curve (Boehm, 1981). Although the details are still debated, the general principle is that the later in your project you discover any deficiency, the more it costs. This is sometimes known informally as the 1:10:100 rule because the cost line is not linear. It is when the mistake is first made that matters most, and then how long it takes to find it. Because errors in requirements usually occur early, they lead to the biggest rework costs.

During an evaluation, the progressive shortlisting of candidates avoids over-investment in unsuitable ones, thereby cutting overall costs. Better still, deep due diligence into the strongest two candidates avoids nasty surprises during implementation – cutting rework of process designs, training material, operational manuals or live data.

I.5.3 Risk is mitigated

Like all due diligence processes, the approach mitigates risk. It engages stakeholders, including senior management, operational users and IT staff, so your project is deeply rooted in the organisation. It gathers support for your project. It manages expectations about it. With multiple feedback mechanisms, risk is detected, giving you an opportunity to mitigate it.

Consistent with the sound principles of formal decision-making, the method dependably creates the 'basis of decision' before applying it. In other words, you agree what success looks like before you go looking for successful candidates.

At the higher level, agreeing the basis of decision before making one helps to reduce the likelihood of causing controversy if your choices are unpopular or divisive (in the sense of different camps supporting different decisions).

At the lower level of operational project process, the basis of decision (as extracted from organisational requirements) is established before contact with suppliers. This safeguards against them influencing the basis of decision in their own favour (see Chapter 2).

I.5.4 Candidates are measured against a yardstick, not each other

The process avoids comparing candidates with each other (which is impossibly complex), but measures all candidates against the same yardstick of your requirements or criteria.

For every selection stage, the method uses a suitable form of scoring. This makes explicit the strengths, weaknesses, benefits and gaps for each candidate that is measured (see Chapters 7, 9 and 10).

I.5.5 Processes are robust to subversion

The interlocking processes are robust to subversion or derailment by internal factional interests or misbehaving suppliers. The method features multiple checks and balances.

Influence is deeply rooted in multiple groups. Somebody who believed their interests would be served by a failed project (or an ill-fitting winner) would have to corrupt several groups in order to subvert your process.

The method exhibits transparency. Information and decisions are crystallised into documentation. Therefore, it is possible to audit the project, decision-making process and material.

I.5.6 Approach delivers peace of mind

The method entails 'doing your homework', so it is a hefty insurance policy. By following the process, you are much less likely to make a disastrous choice.

There are multiple internal crosschecks to verify factual accuracy (see Chapter 9, Section 9.12.4).

Verbal responses from suppliers have contractual significance (see Chapter 12).

I.5.7 Project process is more manageable

The method makes the process of your selection project less complex and more manageable. The evaluation is broken down into understandable steps with clear tasks, each with defined inputs and outputs.

The time commitment by participants is limited and predictable, so you are more likely to enlist the right people. By having different roles in a decision-making framework, people can make short, part-time contributions that nevertheless have traction in the overall decision.

I.5.8 Approach is proven

The method integrates multiple techniques, such as limited-response questionnaires or the weighted attribute scoring matrix. Such techniques are themselves well proven.

This method has itself been tested multiple times (over 50 at the time of writing) and improved by feedback, reflection and learning.

I.6 CHAPTER SUMMARY

TAKE-AWAY POINTS

Software (especially enterprise software) has an enormous influence on the organisation, so you should adopt a **robust** selection approach. It must reflect the realities of software and its selection, especially the need for stakeholder engagement and collaboration with commercial suppliers.

Because large software products are too complex to compare with each other, you should measure all the candidates against the same yardstick of your organisational need. This process of requirements definition is an important aspect of your project in its own right.

Requirements gathering also means that you identify and consult stakeholders. That consultation gives reliability to the result, which is a huge dividend. Most importantly, it encourages 'buy-in' or acceptance of your project by the organisation.

I.6.1 The next chapter

The next chapter examines off-the-shelf software – its nature, the motivations for adopting it and the main pitfalls when doing so.

I.7 REFERENCES

Boehm, B. (1981) *Software engineering economics*. Prentice Hall: Harlow.

Eskerod, P. and Jepsen, A. (2013) *Project stakeholder management*. Gower: Farnham.

Smith, A. (1776) 'An inquiry into the nature and causes of the wealth of nations'. Project Gutenberg, PGLAF. www.gutenberg.org/ebooks/3300 (10 November 2014).

I.8 FURTHER READING

I.8.1 Books and articles

Association For Project Management (2012) *APM body of knowledge*, 6th edition. APM: Princes Risborough.

Axelos (2012) 'Common glossary'. Global Best Practice Portfolio, AXELOS. www.axelos.com/glossaries-of-terms.aspx (10 November 2014).

Enock, K. (2006) 'Motivation, creativity and innovation in individuals, and its relationship to group and team dynamics'. Health Knowledge, Department of Health – Public Health Action Support Team (PHAST). www.healthknowledge.org.uk/public-health-textbook/organisation-management/5a-understanding-itd/motivation-creativity-innovation2 (10 November 2014).

Goldratt, E. and Cox, J. (2004) *The goal: A process of ongoing improvement*. Gower: Farnham.

Harrin, E. (2013) *Shortcuts to success: Project management in the real world*, 2nd edition. BCS, The Chartered Institute for IT: Swindon.

Hawkins, D. (2013) *Raising the standard for collaboration. Harnessing the benefits of BS 11000: Collaborative Business Relationships*. BSI: London.

Heller, R. (2001) *Roads to success in business: Eight leading gurus whose achievements transformed the business world (Business Masterminds)*. Dorling Kindersley: London.

Jenner, S. (2012) *A senior manager's guide to managing benefits: Optimizing the return from investments*. TSO: Norwich.

I.8.2 Useful websites

Tech Republic. 'Buying cycle for tech decision-makers'. www.techrepublic.com/buying-cycle.

Change Management Institute. 'Organisational change maturity model'. www.change-management-institute.com/organisational-change-maturity-model-2012.

ISACA. 'COBIT for IT governance and alignment'. www.isaca.org.

Change Management Institute. 'The effective change manager: The change management book of knowledge' (CMBoK). www.change-management-institute.com/buycmbok.

I.8.3 Related formats by download

Related articles from http://shop.bcs.org/offtheshelfextras.asp.

1 INTRODUCTION TO OFF-THE-SHELF SOLUTIONS

'There is nothing so useless as doing efficiently that which should not be done at all.'

Peter Drucker (1909–2005)

1.1 WHAT YOU CAN LEARN FROM THIS CHAPTER

- Appreciate that major software implementations are heavily intertwined with organisational strategy.
- Understand the impact that off-the-shelf solutions have upon IT.
- Be aware of some of the common myths, false assumptions and pitfalls that you might meet. This includes recognising some of the ill-advised reasons to buy an off-the-shelf solution.

1.2 INTRODUCTION TO OFF-THE-SHELF SOLUTIONS

Off-the-shelf solutions have had a profound impact upon IT (Bray, 2014). They are part of a trend away from bespoke or tailor-made software that is intended for only one organisation. Off-the-shelf software products are often called **COTS**, for commercial off-the-shelf. This means a developer (usually a software house) creates a software product that is specifically intended for deployment by multiple user organisations. Their customers may be commercial companies or public sector organisations (such as a fire service buying an HR product).

Within the public sector, a variant termed **GOTS** stands for government off-the-shelf. This is where one government agency or department builds (or funds) a software product, which is made available to other parts of government – sometimes without cost. Several national governments have stipulated that their agencies or departments use COTS or GOTS solutions whenever possible and often as first choice rather than last resort – for instance the US Cloud First policy (GSA, 2014). As well as the costs and risk of the initial build, bespoke software carries the whole burden of continuing maintenance. Organisations have often found that shortages of skills and money means they own a system that is not adequately supported or maintained. Procuring a solution off-the-shelf avoids in-house construction (or funding one-off development by external software authors). This spreads both development and maintenance cost and improves resourcing because a broader customer base creates a better-funded and more sustainable development environment.

Indeed, there are now areas where off-the-shelf solutions dominate to such an extent that is out of the question for an organisation to write its own software.

AREAS SERVICED BY OFF-THE-SHELF SOLUTIONS

(See the Glossary for acronyms). A list of areas where off-the-shelf solutions are available might be shortened to 'almost anywhere'. There is some form of COTS available for most things. Uptake often grows with more cloud-based working. While this list is not exhaustive, note that evaluation projects using this method have covered all these software areas.

- finance, general or nominal ledger, contracts or project ledger, job costing, fixed assets and depreciation;
- asset intelligence, asset management and service management;
- sales, marketing, CMS and CRM;
- procurement, inventory, MRP and ERP;
- demand planning, SCM, distribution, warehouse management and EDI;
- CAD, building information modelling, stress analysis and visualisation;
- PDM, requirements management and PLM;
- HR, payroll, resource planning and rotas;
- ID cards, access control, time, attendance, work-booking and time charging;
- training, LMS and LCMS;
- document management, content management and DRM;
- web retailing and eBusiness;
- desktop tools, reporting, management information and business intelligence;
- CSCW, support desk and service desk;
- operating systems and middleware.

1.3 INTERACTION OF STRATEGY AND SOFTWARE

Strategic decisions change the business, responding to external forces and the internal planning process. You should recognise that some of your current, and most of your proposed, software solutions are wide-ranging and have a powerful effect on the operation of your organisation. Such software is generally called enterprise software or enterprise-class software. Adopting enterprise software is a strategic decision;

it heavily influences your organisational strategy; it makes this strategy concrete. Consequently, strategy and enterprise software are inextricably intertwined, meaning that the installation of unsuitable software will set back your strategy (Galorath, 2012).

When selecting off-the-shelf solutions, a solid frame of reference assumes that this is not an IT project, but a business project to select IT, which keeps the project rooted in the organisation. As argued in *Good To Great* (Collins, 2001), good technology will not make you great, but bad technology will hamper your operations – meaning that software that fits is not enough by itself.

The method presented in this book will help you avoid bad technology, because an approach driven by requirements, with progressive shortlisting, is intolerant of unsuitable candidates. The process to find suitable technology also helps successful implementation (see Chapter 13).

1.3.1 Organisational strategy and new software

A new organisation-wide solution (enterprise software) is a major investment in, manifestation of, and commitment to your organisational strategy. It is an expensive part of that strategy. It is highly significant to your organisational strategy, especially when adopting software that cuts across multiple organisational silos. It is also highly significant to your IT strategy in that it will consume a significant portion of your IT capital budget. It will deliver a significant lump of the automation requested by your organisation (Frese and Sauter, 2003). This means that you had better get it right.

1.3.2 Organisational strategy and incumbent software

Alternatively, your organisation may have made an earlier considered decision to replace the incumbent software, because it no longer fits your organisational strategy, and to replace it with an off-the-shelf solution. However, the gap between your incumbent solution and the best available off-the-shelf might be close. If so, it is generally not worth the disruption to change a major piece of software. It will be better to invest in your incumbent solution to improve it. See Chapter 9 for gap analysis and Chapter 13 for implementation.

This means that, during your evaluation, you may decide to longlist one or more of your incumbent (current) solutions and it might even go all the way through your process to win. This is discussed in more detail in Chapters 7 and 9. By formally evaluating it, you are not revisiting or overturning the earlier decision, but formally checking whether your incumbent system meets your strategy. This is to validate the strategic decision in case it was misinformed by poor understanding of your current software. It might be much better than its reputation. There might be a newer version that you have not yet adopted.

1.4 IMPETUS – THE PROJECT PRE-CONDITIONS

Organisations have many motivations to change software. Such change is often dreaded, painful and deferred as many times as possible. Enterprise-class software that is embedded into your organisation is usually the most painful to replace. One or more of the reasons that follow will usually apply in providing the impetus. They are generally either major changes to your organisation or inadequate IT.

1.4.1 Changes to strategic direction

Your strategic direction as an organisation may have changed. For a commercial business, it may be an acquisition or perhaps the major expansion of a branch network. For a public sector organisation, it may be a significant change of legislation, departmental structure or reporting needs.

1.4.2 Changes to requirements for compliance

There are external pressures when legislation changes. Improving statutory reporting usually needs more detailed tracking. This directly affects how capable you consider your incumbent software to be.

Also, there may be changes to your approach to compliance. Your external auditors are increasingly aware of the impact of software on the organisation. Their financial and quality checklists will include entries to test aspects such as data integrity or the segregation of duties. Whether you adhere to such principles can often be found out from the set-up of your IT solutions.

1.4.3 Changes to technology or adoption policy

As part of a wider IT strategy, or seizing a specific opportunity, your organisation may decide to adopt specific technologies.

You may face a new policy on provision, for example for certain areas of your organisation to adopt cloud subscriptions (software as a service, SaaS).

1.4.4 Replacing inadequate processing

Your organisation may have recognised that it is time to replace current processing and IT solutions. Technology is often the last aspect to catch up with strategy.

Processes may have become too labour-intensive, making them expensive, not responsive enough and prone to human error. Therefore, your organisation wants more work automation. A common indication of this state is the need to replace semi-manual IT processing, such as spreadsheets, with a more automated solution that can carry out rules without being driven by an operator.

Legacy software may be nearly obsolete. It may have become uneconomic to maintain, or it may be formally at end of life because your external supplier has announced the date it will become unsupported.

You may be replacing ineffective IT. Whatever its age, the solution does not meet your needs. Possibly, it never did because a software development or selection fell short.

EXECUTIVE PERSPECTIVE: AN IT MANAGER'S EXPERIENCE OF MAKE VERSUS BUY

Often IT is challenged with the decision to either build its own software or buy something in. I work with a large population of engineers, so you will always get 'nobody can build this better than us!' Which may have stood true at some point back in time.

The software market has matured enough for good solid off-the-shelf software to be available. The problem is how do you bring the diehard in-house engineers along with you in the decision that off-the-shelf is the right answer. When faced with exactly that problem, the IT selection process in this book involved all key stakeholders. It let even the most troublesome people have their say and know their input will go into the final decision.

Developing in-house software is like a never-ending story with too much temptation to change, over-ambitious developers and constant bug fixes and maintenance. If we had gone down the development route, I am sure it would have ended in disaster, as a later and unexpected reduction in our capital programmes meant we would have never been able to complete a multi-year development project with anything meaningful to use.

The software selection process enabled us to really put the software vendors to task, comparing apples to apples and putting us in a very strong negotiation position. We had all the benefits of spreading the enormous development costs over multiple customers by buying off-the-shelf. Having been involved in this process from end to end, I can honestly say that you will never have any second thoughts of whether you made the right decision as this process puts the decision in everyone's hands.

1.5 WHY BUY AN OFF-THE-SHELF SOLUTION?

Some of the main motivations for adopting off-the-shelf software products include cost savings, improved quality, greater reliability (because other customers have tested it), better documentation, greater sophistication (than you could otherwise afford), faster implementation and the continuing upgrades.

1.5.1 Development costs are spread

An off-the-shelf solution means you are adopting software with a high development cost that is spread over a large customer base. The customer base has funded original development (for major software products this may be decades ago) and all subsequent enhancements.

The funds available have also meant progressive adoption of modern construction tools with up-to-date software development and test environments. This matters because modern tools usually build a more modern user experience.

1.5.2 Extensive specialist knowledge is encapsulated

You are buying encapsulated knowledge – a type of Economic Complexity (Center for Economic Development, 2014). The developers, to be effective, need to understand their niche, such as the business vertical market or the public sector field. They also need to understand the software development process, with professional design, coding, testing, documentation, distribution and training.

You are avoiding the risk of internal 'gifted amateurs' creating DIY software, sometimes called under-the-desk (in contrast to off-the-shelf). With modern tools, it can be dangerously easy to start constructing unique software, but discover too late that you do not have the resources, skills or authority to build a good solution.

1.5.3 Infrastructure for support and maintenance

When you buy a software product, you are also connecting to an extensive support infrastructure. Like the initial development, the cost of supporting and maintaining the product is also spread over a large customer base. There will be dedicated support infrastructure as well as the original software development environment.

This infrastructure aims to keep all installations of the product (including yours) healthy and protected from disaster. It will have automated processes, such as 'harvesting' snapshots of your working environment.

As well as the teams of coders and testers, there will be an extensive network of implementation consultants and support desk staff. As well as their knowledge of the product and previous customer issues with it, you are also benefitting from their support technology, such as knowledge bases or remote support and monitoring tools.

Of course, a crucial part of support is the release of updates. These will respond to changes of regulation, compliance needs, technologies and norms in your sector, as well as fixing bugs. With the right supplier, you can rely on an external team to keep on top of these changes.

Software renewal involves great experience. While software does not 'wear out' like a mechanical device, it does eventually become unmanageable. It reaches end of life when it is no longer economic to maintain the code base.

This is why you expect superseding major versions, which possibly exploit much more up-to-date construction technologies, such as to build apps for smart phones.

1.5.4 Teams provide safety in numbers

You are seeking safety in numbers. Adopting a large software product avoids a single point of failure. You avoid the situation where the person who developed an application (and is the only one who understands it) goes on holiday or quits. Behind the off-the-shelf software product, there are multiple teams – teams to develop it and teams to support it.

1.5.5 Standards and best practice are imported

You are adopting a standardised approach. Assuming the software product encapsulates best practice, your organisation is 'importing' good processes. Since the standard interface is used by a large pool of workers, you can recruit staff who already understand how to work your main IT solution. This makes ownership cheaper.

1.5.6 More choice is available with provision

Off-the-shelf solutions usually have more options for provisioning – meaning the hardware platform to run them. Also, up-to-date software products can often run in multiple environments. For instance, some are designed to connect to more than one database product, so you can stick to technologies where your organisation has mature skills. Alternatively, products may be designed to install on the desktop or server, but optionally run web-based.

Adding these alternatives is technically complex and more expensive. However, such options are attractive when they allow you to choose the platform that is most relevant to your organisation, such as the cloud. Once again, because the product has a sizeable market, the overhead of developing the product for multiple platforms is spread. An in-house software development probably could not afford to carry such overhead.

1.6 AVOIDING COMMON PITFALLS WHEN PROCURING OFF-THE-SHELF SOFTWARE

An off-the-shelf solution can bring its own temptations. As you are buying a pre-existing solution, there is a significant risk of false assumptions. The following points will help you make good choices on your project.

1.6.1 Complex software is not a simple artefact or project

Adopting a software product that has been created by an external supplier does not give you the right to abdicate customer responsibilities for a successful project and a quality IT estate.

Your organisation might assume that technology delivers benefits – it does not; people do. Your project will simply give them tools that are more powerful. Your project process should ensure that the required benefits are clearly articulated and the team are motivated to use the tools to deliver those benefits.

You are not buying 'success in a box' that avoids risk or eliminates customer effort and management attention. Your managers might assume that this project is easy, quick and low risk. It is none of these. The wider your project, the greater the risk, because many of your risks are outside the software itself.

It is generally damaging to buy a large software product simply on perceived brand reputation. The fact that decision-makers have heard of a product because it has a large marketing budget does not make it inherently suitable for your organisation. Picking the biggest player in the market, the software product used by your largest competitor or the product installed at your last employer are not quick shortcuts to an easy decision or an effective implementation.

Your colleagues (especially procurement specialists) might assume that, because you are buying an 'artefact', this means you can treat the procurement like buying any other off-the-shelf item – say a new component for a manufactured item. However, procuring a new software solution is not like procuring a commodity. Your buying behaviours must be different, for instance the contractual assurances you seek. See more in Chapter 2 for supplier psychology, Chapter 6 for finding candidates, Chapter 10 for the demonstrations, Chapter 11 for reference sites and Chapter 12 for negotiation.

1.6.2 Standard software still means managing stakeholders

Decision-makers can mistakenly assume that you can transfer risk to the suppliers, making your project success their responsibility. This ignores the huge customer responsibilities. Your customer responsibilities have far more impact on the project success than the supplier contribution. The shiny new software is no justification for neglecting stakeholder management.

A software product, however capable and well presented, does not automatically yield a user base that is motivated to use and exploit your new solution. Managing expectations, change, doubts and fears remains paramount. Failure to do so is usually curtains for your project. See more in Chapter 3 for project initiation and Chapter 13 for implementation.

1.6.3 Your best people will be needed

Adopting new software is a major project and, normally, will affect the profitability or efficiency and service levels of your organisation for years, possibly decades. This means that you should enlist your most talented people to help decide which is the most suitable product. In a 'survey of surveys', the calibre of the team is a significant factor in determining IT project success (Charette, 2005). In your case, this means the calibre of your evaluation team.

It is also important to remember that the ethics, behaviour and 'character' of your evaluation team members make a difference to the outcome, because they trigger behaviours both internally and at candidate suppliers. See Chapter 2 for supplier talent management and Chapter 8 for evaluation conduct.

1.6.4 Diffused knowledge makes collaboration essential

With all IT projects, the knowledge necessary to make a good decision lies in multiple heads. The subject is large, fast changing and needs command of intense detail: one person cannot expect to know everything and command.

Worse, in terms of organisational challenge when exploiting off-the-shelf solutions, the knowledgeable heads work for different organisations. The candidate IT suppliers understand their software, the project management of its installation and the operational management of its support and maintenance. The prospective customer understands their organisation, its strategy, goals, processes and the project aims.

The critical effect of this is that your entire project involves more than teamwork – it involves collaboration. The organisations involved have different chains of command, goals and, usually, cultures. Successful collaborations require specific mindsets, skills and behaviours (Archer and Cameron, 2014). Collaboration is now so important to commercial operations and public administration that 'the policies and processes, the culture and behaviours required to establish successful collaborative relations' are incorporated into the BS 11000 standard 'Collaborative Business Relationships' (BSI Group, 2014).

Diffused knowledge during decision-making creates an inevitable tension between the experts representing the technology and those representing the organisation. However, the two sets of experts are reliant on each other for a successful project. During a software selection exercise, the customer does not have time to understand in detail the capabilities of the software from multiple suppliers. On the other hand, suppliers cannot know your organisation in depth. If they are to meet your needs, you must understand and express your requirements.

1.6.5 A lack of commitment never works

Adopting a new solution should not be an empty exercise in compliance to satisfy auditors or shareholders. If your organisation is aiming for a quick 'tick in the box' they are unlikely to get the desired benefits, and possibly will lose all benefits if your project fails to deliver.

1.6.6 Competitive advantage comes from exploitation not programming

Naturally, you are not in control of the software development or its adoption by other organisations. Any competitive advantage from off-the-shelf IT does not come from features that only your organisation has. It comes from effectively selecting, installing, understanding, configuring and exploiting the product, and then continually populating it with your own high-quality data and surrounding it with good processes.

1.7 IT CONSULTANCY FOR IT SELECTIONS

Many organisations regard their software selections (especially of enterprise software) as so important that it warrants involving external IT consultants. You executed a make–buy decision when you decided to buy the software off-the-shelf. Sometimes, you also execute a make–buy decision and decide to buy the specialist evaluation and procurement expertise off-the-shelf as well.

Before choosing a consultant, make sure your organisation is clear what they are buying. Typically, this is knowledge of selection projects, organisations of your type and the 'software space' – meaning the nature of the software, typical high-level requirements, the marketplace and some of the suppliers within it.

Usually, the role of the IT consultant is to provide process expertise of software product selections. Specific product expertise can be gathered from the candidate suppliers.

If you are involved in selecting consultants, make sure their interests are declared. Look for proven impartiality.

1.8 CHAPTER SUMMARY

TAKE-AWAY POINTS

Strategy and software (especially enterprise software) need to be considered together. This interlock means that the gulf between a successful project and an unsuccessful one is enormous.

For most business and public sector organisations, there are areas where an off-the-shelf solution is now the only realistic way to access enhanced software capabilities.

Ordinary procurement processes intended for goods are inadequate for large software products with their associated IT services.

1.8.1 The next chapter

The next chapter is a thematic chapter from an unusual perspective. It argues that talent management is important to a successful project. Your evaluation project is necessarily a collaborative effort. Candidate suppliers repeatedly make crucial contributions to your process.

1.9 REFERENCES

Archer, D. and Cameron, A. (2014) 'One city: Two stadiums. Lessons learned in megaprojects'. *Project Manager Today*, XXVI Issue 3 (Apr 2014), 16–19.

Bray, M. (2014) 'Bespoke vs. off-the-shelf software'. BCS, The Chartered Institute for IT. www.bcs.org/bespoke-shelf (10 November 2014).

BSI Group (2014) 'Introduction to BS 11000'. The British Standards Institution. www.bsigroup.com/en-GB/bs-11000-collaborative-business-relationships/Introduction-to-BS-11000/ (10 November 2014).

Center For Economic Development (2014) 'The atlas of economic complexity: About – glossary'. Harvard University. www.atlas.cid.harvard.edu/about/glossary (10 November 2014).

Charette, R. (2005) 'Why software fails'. Spectrum, IEEE. http://spectrum.ieee.org/computing/software/why-software-fails (10 November 2014).

Collins, J. (2001) *Good to great: Why some companies make the leap and others don't.* HarperCollins: London.

Frese, R. and Sauter, V. (2003) 'Project success and failure: What is success, what is failure, and how can you improve your odds for success?'. UMSL, University of

Missouri – St Louis. www.umsl.edu/~sauterv/analysis/6840_f03_papers/frese/ (10 November 2014).

Galorath, D. (2012) 'Software project failure costs billions. Better estimation & planning can help'. Galorath, SEER. www.galorath.com/wp/software-project-failure-costs-billions-better-estimation-planning-can-help.php (10 November 2014).

GSA (2014) 'Cloud IT Services'. US General Services Administration. www.gsa.gov/cloud (10 November 2014).

1.10 FURTHER READING

1.10.1 Books and articles

Castellina, N. (2012) 'ERP in manufacturing 2012: The evolving ERP strategy'. Aberdeen Group. http://aberdeen.com/research/7812/ra-enterprise-resource-planning/content.aspx (10 November 2014).

Eoyang, G. (2013) *Adaptive action: Leveraging uncertainty in your organization*. Stanford University Press: Palo Alto.

Hushon, D. (2014) '6 IT trends you can't ignore in 2014'. Computer Sciences Corp (CSC). www.csc.com/innovation/publications/91590/105101-6_it_trends_you_can_t_ignore_in_2014 (10 November 2014).

1.10.2 Useful websites

BCS Practitioner Certificate in Integrating Off-the-shelf Software Solutions: www.bcs.org/integrating-oss

2 TALENT MANAGEMENT: SUPPLIER PSYCHOLOGY

With Cathy Humphreys

'Nearly all men can stand adversity, but if you want to test a man's character, give him power.'

Abraham Lincoln (1809–1865)

2.1 WHAT YOU CAN LEARN FROM THIS CHAPTER

- Understand the people occupying 'the opposite side of the table'.
- Realise the ways in which your behaviour can affect the behaviours and responses of your candidate suppliers, and consequently your project outcome.
- Comprehend what a good sales prospect looks like to a candidate supplier.
- Recognise it is in your interests to be a good customer, and how to be one.

2.2 OVERVIEW

For most organisations, selecting an off-the-shelf solution should be deliberately different from 'conventional' procurement exercises such as bulk stationery. Organisations that do not recognise this usually miss opportunities, or even experience project failures.

The philosophy of a successful off-the-shelf selection reflects the Charles Handy view that modern organisations are communities. They should compromise to reach solutions that satisfy all stakeholders, including suppliers (Heller, 2001).

Organisations miss out if they do not fully recognise the candidate suppliers as professionals and motivated knowledge workers. They are stakeholders with an enormous contribution. They are talent that needs managing. They need to be harnessed rather than stifled or ignored. It would be a mistake to expect them to dutifully follow instructions without thinking. By working within a proper partnership, collaboration contributes profoundly to the success of the project (Archer and Cameron, 2013).

Furthermore, your project works best if it consciously shares risk. Formal risk management is a huge subject, which links into project, operations and contract management. It is too large a topic for this book. However, be aware of one specific pitfall for your evaluation project. Some organisations believe they can transfer risk to their solution supplier, whereby the level of risk accepted then becomes part of the decision criteria. This usually leads to a project with an underlying blame culture or a perception of protection through contractual responsibilities – the 'cast iron' contract (see also customer responsibilities in Chapter 1, Section 1.6.1). The most successful projects are those where both customer and supplier share interests in common goals and the motivation to work together towards them.

This chapter is unusual in the book in that it is written with the candidate supplier perspective in mind, rather than only the view of the prospective customer, you. Accordingly, writing this chapter involved consulting some of the candidate IT suppliers who have experienced the method from the selling perspective, and the Executive Perspective panels are quotations from IT suppliers.

2.2.1 This chapter's position within the book

This chapter relates to your contact with candidate suppliers. It is positioned here, near the start of the book, because suppliers are crucial to your process and there are stages when they are heavily involved.

- **Initiation:** when you may ask representative suppliers for estimated costs as part of your early feasibility study. See Chapter 3.
- **Trawling the marketplace:** when you are searching for software products, and, therefore, for their suppliers and the best sales contacts within them. See Chapter 6.
- **Assessing longlist candidates:** when you rely on suppliers to complete your preliminary shortlisting questionnaire, the request for information (RFI). See Chapter 7.
- **Detailed evaluation:** when you have intense meetings to discuss your requirements. See Chapter 8.
- **Scoring:** when candidate suppliers validate their own scores for fit. See Chapter 9.
- **Demonstrations:** when the two strongest contenders show their product to large audiences you have pulled together. See Chapter 10.
- **Contracts:** when you have identified the one or two suppliers for negotiation. See Chapter 12.

Therefore, you might skip this chapter for now if your costing for the feasibility study will be compiled internally; that is, by a pre-existing team without contacting software suppliers. If you do skip ahead, you should come back to this chapter before going to market at Chapter 6.

EXECUTIVE PERSPECTIVE: A SENIOR SALES EXECUTIVE'S EXPERIENCE AS CANDIDATE SUPPLIER

Software suppliers love projects where there is a good technical fit, a short sales cycle with a low cost of sale, painless win–win negotiation and a successful implementation leading to fantastic benefits. This leads to healthy revenue, and a good PR story and a reference-able customer, which, particularly in the UK, is paramount to building further success.

Too often, we enter sales cycles where we have to do a lot of work to find out what the actual question is. What do they want? How are they going to make a decision? Who is the competition? Has anyone already influenced the basis of decision? Do we have a fair chance of winning?

When I came across a prospective customer using the method in this book, I knew it would be a well-run, open and fair process, and I wasn't wrong. We received clear documentation on the consensus requirements, including critical areas, how the decision was going to be made, the timeframe, who we were up against and what was expected from us to demonstrate evidence. This made it an easy decision on whether to participate, the risks were known and we knew what we needed to do to win. The rest was up to us.

With any opportunity using a systematic method, if we are not selected, but the basis of decision is clear, we have to admit we were not the right partner and learn from this for future projects. It helps knowing it has been open and fair, and it was our decision to participate with the risks we identified. Either way, knowing the question early in the process ensures we can be efficient in our use of resources and maximise the opportunity of winning for a low cost of sale.

2.3 CANDIDATE SUPPLIER CONSTRAINTS

When dealing with candidate suppliers, it is important to recognise that they have several constraints. However large their organisation, they still have limited resources and decisions to make about which opportunities to prioritise and how to service them. It would be a mistake to assume that your software supplier wants your order on any terms. You need to ensure that you understand their constraints and work with them to get the best service.

A common model is for the sales effort to draw on implementation consultants for their product expertise. They make good presenters and demonstrators, especially to address those questions that cannot be predicted by the demonstration script. Other models do separate pre-sales from post-sales, or have one pool of resource, with a consultant primarily working pre-or post-sales at any one time.

Whatever model is in place at candidate suppliers, technical consultants are an expensive resource. They have high daily charge out rates on external work. When they support sales, substantial revenue is lost. They might be committed to existing customer contracts and have to be released to your opportunity. The candidate suppliers will struggle to cooperate if you require resources at short notice or your dates often change. If you became their customer, you would not like consultants being pulled away from your project with no notice.

Your project succeeds when the best people at candidate suppliers contribute their knowledge to decide how to best meet your requirements. But the best consultants are not sitting on the bench, so you improve the chance of project success if you show them that it is worth allocating the good people to your opportunity. You need to demonstrate that your project is worth more than other commitments, give plenty of notice for mobilisation and be flexible with dates.

2.4 ATTITUDES AND RELATIONSHIPS

2.4.1 Culture of knowledge workers

The implementation consultants seconded to your sales meetings are knowledge workers. To be effective in their main role, they will be intelligent and perceptive. They will want to deliver a professional result, which means that they need relevant, quality information and preparation time. If you regard any contact with suppliers as a form of talent management, you will be in a stronger position as a prospective customer.

You will benefit from any safeguard that means that you and your evaluation team act accordingly. It can be tempting to set aggressive dates, in order to 'see who wants the business badly enough to drop everything'. However, this is counter-productive and should not be one of your criteria. It simply results in scant preparation time. If large meetings require a couple of weeks' notice, remember that you probably will not execute this sort of project again for another ten years or more. Next year, when you are struggling to install an ill-fitting solution, nobody will congratulate you on your tough tactics.

2.4.2 Provide information about your organisation and project

You should not risk treating your project as a secret and keeping candidate suppliers in the dark. You will need to provide plenty of information, rather than assume suppliers will know your specifics.

Software suppliers sometimes say that they feel their prospective customer insisted they guessed the requirement, and then awarded the contract to whichever supplier had the luckiest guess.

You might hope that candidates understand your market sector from previous experience (especially if they claim to dominate the niche), but they are unlikely to know where your organisation is going, how you are conducting your project or the business context (such as your rationale for changing software). Before you go to market, it is best to address this risk by preparing a supplier briefing document with such background facts. You must also be prepared to allow suppliers to 'interview' you. Candidates need to ensure that they have the necessary information to propose the best solution for your business change. Likewise, do not hide the decision criteria (see also Chapter 7, Section 7.6).

2.4.3 Your project as a strategic sale

It is valuable if all candidate sales teams, and especially their management, are convinced that your opportunity is a potential strategic sale. This means your contract will open up an important new market niche for them.

If a candidate supplier is of this view, or you can convince them of the strategic importance of your project, they will take your opportunity more seriously. Their service level will be higher and they will be less conscious of their cost of sale – because that cost will be spread over both this contract and subsequent future opportunities.

If you believe you will be a significant new customer, prove this is really the case. You may become the successful supplier's index customer – the first in a new field. You may be the biggest or most dominant organisation in your field – now, or in the future, as you grow.

You will balance this against the potential risks. If they do not know your sector, you will be training them. You might be a much bigger organisation than they are used to dealing with. However, try to discover similarities between your project and their experience. In essence, before the candidate suppliers sell their solution to you, you should sell your project to them.

2.4.4 Potential for customer and supplier cultures to clash

Cultures can clash between you, as prospective customer, and the candidate suppliers. Your buying culture and procurement process usually relate to the culture of your industry. This means your philosophy when buying will usually be shaped by your internal procurement department, your IT department or your organisational culture. You should be mindful of the risk of tacit cultural assumptions.

Your organisation's procurement philosophy might not automatically incorporate the most productive approaches to software suppliers. Your organisation's stance may be that suppliers are interchangeable and therefore powerless. If your organisation mainly buys commodity items – meaning products that can be fairly easily substituted and that can be bought against a rigid technical specification – your procurement culture might be shaped by the attitudes that prevail when dealing with less potent suppliers.

You can defend against this risk with a specific procurement process for your project that reflects the specifics of procuring off-the-shelf software solutions. You can portray your evaluation process to your organisation as fit for purpose and proven, but separate from 'normal' procurement until later in the process – perhaps at the negotiation stage.

2.5 THE SALES PROCESS AT THE SOFTWARE SUPPLIERS

It will not be a surprise that suppliers have a sales process. Naturally, the approach varies between suppliers. The overall project process is an exercise in 'match making' the best product to your needs. Nested inside your project is the sub-process of matching your project method to the sales methods of multiple candidate suppliers.

2.5.1 Lead qualification at suppliers

A software supplier of any maturity will have an authorised process for handling leads. They need to conduct their own due diligence and will qualify your opportunity to make certain that they are not squandering resource (see Section 2.3). Their decision varies with market conditions: in a buoyant economy they may pass.

One of the first things suppliers will check is your organisation's turnover (if commercial) or annual budget (if public sector). If information is limited, they may misconstrue your true value as a prospect. If you are small but growing fast, historically published figures will be misleading. There may be special circumstances when your IT spend is much higher than pure size would suggest – such as your policy of technology leadership. Suppliers may have a turnover threshold, where a different internal division or partner cuts in. Ensuring candidate suppliers have the right valuation of your company will lead to the best service for your project. See Section 2.4.2 for your supplier briefing document.

Candidate suppliers may request additional information because they have other qualification criteria (or indeed special insights) not covered by your briefing document. Do not refuse on the basis that you are managing a level playing field and the other suppliers have not requested the same. Send these extras to all candidate suppliers at the same time.

You may learn more by the questions suppliers ask. Again, the analogy to recruitment applies – the strongest job applicants can be those that ask the most insightful questions. So do not deny yourself this chance to evaluate and suppliers the chance to clarify.

2.5.2 Aspects that suppliers need to know

Candidate suppliers need to understand you and the opportunity you are presenting. It drives their sales strategy. They need to answer the classic question – what is in it for them? Does your opportunity lead to a high-value contract? Will it be their entry to a new market? Will it allow them to keep their market dominance, by keeping out potential competitors from a niche they believe they own?

Therefore, it is best if you can think through how important you are to a supplier. As your evaluation progresses and your shortlist becomes shorter, you will learn more about what is important to each candidate and will have more insight about how important you are to each supplier.

A candidate supplier needs to forecast the value and timing of future revenue opportunities – just as you will forecast your own sales. If each supplier has realistic schedules and can estimate their own revenue expectations, it will help them manage their delivery capability. It also sets commercial expectations internally, enabling them to focus on delivering against your expectations. Just as you may measure supplier delivery performance in your normal business, sharing quality information on what is expected from your software supplier, and when, improves their ability to deliver. They also need to understand your decision-making process and buying influences (Miller Heiman, 2013).

Help the sales executive at each candidate supplier manage upwards. When you buy wide-ranging software, especially enterprise software, products come from large organisations. The candidate's sales executive will have layers above who manage partly by the numbers. Providing them with the means to estimate these will ensure that they obtain management support.

The supplier needs to understand the likely size of your contract, the likelihood of winning it, and the probable cost of sales. The staged decision-making in this method is useful to your organisation, and you can make it work for candidate suppliers. You do not have to divulge your budget, or name the competitors – it is not necessary (or desirable) to do so. Instead, always let them know the number of contenders at any stage, what work is needed to get to the next round and how many will be left by your next stage. If a supplier is one of 20, but only needs two days' effort to become one of three, they will commit the resource.

2.5.3 The importance of documentation

The pre-sales phase of a selection can run for a long time, with the gap between initially contacting a supplier and eventually signing a contract anywhere from three to 18 months. (Note that this method aims for an aggressive close, with your pre-sales phase at the low end of this range.)

As well as a long sales process, an IT selection project is a clear example of team-to-team selling. Candidate suppliers often involve many individuals and indeed handover to a different team entirely. Transfers are likely for your implementation. Moreover, your later stages may be handled by external subcontractors, such as approved training organisations. This all means that you should not rely on purely verbal information.

- Verbal information may not be passed on during handovers, or may be distorted in transmission.

- Consistently using verbal briefings condemns your implementation team to repeating themselves when fresh faces join your project.

- The eventual solution design may have gone through several iterations in thought development. It is important that you apply version control throughout your process, to ensure that you effectively communicate the latest position to all stakeholders.

This all means you need up-to-date documentation. You need briefing documents about your organisation, your project and its objectives. State the key staff, especially your project sponsor, your project manager and the principal evaluation team members. See Chapter 6.

You also need documentation on your selection process, so that candidate suppliers (and of course your internal stakeholders whom they meet) understand how, where and when you intend to make a decision.

Naturally, you also need a requirements document. This will be a major deliverable that encapsulates many hours of effort and many years of business experience. See Chapters 4 and 5.

2.5.4 Suppliers want to influence your process

Bear in mind that the sales process at the candidate suppliers will normally attempt to shape your basis of decision and your project process to their advantage. That is part of the job of their sales executives.

You will need to consider all points being promoted by each candidate supplier in the context of your overall requirements. Some points will be relevant and justified, and they might alert you to a gap in your requirements document. It is important to examine thoroughly those points that would change your basis of decision.

Suppliers will have financial pressures to recognise revenue in a particular financial period by closing the sale in a timely manner. Candidates will therefore look to accelerate your decision-making process with strategies that affect your schedule, such as concessions with a short expiry date. This can work to your advantage – when there is obvious commercial pressure, you can win the best deals. However, do not cut short your process to take advantage of a great deal. First, ensure you select the best supplier to meet requirements. If there is a special deal on the table, this may attract attention in the short term, but will probably have marginal impact on your long-term financial commitment, say over 10 years.

For more information to safeguard against these effects, see Chapter 6, Section 6.4.

2.6 POWER, PARTNERSHIPS, FAIRNESS AND GOOD LOSERS

2.6.1 Relative power positions

There might be temptation for you (or some of your more 'hawkish' colleagues) to treat suppliers as a disposable resource to exploit, gaining free knowledge and advice. Do not assume this is risk-free. In fact, the power relationship needs to be evenly balanced if you are to establish and retain a good, long-term relationship. It is not safe to assume that the supplier has more to lose than you do.

Software suppliers have a concept of 'qualifying out'. If the commercial or reputational risks outweigh the prospective benefits of a project, a candidate supplier can choose to eliminate those risks. If a software supplier walks away from your project, they drop some revenue in the short term, but they can divert resources into other opportunities – possibly more lucrative ones. However, if your organisation picks the wrong software, it will hold you back – possibly for years.

A sales executive does not damage their career if they withdraw with a justification. However, a manager responsible for heading a failed IT selection will probably damage their career.

2.6.2 The software supplier as critical partner

The successful supplier on a wide-ranging software contract immediately becomes one of your most important IT partners and sometimes the most important business partner. They need to be motivated to serve you well. Their pre-sales experience is usually a respectable indicator of how your implementation project will proceed. If your procurement has been tortuous and has demoralised them before signing your contract, they will not be motivated to excel in project delivery and consequently their service level will likely be poorer. You may never know what you lost.

Sometimes, people in power talk about other people 'that they need to be nice to'. During an IT selection, you do not know who your winner will be until you have an agreed contract. So, on this cynical basis, you should persuade your organisation to treat everyone as a prospective winner since anybody could be your successful supplier.

Selecting the best candidate for partnership is similar to recruiting talented individuals. You would expect a job applicant to interview their prospective employer as much as they were being interviewed. They want to ensure a match of values, expectations, level of responsibility and chemistry. It is little different when choosing the best IT supplier. You need to respect that they want to work on the best projects for the best companies.

To secure the best talent, you need to demonstrate that you will be a good customer. Your conduct during the pre-sales process will indicate how you will approach them as your implementation supplier. It is important to look at it as a two-way partnership from the outset.

2.6.3 Fairness is pragmatic, not philanthropic

If a supplier develops the perception that they are being treated unfairly, that other candidates are being obviously favoured or if they predict a high risk of losing, they may change their behaviour. They might withdraw from the race, and you might lose your strongest candidate. They might stay in the race, but change their behaviour to become 'anti-competitor', meaning that their focus moves away from requirements towards behaviour that enables them to win against the competitors. This is like the two people in a forest being chased by a bear. One dons running shoes, the other says 'you can't outrun a bear'. The first says 'I don't need to outrun the bear, I only need to outrun you'.

Suppliers might adopt spoiling tactics if they get as far as your shortlist for negotiation but feel they are a 'make-weight' or 'filler candidate'. For instance, they might hint at price reductions (expecting they will never need to honour them) to encourage the competitor who eventually closes the deal to undercut, driving down your contract value to a less profitable level. The customer rarely wins if the project runs out of profit.

More subtly, a disheartened supplier may concentrate on their unique selling points – the areas where they know they are stronger than the other products in this market niche. This is to your disadvantage, because you want to keep the focus on your customer requirements, not on specific features in one product offering. You do not want to lose control over your basis of decision.

2.6.4 Effective behaviours that are in your interests

Throughout the IT selection process, you need to be conscious of your staff behaviour, observing good etiquette and healthy ethics with candidate suppliers. The reputation of your organisation is at stake, and you need to gain or preserve a good reputation in the marketplace. If poor treatment by an evaluation team member or senior manager occurs, it is at best unproductive and arguably counter-productive.

- You should be civil, professional and collaborative. This does not mean that you are a weak customer who suppliers can bully. You can know what you want and strive determinedly to get it, while still recognising that your two organisations have different motivations and the people involved have different understandings.
- You should answer questions as clearly and honestly as you can, without hiding behind artificial claims about confidentiality.
- You should take candidate staff time seriously. You should prepare for meetings, being alert and attentive during them. Communicate effectively and consistently, because understanding candidates naturally requires a joint effort.
- If you create the impression that your organisation is not committed to your project or is poorly organised, your candidates might decide that implementation will be difficult. Problematic projects usually reduce or eliminate profit and risk reputational damage. Good candidates may withdraw.

In summary, deliberate or unconscious poor behaviour towards potential suppliers can mean your project becomes regarded as 'the bullet to dodge' or 'the poisoned chalice'. Therefore, you should aim to demonstrate the behaviours of an organisation that it is lucrative and even enjoyable to service. Also see Chapter 8, Section 8.5.1.

2.6.5 Avoiding unhappy losers

When a candidate supplier loses an evaluation, they mind less if your process was fair. If they were treated even-handedly and the basis of decision was clear and consistent, they are much more likely to accept a rejection and, more importantly to you, have no recourse to challenge your decision.

With emphatically 'black hat thinking' (de Bono, 2009), in certain circumstances, one or more unsuccessful candidates can take legal action against a provably unfair contract award.

For instance, after a large purchase under European Public Procurement Rules, unsuccessful candidates might believe the tender process was 'ineffective'. Examples include the criteria being applied differently so that the winner experienced favouritism. Losers can take court action to challenge the contract award and have the purchaser fined (Whitehead and Pender, 2012).

If you use the method presented in this book, your evaluation will be rigorous, your basis of decision explicit (as requirements) and your scoring process transparently fair. Together, this should eliminate the likelihood of legal challenges.

2.7 CHAPTER SUMMARY

TAKE-AWAY POINTS FROM THIS CHAPTER

It is in your interests to respect the culture, constraints and processes of each candidate supplier. Any one may ultimately become your partner, and a long-term partnership starts at first contact.

- Respecting constraints, sharing information and valuing all contributions will improve the quality of your evaluation.

- Candidates have processes to qualify your enquiry. They decide whether it is serious (not time wasting), relevant to them and whether it meets their success criteria.

- You help yourself if candidate suppliers perceive your project as an important potential sale – one where it is worthwhile allocating scarce resource.

- Your professionalism when dealing with candidate supplier staff will pay dividends to your project and ultimately your organisation. Make sure candidate suppliers know that your process has been fair. Ensure each perceives you as a prospect who is organised, professional and commercially attractive.

2.7.1 The next chapter

The next chapter is the first 'method chapter'. It is about determining the boundaries of your project, its feasibility and its resourcing, including sponsorship.

2.8 REFERENCES

Archer, D. and Cameron, A. (2013) *Collaborative leadership: Building relationships, handling conflict and sharing control*. Routledge: New York.

de Bono, E. (2009) *Six thinking hats*. Penguin: London.

Heller, R. (2001) *Charles Handy (Business Masterminds)*. Dorling Kindersley: London.

Miller Heiman (2013) 'Blue sheet: Buying influences'. Knowledge Center, Miller Heiman Group. www.millerheiman.com/Knowledge_Center/Knowledge_Center_Articles/Alumni_Materials/Blue_Sheet_Buying_Influences (10 November 2014).

Whitehead, A. and Pender, V. (2012) 'A guide to the European public procurement rules'. SGH Martineau. www.sghmartineau.com/publication_event/updates/A-Guide-To-The-European-Public-Procurement-Rules.pdf (10 November 2014).

2.9 FURTHER READING

2.9.1 Books and articles

Business Application Software Developers Association (2007) 'The BASDA request for information (RFI) selection process'. http://myfiles.uk-plc.net/c372982/documents/ BASDA-Publications/BASDASelecting a Business System 2007 final.pdf (10 November 2014). This is a proposal from the trade association for software developers to reduce their tendering costs.

Hawkins, D. (2013) *Raising the standard for collaboration. Harnessing the benefits of BS 11000: Collaborative Business Relationships.* BSI: London.

Nickson, D. (2012) *Bids, proposals and tenders: Succeeding with effective writing.* BCS, The Chartered Institute for IT: Swindon. This is about bidding from the supplier's point of view.

3 INITIATION: SHAPING AND AUTHORISING THE PROJECT

'If you don't know where you are going, you will probably end up somewhere else.'

Laurence J. Peter (1919–1988)

3.1 WHAT YOU CAN LEARN FROM THIS CHAPTER

- Understand the crucial role of project scope in off-the-shelf IT selections.
- Realise the power of a clear scope and the relevance of scope to every subsequent stage in the method.
- Appreciate techniques and approaches for determining and agreeing scope within a straightforward, effective scoping workshop.
- Recognise some techniques for the feasibility study.

3.2 OVERVIEW

What is scope? Put simply, scope in the context of IT selections is the coverage of your project – its extent, its latitude or range, with associated boundaries. Scope establishes what can be changed by a project – or at least investigated with a view to change.

As well as recording what is included or covered, it is important to explicitly record and publicise areas to be excluded.

If an area is within your project scope, you are authorised to change its processes, procedures, clerical systems or IT solutions. However, you might not – you are allowed to investigate, but you are not committed to change everything inside scope.

A firm scope will yield benefit all the way through your project. However, scope is often difficult for business staff to articulate, unless you provide a framework or process.

Once you have a clear scope, you understand the area for investigation and automation, so you can progress to feasibility study.

3.2.1 Special note on scope and feasibility within a wider framework

This chapter addresses scope and feasibility because they are so important to your evaluation project. Bear in mind that scope, feasibility and project authorisation interact. Also, the scoping, feasibility and business case may be outside your specific evaluation work because your governance, IT strategy or project approval mechanisms cover them. (For the interaction of this evaluation method with other approaches, download the article from the supporting BCS page at www.bcs.org/offtheshelfextras.)

3.3 DETERMINING SCOPE

Since a scope statement confirms what can be investigated by a project, it should be top priority for any new project. Yet, unclear, badly delineated scope is surprisingly common – and highly damaging. It is a common reason for projects failing to meet expectations (Frese and Sauter, 2003).

When determining scope, it is important to agree aspects both **inside** your project and those that lie **outside**. Therefore, by definition, coverage involves constraints. These are things that your project must recognise and respect, but not change.

Before the scoping phase, some exclusion may have been fed into your project as a constraint. An example is an incumbent solution (one of your own, or possibly at a major supplier) that must **not** be replaced by the new project, but will require data feeds as part of an interface from your new software. However, additional exclusions will definitely be a worthy output from the scoping process – see Section 3.4.3.

Agreeing scope involves drawing boundaries. The project needs to be clear on where its boundaries lie – for instance between territories, divisions or departments to be covered or not, products or services to be included or excluded and the business processes to be automated or left alone.

Note the distinction between project scope and functional scope. Project scope (such as managing organisational change) will be wider than the functions automated by the new software product. It is crucial that people working in the project understand so. The relevance to this book is that the evaluation process concentrates on the **technology**, but other activities will cover organisational impact – the **people** and **processes**. These 'soft' aspects still need to be addressed within the project, or the hard and soft areas should be addressed under a common governance structure (see Chapter 13).

EXECUTIVE PERSPECTIVE: A FINANCIAL IT SPECIALIST'S EXPERIENCE OF FORMAL SCOPING

Back in 2008, when our company was relatively small, we decided to replace our fragmented business systems with a new ERP system. Time was short, the budget was tight and – as we urgently required a solution – we selected an ERP system that fit our budget and met our basic requirements at the time. Within three years, our company had grown significantly and we found that our ERP system could no longer cope with the demand.

We realised that the first system selection lacked long-term consideration for business strategy and forecasted growth. In addition, we didn't properly evaluate the functionality that was required across the business and the integration between the various parts of the organisation. We therefore agreed to implement a more methodical and comprehensive evaluation, one that would look at both immediate and long-term requirements.

During formal consideration of project scope using the method here, the team spotted an opportunity to merge two selections and attempt to find one solution. We did so. A year later, supplier estimates showed the external cost with this approach would be roughly £18 million less over 10 years.

3.4 SCOPING WORKSHOPS

While scope is important, it is typically difficult for the prospective user community to agree 'how big' the project should be, or what areas it should cover. In practice, the boundaries between included and excluded areas tend to be fuzzy, and differ depending on who is speaking.

This is partly due to the length of some kinds of projects. For example, with enterprise software, you will probably be looking at a planning horizon of around 10 years. The thought of planning 10 years ahead, or the sheer size of some enterprise initiatives, can freeze even the best people.

Whatever the scale of the solution, a workshop is effective if fuzzy scope will damage a project that is critical to the organisation. This means that applying rigour should be based on the value of the project, not its cost or size.

The aim of a scoping workshop is to establish the scope boundary by asking one simple question, repeatedly, about many potential topics. This will engage stakeholders, and elicit knowledge of future states, the organisation, its processes, IT solutions and requirements. Almost without noticing, participants will determine the scope of your selection project (and possible other projects as a by-product).

3.4.1 Who should attend the scoping workshop?

You should seek a spread of attendees to represent different areas and to root your project in the organisation. They should be senior enough to have a perspective across the organisation.

It is difficult to be more specific about attendees, because you cannot exclude people by department if you do not yet know if the department will be affected by the scope of your project.

However, you will probably have insights about the people likely to be affected by your project. If you are having difficulty with your invitation list, formal stakeholder analysis will help (Eskerod and Jepson, 2013). Indeed, most formal project management methods actually mandate it.

The facilitator might be you, the project manager or someone external. They should combine meeting management with facilitation skills. They must be confident about using the spreadsheet software you will use during the meeting (see Figure 3.3), because participants will be watching live updates. However, they do not need to understand the full breadth or detail of your organisation – the participants hold that knowledge.

3.4.2 Preparing inputs to workshop

Levels of decision to take

The entries (subjects or topics) presented for the scope decision have different sizes or scale in terms of impact (shown in Figure 3.1).

Figure 3.1 Types of entries for scope decisions

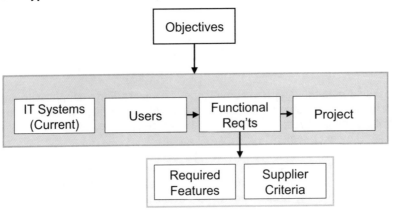

The highest level and largest decisions concern the **objectives** of the organisation, off-the-shelf solution or project. These will cascade from your organisation strategy, although your specific project may only support some of them.

Below this top level there are a group of related decisions of similar impact concerning:

- the current **IT systems** (hardware and software to be potentially replaced by this project);
- the type of **users** serviced by the new software;
- the major business **functions** that could be automated by the new solution;
- the **project** coverage (beyond IT processing) including supporting actions needed, such as process redesign.

At the lowest level of scale and impact are **required features** in the new off-the-shelf solution and the **supplier criteria** such as the calibre of the support they offer.

Scoping workshops operate best at the top and middle levels – this is fine-grained enough to be understandable, while the subjects are significant enough to shape your selection project. The lowest level is covered later in the project, by your requirements document (see Chapter 5).

WORKED EXAMPLE OF TOPIC LEVELS

This worked example is from a project at a fire service to evaluate new software for training management – both course administration and content management.

Referring to Figure 3.1 and the list that follows, one **O** entry will have several **I**, **U**, **F** and **P** entries. There should be consistency between them – for example, if one **function** concerned booking a course, you would expect one of the **user** groups to be course administrators.

O	Must support a safer place to work, including observing legal directives.
I	Existing web-based service for holding and distributing health and safety material.
	[Need to decide if this project replaces it, or it stays, probably with an interface.]
U x4	Health and safety officers.
	Firefighters.
	Course Directors.
	Course Administrators.
F	Track course content, so that staff know what H&S training material is available and they get the latest version, unless they actively seek a superseded one.
	[**What** to do.] [There will be other related **F** entries.]
P x2	Ensure our quality scheme registration is aware of our project and receives an up-to-date list of our courses that embed H&S material.
	Educate towards safety mentality, if not prevailing.
	[These are not criteria for selecting an IT solution. They appear as part of a consistency check, perhaps revealing that some users were missing, or the health and safety officers.]
R	Automatic numbering and supersession to manage version control of material, at course and module level.
	[**How** it is done.] [There will be other related **S** entries.]
S	The supplier's training courses must cover managing documents that are authored outside our new solution, but referenced by it.

Preparing workshop input lists

Depending on project size and risk, you should prepare a list of 50–150 topics, across the top two levels, with a mix of the five types **O**, **I**, **U**, **F** and **P**. These entries come from multiple sources.

- Any documentation with reasons the project started – see Chapter 1, Section 1.4.
- Studying documentation on objectives, such as your marketing, organisational strategy or IT strategy plans.
- The experience of team members and other subject matter experts.
- Prior projects, perhaps including lists from earlier scoping workshops.
- By reverse engineering publicly available material on software products (to turn major features or module lists into topics of potential interest).

You should not agonise over these topics. There should some deliberate redundancy because it reduces risk, and the workshop process is normally self-cleansing and self-directing. If you add an irrelevant topic, it will be excluded – scoped out. If you miss one, a workshop attendee will normally prompt you from their experience, when triggered by a related entry, or sometimes by an unrelated one.

3.4.3 The workshop process

The overall objectives of a scoping workshop are to determine project coverage, as well as to engage stakeholders and to improve 'buy-in' (organisational acceptance). The objective of the workshop process is to avoid the attendees freezing when presented with a blank scoping canvas. Making a 'swarm of small decisions' is safer and easier than making one large decision. In this context, 'lots of little guesses' are less risky than 'one big guess'.

You may need an address by a very senior stakeholder to open the meeting and introduce the project. This depends on how well the workshop attendees know each other and how close they are to the project. Alternatively, you may need something circulated in advance.

You should brief the group on the project context and status. Explain your workshop objectives and process. To heighten credibility and understanding, cover the sources of the topics on your input list (especially the study of best practice) without showing the detail.

The conceptual diagram at Figure 3.2 may help you to explain the process. The X marks are a 'cloud of points' representing the topics. If you can establish (see top right) three topics that are in, out and (just) out of scope, you can draw one segment of the scope line. Continuing this process eventually establishes the scope boundary. It is like the story of carving an elephant by starting with a block of stone, and cutting away everything that does not look like an elephant (Rahaman, 2002).

Decision-making cycle

Workshop attendees are invited to allocate the topics from your input list into one of three classifications:

- **In scope:** we will investigate and include this in the new IT solution, subject to technical feasibility, organisational requirements and cost.

Figure 3.2 Conceptual diagram of process to establish scope boundary

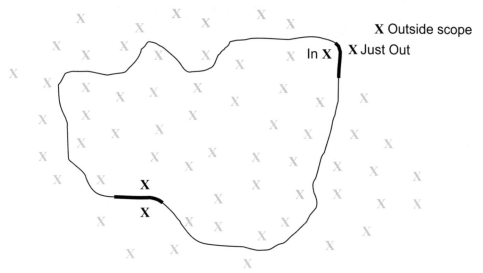

- **Not needed:** this is not required anywhere in the organisation within our planning horizon.

- **Another project:** necessary for the organisation, but outside the scope of our own project.

In the spreadsheet (Figure 3.3), these can be shortened to **In**, **No need** and **Other** to make the values visually distinct. Also, you should have extra work-in-progress values including **Refer** (follow up with someone outside the workshop) and **TBD** (to be determined, the initial value for all entries).

Note the 'rejections' into **No need** and **Other** are important. The scoping process is probably not finished until you can agree some areas as outside scope that were not established as such before the workshop. If every entry is deemed in, you are not in a position to draw a line.

Flexible content

It is important to recognise that the start-up list at the beginning of your workshop is simply the start-up agenda and not a constraint upon the workshop. New topics (potential areas of coverage) will be triggered by the debate. Each new area should be added to your spreadsheet and subject to the normal triage mechanism.

Finishing the meeting

When you have made the first pass, reached the end of your list and triaged all entries, you need to go through a final review. A good final review is to filter the list to show the three outcomes separately – In, Not, Another. Seeing an entry alongside its peers might trigger further debate and a few adjustments to classification.

Figure 3.3 Spreadsheet for scoping workshop with drop-down triage values

Agreed	Type	Title		Ref	Reqts Section
In	Obj	Reduce product liability risk		10	Introduction
In	User	Users - customer services		20	Introduction
In	User	Users - engineering		30	Introduction
In	User	Users - PMO		40	Introduction
In	User	Users - sales & business development		50	Introduction
In	Func	Sales Contract Management		60	Marketing
In	Func	Service Contract Management		70	Marketing
No need	Func	Call Centre		80	Marketing
In	Func	Sales Configurator		90	Marketing
In	Func	Event Management		100	Marketing
In	Func	Organisation (partner) details / contact (people) details		110	Marketing
Other	Func	Risk assessment & risk management during tenders		120	Marketing
In	Func	Contracts including versions & revisions		130	Marketing
In	Func	Sales order invoicing		140	Marketing
In	Reqt	History log of letters, calls & appointments		150	Marketing
TBD	Func	Enquiry, quotation, costing, proposal		160	Marketing
In	nc	Sales cycle management including prospecting		170	Marketing
No need	eqt	Standard price lists (tariffs)		180	Marketing
Other	nc	Customer details		190	Marketing
Refer	nc	CAD model control		200	Lifecycle
✓ TBD	nc	Engineering Change Management		210	Lifecycle
TBD	Func	Asset Data Management		220	Lifecycle
TBD	Func	PDM Configuration		230	Lifecycle
TBD	Func	Other design processes - changes/modifications		240	Lifecycle

There may be a few entries you cannot process as group, but make a provisional decision (best guess) and a note to escalate them for ratification.

3.4.4 Outputs from scoping workshop

Generally, the output from your scoping workshop will simply be the following three lists:

- Those topics that will be included within scope.

- Those topics explicitly excluded.

- Those areas that are to be tackled by another project.

Check the lists back to the reasons for starting the project and reconcile any inconsistencies you find. As part of stakeholder management and gathering support for your project, it is important to circulate these lists and invite comment. They should be distributed not only to workshop attendees, but also more widely. The more senior the people that you can get to comment, the better.

Check your scope is acceptable to your sponsor now, if in place, or as soon as they are appointed. Either escalate the lists to the senior management team, or get your sponsor to explain the process and stress the scope is now formally agreed.

EXECUTIVE PERSPECTIVE: A DIRECTOR'S EXPERIENCE OF EARLY, FORMAL CONSULTATION

The most successful changes start with winning the hearts and minds of people. I sponsored the implementation of a new set of business tools and wanted to start engaging people early. This methodology met that need as people were asked their opinion at the very start of the process.

I soon found that many of the most vocal, and historically those people most resistant to change, became the greatest advocates for the solution chosen. This is because they felt that they were instrumental in making the change, rather than it being done to them.

Harnessing the intellectual power within the business also produced a far better understanding for what was needed by the business than anything I could have produced in isolation.

3.5 STUDYING COSTS AND FEASIBILITY

Once scope is clear and formalised, you can progress to any necessary feasibility study. Remember, this chapter assumes feasibility is addressed within your evaluation project (see Section 3.2).

You can treat feasibility under four headings: strategic, technical, economic and organisational.

Although they interact, it is often best to consider them in this order, since the earlier dimensions shape the later ones. The order does not imply descending importance – it is simply logistically easier to sequence your investigation this way.

After these considerations, you will need authorisation to commit, given competition for resources of funds and time (see Section 3.5.5).

3.5.1 Strategic

The strategic questions will again refer back to any project terms of reference, plus the existing marketing, organisational strategy and IT strategy plans. Strategic questions include:

- Is the new project a strategic fit?
- Does it align with the intended direction of the organisation?
- Is it appropriate to our current or planned size and international presence?
- Is the project looking far enough ahead, given the rate of change and the lead-time to implement?
- Have we looked across other industries or sectors for ideas? Have we studied best practice? (See Chapter 4, Section 4.4)

Such questions typically inform the decision as to whether you should be going ahead with a proposed project at all. A surprising number of projects are instigated after an off-the-cuff conversation when a senior manager and a formal or informal IT person bump into each other. Personal enthusiasm by a senior individual for some new software does not mean official sanction for a project. Where an executive champions a project that aligns with individual goals, but not necessarily with the strategy of the whole organisation, this is better termed a pet project (Axelos, 2012).

The considerations of strategic fit will not only inform the decision to go ahead, but will also have a major impact on the people who are affected by the project. They also shape the next dimension, the technical feasibility, because you now have a clearer idea of what you are actually attempting to automate.

3.5.2 Technical

There are several critical questions about the technology area.

- Do off-the-shelf solutions exist in the software space of interest?
- Is this a vertical market with mature players and a range of providers, ideally including companies and individuals who are independent of the original software author?
- Are we sure, given our likely deal size, that we will be an attractive prospect to suppliers? Given the marketplace, might we be dealing direct with the software author? Or would we be dealing with a local reseller?

Establishing that there is likely to be an off-the-shelf solution with interested suppliers has a major impact on the shape and feasibility of your project.

3.5.3 Economic

An off-the-shelf solution reduces the costs and therefore improves the affordability of the new software. You are now ready to ask questions about the financial impact.

- Can we afford it, given the rough estimates of cost? (See feasibility costing in the sub-section that follows.)
- Are we expecting financial benefits such as cost reduction, as well as non-financial benefits?
- Is the solution cost justified?
- Does our cash flow allow us to contract as soon as we have selected the preferred supplier?
- Do we need to phase the purchase?

Feasibility costing

When compiling your feasibility costing, the first important decision is whether this will be created only with internal expertise without reference to suppliers, or whether you approach the marketplace now for supplier input to joint figures.

Internal costing involves knowledgeable people in your organisation compiling their best estimate of the hardware, software, services and expenses costs for both the project itself, and the solution that it eventually procures.

Joint costing involves the project manager (or an early evaluation team member) establishing costing parameters and contacting some suppliers for their estimates. The suppliers are ones that you believe to be representative. Their figures can never, of course, be contractually binding, but their informed guess is better than yours.

In return, as a thank you, you offer a place on your longlist – although this is not actually much of a concession as they take their chances alongside other candidates, and they would probably be longlisted anyway. At least 'the costing candidates' get early warning of your project.

In order to make such costings as accurate as possible (however high-level and roughly estimated they are), you should control as many of the variables as possible. Not all variables will be applicable to all candidates' suppliers. However, it is better to have a standard estimating harness, where they ignore any parameters that do not apply to their pricing model.

- For instance, you would nearly always establish the number of users or seats that will be required on the new solution.

- You will indicate broadly the scope of supply, such as the departments covered or the high-level business processes to be automated, so that the suppliers can map this onto their list of products or optional software modules.

- To be safe, state the number of currencies, languages and countries to be covered, because some software pricing models are affected by these cross-border considerations.

- Request likely extra license costs for any new database software. The solution will normally sit on a bought-in database and the candidates may be resellers of it, so they know the list price.

- You might include requests for typical hardware costs, such as extra servers to run a conventional installation of an 'on-premises package' (unless the machine capacity is a general overhead rather than specific to your project).

- Request list prices for obligatory maintenance charges – the recurring subscription cost or a percentage of initial software cost paid annually. Over 10 years this forms the largest portion of the lifetime cost – at 20 per cent, you buy the software anew every five years.

- Request list prices for support costs. If you know your needs, state whether you need 9–5 Monday–Friday helpdesk cover, or 24x7.

- Request very rough estimates of services costs for implementation support, training, data migration, project management (if resourced externally) and possibly writing interfaces. (Or use a standard multiplier, such as service cost at a 2:1 or 5:1 ratio of software spend.)

Some initial business cases are based purely on the costs of the external supply, with no accounting for internal resource costs. This means that the business case understates the cost and impact. Establish whether you need to factor in the opportunity cost of internal labour diverted to your project. What internal charge-out rates apply to staff working on in-house projects? Your organisation may even have a formula for calculating the equivalent money cost of risk, or the opportunities lost while focused on the new solution project.

Once you are more confident that the project will go ahead, and off-the-shelf software is feasible and affordable, you can move on to considering the impact of implementing the software product on the organisation.

3.5.4 Organisational

While listed fourth in this section, the organisational dimension is usually more important than the economic dimension. However, it is simply easier to assess the organisational impact of the project after you have considered the other dimensions and have a better understanding of the shaping forces of strategy, technology and affordability. Questions concerning the organisational dimension include:

- Are we organisationally ready to tackle this project, with relevant skills, resources and approvals?
- What are the internal resource implications where organisational change is needed? Should this be an element in our evaluation? Do we need to add internal cost to our economic feasibility?

Your organisational feasibility should also address cultural dimensions.

- Can we change to get the benefit of the new solution?
- Can we change our processes, our reporting lines, our accountabilities, our relationships and possibly our mindsets?

NOTE ON ALTERNATIVE SEQUENCES TO INVESTIGATE DIMENSIONS

Of course, it is possible to research the headings above in a different order. In some situations, the organisational dimension might be the one to consider first.

- Culturally, is this the sound thing for you to do?
- Ethically, is this the right thing for you to do?
- Are you organisationally ready to do it – now?
- If not, what do you have to do to get ready for the technology and process change?

3.5.5 Stop/go decision

Having discussed, documented and circulated findings against the four dimensions of feasibility, the senior management team are in a position to make a stop-go decision about your project. There is often a standard approval mechanism with a specific proposal form such as a project initiation document (PID) or authorisation request (see Section 3.8). Approval usually involves iterations and successive refinement of the submissions.

Note that this work, including estimating costs, is an educational process. As well as getting the project approved, it will have benefits later: you will ask smarter questions of interviewees during the requirements capture (see Chapter 4); you will also create a better RFI with more measurable questions that find the differences between candidates (see Chapter 7).

3.6 ESTABLISHING PROJECT PHASES

As part of agreeing scope, it may be wise (even necessary) to establish at a very high level some project phases.

An important technique is to break down your project into 'minimum success units'. This means you can have a roadmap of the entire project, but still have a clear idea of the first steps. It may mean that you plan, in a very large project or programme, to improve automation in particular departments or countries first. It may mean that you intend to install certain foundations, such as the financial module, before you install the processing that depends upon it. Even without a software product in mind, there will be some dependencies in the information flows. Usually, staff in Sales cannot raise a sales order for a brand new customer before credit checks by Finance.

Even before you study specific products in the marketplace, it is highly beneficial to educate yourself. Improve your understanding as to the types of processing you can buy off-the-shelf, or consult a subject matter expert. This will help you to match solution capabilities with the needs of your organisation, and to recognise inter-dependencies within the project or the solution. These inter-dependencies might influence how you sequence multiple evaluations or multiple project phases.

There is a blunt but expressive question in IT project management: Would you rather have your name on a small project medal or a large career gravestone?

Once your scope is clearer, you may realise that other projects may affect yours. This is often about relative timing, or data availability. This chapter cannot begin to address the disciplines of coordinating across projects, but can only mention the fields of Programme Management and Portfolio Management (Axelos, 2012).

3.7 THE EXECUTIVE SPONSOR

A crucial aspect of setting up or initiating any project is to secure the senior or executive sponsor. Normally, they are the most important person on your project (James et al., 2013).

The executive sponsor is 'the main driving force behind a programme or project ... equates to executive or senior responsible owner (SRO)' (Axelos, 2012).

The role of the sponsor is to ensure that resources are allocated and to monitor outcomes. The following summary of their contribution is taken from *The Sponsorship Checklist* (James et al., 2014):

- provides direction and guidance for strategies and initiatives;
- works with the project manager to develop the project charter;
- identifies and quantifies business benefits to be achieved by successful implementation;
- negotiates funding for the project;
- makes stop-go decisions;
- evaluates the project's success upon completion.

You can see that it is not the sponsor's role to supervise the detail of the project process.

Inconveniently, scoping and sponsorship interact. There may be a couple of iterations to establish both the agreed scope and the appointed sponsor.

For example, you may have to address circular dependencies: you may need a sponsor before the scoping workshop to allocate resource in the sense of inviting attendees with some authority; alternatively, the scoping workshop will make it clear from the coverage who your sponsor must be.

Again, like the invitees to your workshop, rigid guidelines are rarely necessary because the ideal sponsor is often obvious. It is securing them to service the project that can be the tricky part. It helps greatly if the organisation understands – or can be made to understand – the impact of effective project sponsorship (PMI, 2006).

3.8 PROJECT INITIATION OR TERMS OF REFERENCE

Usually, the most important document associated with scoping is the 'project terms of reference' (ToR) document. An alternative name is the 'project initiation document' (PID), which is the term in PRINCE2 (Prince2.Com, 2014).

You should view this as an agreement (a word with better connotations than contract) that has been forged between your project and your organisation. Some generic examples of the project dimensions to cover include the following:

- business case, featuring objectives, major deliverables and expected benefits;
- project approach and controls, including boundaries for the project and limits on authority for its people;
- locations covered, with work or business areas excluded;
- roles and responsibilities, especially for the project manager and project sponsor;
- communications, points of contact, team structure and reporting lines;

- initial project plan or schedule, possibly supported by work breakdown structure (WBS), milestone plan, decision points or Gantt chart;
- risk management, statements and assessment, usually with the necessary mitigating steps, a formal risk plan or supporting FMEA – failure mode effects analysis (Stunell, 2014);
- staff hours expected, often termed (human) resource requirements, possibly with soft staff allocations and initial resource estimates (forecasts, histograms or impact statements, such as new staff or contractors needed);
- monetary cost and revenue estimates, maybe with cash flow forecasts;
- exception conditions, such as handling the implications of external events, for instance the response if seconded staff are pulled back to their original role;
- applicable standards for, say, documentation or budgetary control;
- outstanding actions, such as feasibility study results awaited or risk reduction actions in progress;
- various recorded approvals and authorisations, such as budget allocations, permissions to allocate/recruit staff and nominated signatories for the project stop/go decision.

Note the distinction between **project** terms of reference (or PID) and **personal** terms of reference for people contributing to your project – perhaps seconded evaluation team members. Project terms of reference may be the parent of a set, shaping agreements that are more individual for the most significant contributors. For instance, the project terms may give outline project dates, while the individual documents may guarantee any seconded person their old job back at the date representing the end of the selection project.

Separately, there may also be 'cascading' terms recording commercial agreements (such as responsibilities or expenses policy) for external consultants who are advising your selection project.

3.9 LAUNCH EVENTS

Change management should start right at the very, very beginning of any major IT project – if not sooner. When the selection project is becoming well formed, your organisation needs to be updated with intentions and reassurances.

One way is a launch event or, even on the largest projects, a series of launch events such as a road show. This gains support or 'buy-in'. Events must feature, and preferably be led by, the project's executive sponsor.

An alternative (or supporting) approach is a series of low-profile personal chats with a wide sample of stakeholders, both senior and junior. This may appear labour-intensive, but can be extremely effective, especially if a project is controversial. The meeting participants can discuss sensitive issues more freely when in very small groups or one-to-one.

3.10 CHAPTER SUMMARY

TAKE-AWAY POINTS

People involved in IT projects sometimes complain that the customer moved the goalposts. The scoping exercise during project initiation is all about making sure you have marked out the pitch before you begin to play the game.

Major software solutions that cut across organisational boundaries – often referred to as enterprise software – have a complex life cycle. There are many places where the project can go wrong. The earlier you get it wrong, the more likely it is that your whole project fails, so it is important to set off in the right direction.

Scope shapes everything.

- the people involved – departments, the sponsor, the supervising management group and the interview list;
- the high-level requirements;
- supply parameters for the candidate vendors, such as which of their software products are candidates, or which modules are relevant within a large solution that has many optional components;
- the budget, which is likely to be higher if a large number of departments will benefit from the new solution, and therefore the affordability of what the project delivers.

During the project, it is important to refer back to your agreed scope as part of defending against scope creep.

3.10.1 The next chapter

Now you know the scope and have strong foundations – an authorised project – the next chapter will guide you through the set-up of the interview programme and capturing requirements.

3.11 REFERENCES

Axelos (2012) 'Common glossary'. Global Best Practice Portfolio, AXELOS. www.axelos.com/glossaries-of-terms.aspx (10 November 2014).

Eskerod, P. and Jepsen, A. (2013) *Project stakeholder management*. Gower: Farnham.

Frese, R. and Sauter, V. (2003) 'Project success and failure: What is success, what is failure, and how can you improve your odds for success?'. UMSL, University of Missouri – St Louis. www.umsl.edu/~sauterv/analysis/6840_f03_papers/frese (10 November 2014).

James, V., Rosenhead, R. and Taylor, P. (2013) *Strategies for project sponsorship*. Management Concepts Press: Tysons Corner.

James, V., Rosenhead, R. and Taylor, P. (2014) 'Strategies for project sponsorship: The sponsorship checklist'. WordPress. http://strategies4sponsors.com (10 November 2014).

PMI (2006) 'Executive guide to project management'. Project Management Institute. www.pmi.org/~/media/PDF/Publications/PMIEXEC06.ashx (10 November 2014).

Prince2.Com (2014) 'Sample project initiation document'. PRINCE2 Download Centre, ILX Group. www.prince2.com/downloads (10 November 2014).

Rahaman, V. (2002) 'The man who could see elephants.' The Free Library, Farlex. www.thefreelibrary.com/The+man+who+could+see+elephants.-a092724641 (10 November 2014).

Stunell, P. (2014) 'Failure mode effects analysis (FMEA)'. Stunell Technology. www.stunell.com/fmea-training (10 November 2014).

3.12 FURTHER READING

3.12.1 Books and articles

Association For Project Management (2012) *APM body of knowledge*, 6th edition. APM: Princes Risborough.

Blackstaff, M. (2012) *Finance for IT decision makers: A practical handbook*, 3rd edition. BCS, The Chartered Institute for IT: Swindon.

Morgan, J. and Dale, C. (2013) *Managing IT projects for business change: From risk to success*. BCS, The Chartered Institute for IT: Swindon. (Particularly the chapter on stakeholder management.)

Pacelli, L. (2009) 'Great sponsor + great PM = great success: Ten truths of an effective sponsor/PM partnership'. Project Smart. www.projectsmart.co.uk/great-sponsor-great-pm=great-success.php (10 November 2014).

Paul, D., Cadle, J. and Yeates, D. (2014) *Business analysis*, 3rd edition. BCS, The Chartered Institute for IT: Swindon. (Particularly chapters 'Making a Business' and 'Financial Case'.)

3.12.2 Related formats by download

From http://shop.bcs.org/offtheshelfextras.asp a scoping workshop input spreadsheet – format to present the list of entries for triage – and sizing questionnaire to scope a software selection project and establish the likely sophistication of the off-the-shelf solution.

4 REQUIREMENTS ANALYSIS: CAPTURING THE ORGANISATIONAL NEEDS

'A new idea is delicate. It can be killed by a sneer or a yawn; it can be stabbed to death by a quip and worried to death by a frown on the right man's brow.'

Ovid (43BC–AD17)

4.1 WHAT YOU CAN LEARN FROM THIS CHAPTER

- Understand the critical differences between collecting requirements for software construction as opposed to requirements for a software product selection. This especially applies if you (or your organisation) normally capture requirements to be passed to programmers to construct bespoke software.

- Be aware of some of the appropriate techniques for requirements definition, and how they affect stakeholders.

4.2 OVERVIEW

Requirements are crucial to all IT projects. Most projects fail because of non-technical complexity – meaning human factors rather than the technologies involved (Krigsman, 2007). The most enduring explanation for IT project failure remains poor communication. This shows up in poor requirements definition and the consequent poor management of expectations (IT Cortex, 2014).

Defining requirements is vitally important to software selection projects. The requirements-capture interviews and workshops set people's expectations for your project and provide important learning for the participants, as they are asked to think about precisely what they want, and as they find out about the capabilities of the technology. The requirements definition process is therefore also an important contribution to stakeholder management, because people are being consulted.

4.2.1 Requirements are essential

The fact that a solution is off-the-shelf does not mean that you can abandon the process of thinking about what you want. You must not become a passive consumer of technology, bowled over by the 'wow factor' at demonstrations. You must stay in control of what constitutes a good feature for your organisation. Your requirements provide the anchor for this stability.

However, requirements for a selection project need to be articulated in a different manner from a specification for software construction. You need to concentrate on the 'what' rather than the 'how' – objectives and outcomes, rather than the detailed processing. For instance, it is a waste of effort (as well as perhaps reflecting an inappropriate attitude) to create screen or report layouts.

Requirements capture is a huge topic, so this and the following chapter can only attempt to address some of the specific knowledge about defining requirements when selecting off-the-shelf solutions. There is an entire discipline referred to as Requirements Engineering, and many books on the skills required of a business or systems analyst. Section 4.11 has some excellent books on these topics.

Note that this chapter concentrates on the process of gathering requirements, whereas Chapter 5 focuses on writing them up for selections. If you are reading chapters of this book in step with your project stages, it is best to read both Chapters 4 and 5 together. The target requirements documentation may inform your manner of requirements capture, such as how you organise your notes.

EXECUTIVE PERSPECTIVE: A PROJECT MANAGER'S EXPERIENCE OF FORMAL REQUIREMENTS CAPTURE

I was first introduced to this selection process by a colleague who had used the method for a different project. As the project manager for the selection of a global internet portal solution to replace a manual process, I was faced with many challenges:

- Coordinating a team of stakeholders from several European countries with local autonomy.
- Merging requirements from varying levels of process maturity.
- Lack of a common vision for the ultimate solution.

While the evaluation team members were already aware of some of the company politics, what made the real difference was the systematic method we followed.

The project team were able to agree a common set of global requirements very quickly. The method had the effect of breaking down inter-cultural barriers. Good documentation and clarity of progress supported a consistent interpretation of the requirements and kept all members engaged and motivated. The less mature parts of the organisation were represented fairly rather than being outvoted by their more mature counterparts.

I was also able to concentrate on managing the project and the team, knowing the content was being taken care of by the method. I had great confidence in the stakeholders agreeing the ultimate decision, since the requirements and weightings had been agreed through consensus, forming a solid basis of decision.

A structured approach was critical in selling the project internally to management for release of funding for the next phase. The team were able to provide evidence that due diligence had been carried out on the decision reached.

4.3 SOME CAUTIONARY NOTES ON REQUIREMENTS CAPTURE

4.3.1 Manage expectations about meeting requirements

Capturing a requirement during an interview or workshop should not be a promise that the requirement will be met. It may not be supported in the off-the-shelf solutions, or may involve optional modules at an unaffordable cost. (Indeed, you might find that there is no solution worth buying, although you will handle that exception later.)

Therefore, it is important that you manage expectations when asking people what they want. Let them know that you may not be able to deliver everything. Most people will recognise that an off-the-shelf solution will never be a perfect fit, but it is better if you declare this early to avoid doubt.

Notwithstanding, your eventual requirement statements can legitimately aim for the stars – if you never test the solutions against the most demanding requirements, you will never know which solutions come closest to a perfect fit.

4.3.1 Sufficiency beats perfection

Defining requirements is an iterative process and an imperfect one. You cannot expect perfect understanding, but you can seek clarity and consistency. It is important to conduct the exercise to understand those requirements that **can** be captured. Many requirements are emerging ones – not known before starting the process, but teased out by conversations. Not all requirements can be captured – for instance, because they will emerge in the future as appetite for the available solutions increases with better understanding of fit. Ultimately, both the requirements and evaluation phases of the method are sampling techniques.

Consistently, throughout the 50 projects that have used this method to date, candidate solutions that fit the requirements known during the evaluation have also coped well when new requirements were presented to the successful candidate after installation. This should not really be a surprise, since candidates that fit well to a comprehensive requirements statement usually have sophisticated processing, a rich data structure and good flexibility (they are highly configurable). These qualities will all help a newly installed solution to 'roll with the punches' when new needs emerge.

4.4 STUDYING BEST PRACTICE

This is an optional but recommended step. It will allow you to ask smarter questions in requirements interviews by asking people if specific facilities would help them. Note, it may have been done earlier or at a higher level as part of justifying the project (see Chapter 3, Section 3.2). If so, you will pick up those points and agree whether it is justified to look deeper or wider.

Looking across other industries or sectors for ideas is well established in strategic thinking. Studying best practice can also help preview your future. Other industries may be a template if they have automated their work because they used to have high labour costs and organisational risks (like yours now).

Within the case studies of other organisations, you might find inspiration for interview questions and proposals. Try to formulate thought-provoking questions that will get people thinking. You might call it requirement clarification by provocation. For example:

- A well-funded organisation in a related sector has adopted radical automation. Do you think this could work for us? In what circumstances? What would be the obstacles? Does it fit our organisational strategy?

- You might decide to ask a member of your finance team whether the organisation could remove the cross-charge mechanism. What would happen to invoicing?

- Another common technique is basic but effective – propose dropping some of the routine reports. Often, reports are created and dutifully filed, but have not been studied for years.

4.5 CAPTURING REQUIREMENTS

Requirements definition is the foundation for all future selection work. If poorly managed, it is a cause of project failure (Frese and Sauter, 2003). Therefore, you should not risk a single point of failure by sticking to one type of source, a single interviewee or one technique. You are trying to understand the organisation at different levels, both the strategic and operational. You are also accommodating multiple perspectives, from the mindset of 'the plodder' or 'slogger' to that of 'the dreamer'. You need a range of techniques. The main ones you should consider follow below.

4.5.1 Digest existing documentation

To read your way into a project, organisation and requirements, study existing documentation, including these sources:

- Relevant senior management documents in your organisation, such as the vision, mission or organisational strategy statements, the marketing plan or the IT strategy.

- Any existing statements of requirement that are available, such as memos about the project or senior management meeting notes that refer to strategic direction or high-level requirements.

- Documentation about existing IT solutions, business processes and procedures. If available, these are the best start point to understand cross-departmental linkages and responsibilities. They often also articulate aspects of the organisation that are unique, which will therefore test the candidates because they demand unusual processing.

- Output from the 'old' (current or incumbent) solution, such as reports that the staff consider useful.

- Lessons from previous comparable projects. (If these are not actually written up, talk to people who were involved.)

Remember when processing 'current' material you are extracting goals and requirements, not detailed descriptions of the incumbent processing. Your eventual requirements statements will concentrate on stating what needs to be achieved, not specifying processing.

4.5.2 Work shadowing

By observing existing systems and procedures, you can identify problems where the information processing is inadequate. Interviewing for requirements at a participant's desk often gives insights. People obliged to augment (or even circumvent) the current information system are indicators. For instance:

- A data capture form where people write in the margin almost certainly lacks important information fields.

- If a person routinely sits down with a printed computer report and a highlighter pen, it means the selection criteria are not good enough.

- If people repeatedly extract information to spreadsheets and manually type or paste extra information to complete the analysis, it yells that the information system is in trouble. This can be the most serious sign of deficiency. People working on screen are less visibly augmenting the incumbent software. Worse, the spreadsheet can be viewed as the solution, rather than the symptom. It is mistakenly interpreted as work automation. It is not, because it constantly requires the operator.

However, as a note of caution about the unintended impact of direct observation, you should be aware of your own effect as an interviewer or observer. Sometimes called the Hawthorne Effect or Observer Effect (Shuttleworth, 2009), watching people while they work can be an intrusive and misleading method. If people feel they are being monitored, it can alter both their behaviour and their performance levels, so you may get a distorted view of processing and therefore the IT requirements.

Because you are capturing requirements for an off-the-shelf solution, ensure descriptions of current IT (say incumbent screens) concentrate on their information content, benefits or shortcomings. Remember you will not be specifying identical replacements.

4.5.3 One-to-one interviews

Individual interviews allow people to cover specialist topics that will not interest a group. Also, interviewees can speak more freely about any concerns and you can gain support for your project with frank answers.

4.5.4 Small workshops

An advantage of the workshop is that you can consult a larger number of people and make efficient use of their time. You may put together functional groups, such as all the regional managers, or you may have a mixed group within one department or function, with representatives of different roles or seniority – for instance field engineers and their corresponding office-based administrators.

4.5.5 Standard requirements

In your finished requirements document (see Chapter 5) there should be some standard or 'imported' requirements, which were not requested by interviewees. You will have extracted them from a formal or informal 'library' of standard requirements that are based on previous projects. Alternatively, they may have come from your best practice research. Some examples are:

- Hardware and software guidelines from your IT department. These improve compatibility with the IT estate.

- Legislation you must recognise. Sometimes fundamental restraints are so 'obvious' that nobody mentions them.

- The impact and cost of organisational change. If this is an element in your evaluation, the wording will be vital. You want to reveal if one product has more or less impact. Your project also needs to decide if less impact is good or bad.

- You might require a solution to have a mature 'eco-system' surrounding it, such as books, training courses, independent consultants and events. This means that your eventual supplier does not monopolise those resources, and either you or they can tap into it. You are likely to go back to this 'well' repeatedly over the years and it does not hurt for the supplier to know that there is competition.

Including standard requirements is a sensible approach. It is protected from bias or accusations of 'nannying' because the process is effectively self-cleansing. If you arbitrarily create a requirements entry that is inappropriate to your organisation or your current project, your weighting meeting will remove the entry (see Chapter 5).

4.5.6 Requirements for services as well as software

Requirements reflect the software type and specific service provision. For instance, your project might have agreed at Initiation stage that a strategic requirement was to go for the cloud, SaaS or subscription model. Alternatively, your evaluation may be of solutions that are inherently cloud-based, such as cloud brokering or cloud enabling (Rouse, 2013).

In these circumstances, you will have many more criteria that address **services**, such as service level agreements (SLAs). It is normal to expect a mix of software product and supplier attributes in the requirements list. If your cloud subscription would fund a combination of software capability, hardware provision and service functions (such as support), you should elicit more requirements about the supplier. You need to establish, say, the acceptable service level for availability or downtime.

Most dimensions of an SLA (capacity, uptime, response and fix times) are less a software product feature and more a supplier attribute. Another example is the opening hours for the help desk.

4.5.7 More information on analysis techniques

This chapter can only attempt to address some of the specifics of defining requirements when selecting off-the-shelf solutions. For more general information, techniques and guidelines for business analysis refer to Cadle et al. (2014). As well as more detail on the techniques above, this covers other supporting analysis approaches, such as surveys.

4.6 SELECTING INTERVIEWEES AND ORGANISING INTERVIEWS

4.6.1 Who – the list of interviewees

The interview programme should be organised to reflect the importance of organisational units by function, number of potential software users, stakeholder status or the size of the opportunity for improvements. The requirements definition process needs to identify and include the key users of the existing software – the acknowledged 'local experts' – irrespective of seniority. These are informal opinion leaders during software selections. If your consultation is seen to exclude them, your requirements definition will not be credible.

For your interview programme, you might exploit a RACI matrix, which stands for Responsible, Accountable, Consulted and Informed (Smith and Erwin, 2011). You can use this to track allocations to interview or workshops.

Alternatively, track interview involvement on a responsibility chart (see Chapter 14, Section 14.4). The strength of the responsibility chart is its ability to track multiple roles without multiple documents. You can also see an integrated view of the contribution by one individual, who may be an interviewee, and later a member of, say, the evaluation and negotiation teams.

Conceptually, the interview plan should 'take a diagonal slice' through the organisation. This means both different functions (crossing silos) and different levels of seniority.

While this is an organisational project not an IT project, it is legitimate (indeed, necessary) to include IT staff in the requirements-capture programme. They are also stakeholders, with requirements such as which database platform the solution should run on. They have to protect the IT estate, so will have technical requirements that ensure the new software product is 'well behaved'. In addition, IT staff are often well placed to put forward products for your longlist (see Chapter 6).

4.6.2 Organising workshop groups and one-to-one interviews

One thing to keep in mind when organising consultations is that senior people are usually best interviewed one-to-one, whereas more junior people tend to work better in small groups where they can support one another and bounce around ideas.

Senior people are often better questioned about the vision of the future. You must look forward, since the new solution will be in place for many years. Ensure your questions are informed by changes to the intended organisational strategy. For instance, there may be mergers on the horizon, or a significant scale change like a new office network.

These plans may not be widely known in the organisation – yet. However, while acting as business analyst to capture requirements, you need to know – now. You then need to think through articulating requirements from new initiatives without compromising commercial confidentiality. (The solution may be to simply state needs, without divulging rationale.)

Junior people are often better quizzed about operational requirements. Good IT support for low-level processing is essential to the productivity of the workforce. There is generally an enormous amount of tacit knowledge in any organisation that is actually hidden from the senior management team. You cannot afford to miss this knowledge. Otherwise, the people whose hands-on effort makes the organisation work will be set targets that can only be met by access to information without effective tools to retrieve it.

The broader coverage of the 'diagonal slice' also inherently mitigates risk. There is less chance that the requirements are dominated by the wrong people – perhaps a powerful individual or faction who almost obliterate other people's statements of need.

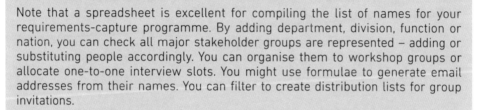

TECHNOLOGY FOR LIST OR MATRIX MANAGEMENT

Note that a spreadsheet is excellent for compiling the list of names for your requirements-capture programme. By adding department, division, function or nation, you can check all major stakeholder groups are represented – adding or substituting people accordingly. You can organise them to workshop groups or allocate one-to-one interview slots. You might use formulae to generate email addresses from their names. You can filter to create distribution lists for group invitations.

The spreadsheet is also a great vehicle to manage your RACI matrix or responsibility chart (see Section 4.6.1). As well as the list management above, you can integrate the interviewee role with other roles and visualise multiple contributions by one individual. You can filter to shortlist the people fulfilling one role, for instance to distribute an update email to this interest group.

4.6.3 Management commitment

You must get commitment from managers that their people will be allowed time to attend the requirements-capture meetings. This can be especially difficult for short contributions (perhaps as little as a few hours) where there is no formal secondment. You may encounter resistance to participate, often because people are worried about their job being eliminated by new IT.

People might book the meeting, but cancel at the last minute. You will need to chase to avoid no-shows, and probably offer rescheduled or follow-up meetings (say, joining another workshop in the requirements programme). Ideally – and especially for people who will make regular inputs to the new project – ensure that their proposed contribution is written into their annual targets and therefore becomes part of their appraisal.

If your requirements-capture exercise covers factories or call centres, it may be necessary to reflect shift working when scheduling meetings. Alternatively, the manager may have to organise shift cover or shift swaps to secure the interviewee or workshop attendee for your requirements-capture programme.

You may need to ask for work re-assignment. People may need 'back-filling' to release them. This means temporary workers, interns or trainees take over while more experienced staff attend the series of meetings.

ADJUSTING THE INTERVIEWEE LIST DURING THE PROGRAMME

Your requirements are shaped by your interviewees, so be sure your interview list (with its grouping to workshops) is a solid foundation. If one interviewee suggests that you have missed somebody important on your programme, you should usually seek permission to extend your interview list. To err on the side of caution do interview them, unless there is a compelling reason to exclude them.

Note some interviews are 'political', to engage stakeholders rather than seeking 'technical' content about requirements.

If you do miss somebody, make sure they get a copy of your draft requirements document with a personally worded invitation to digest it and send comments (see Chapter 5).

4.7 PREPARING ATTENDEES FOR INTERVIEWS OR WORKSHOPS

As part of organising the meetings, send out a standard information pack to brief invitees on what to expect. As well as general background on the project intentions and status, include the following specifics:

- You will be studying both the **operational system** (the organisation and what it delivers) and the **information system** that models it.

- This information system is not just the current software, but also every method of record keeping, including paper forms, visible record boards and spreadsheets. Most organisations can store information – piling paper forms randomly into cardboard boxes would do that. The difficulty with information is how it is classified during storage so that **retrieval** is timely, cost-effective and offers the relevant level of detail.

- Any current information system is to an extent the specification of its own replacement. It is like taking the blown car light bulb into a spares shop to get a replacement – one that works. When defining requirements for the new solution, it can be described rather simply as the current system **less** its problems **plus** business requirements. Problems and requirements are simply two sides of the same coin when articulating need.

- Make it clear that the new off-the-shelf solution will deliver more work automation than the current one, but will not look the same. The project aims to select capable processing off-the-shelf. It is not building an identical replacement.

- Encourage people to prepare for your meeting by: thinking about their needs; collecting samples (to illustrate good and bad); discussing issues with others in their area (so that they are an effective representative).

- Reassure attendees that they do not need to understand the technicalities of software to state their business needs for an off-the-shelf solution. They should concentrate on outputs, outcomes and goals, rather than whether something is technically feasible or affordable. The technology is your job, or at least the job of the evaluation team collaborating with candidate suppliers.

Unless you think it will look unhelpful, let interviewees know that documenting a requirement now cannot be a promise you will meet it (see Section 4.3). Alternatively, leave this point out of the briefing pack. When opening each meeting, address it verbally and in a friendly way.

4.8 PREVIEW OF LATER USE OF REQUIREMENTS

Most systematic methods or due diligence approaches come down to an 'investment-to-dividend' ratio, and a software product selection method is no different. To get the benefits, you first need to put in the work. Partly, your investment in process pays a high dividend because the benefits flow to a large number of people.

Accordingly, it may help to see – now – all the areas where your requirements-capture exercise will deliver benefits. These may include the following:

- The programme to capture requirements will familiarise evaluation team members with organisational processes. This is especially useful for prospective project members who are 'outsiders', such as staff who have been seconded from other departments, divisions or sites. Their 'induction by requirements' will pay benefits for the rest of your project.

- Because the method has multiple roles, such as evaluation team member or demonstration attendee, people will be constantly joining the project to make a defined, possibly short, contribution. Their experience in interviews or workshops means that they are not joining cold. See Chapters 5 to 13.

- The interview process necessarily introduces people to the project approach or method. This usually increases confidence in the process and therefore reassures people about the likelihood of success. See Chapter 13.

- The future evaluation team become more familiar with the other staff, through meeting them at interviews and workshops. This helps to identify (or confirm) key internal users, for instance those people who must attend the later product demonstrations, or the flag bearers for implementation. See Chapters 10 and 13.

- The requirements interviews and workshops engage stakeholders, which is a soft benefit that is incredibly difficult to measure, but enormously important. See Chapter 13.

- Requirements capture fundamentally informs your requirements document, which is the foundation of all subsequent phases. Overall, this will probably be the most important document created during your project. See Chapter 5.

- The requirements statements provide the basis for the later weighting exercise, which will distinguish between the must-have and nice-to-have requirements. See Chapter 5.

- The requirements are used to derive your preliminary shortlisting questionnaire (the request for information, or RFI) based on those requirements that have a high weight for importance. See Chapter 7.

- Later in the process, the full requirements statement informs candidate IT suppliers of your organisational need. See Chapter 8.

- Requirements feed your software gap analysis, because they create a yardstick that allows you to spot the requirements that are **not** met. See Chapter 9.

- Requirements provide the foundation for candidate scoring and therefore selecting the candidate (software and supplier combination) that fit the best. See Chapters 9 and 10.

- Requirements feed your specifications of the demonstrations. See Chapter 10.

- Requirements are one of the critical project working documents that become an attachment to your contract with the successful candidate. See Chapter 12.

4.9 CHAPTER SUMMARY

TAKE-AWAY POINTS

- Consultation is crucial during IT selections and your requirements-capture programme is one of the most important pieces of consultation. You cannot speculate on the requirements. In a modern organisation, no one person can understand how everything works.

- Requirements will be for a mix of software facilities and supplier services.

- Also essential, but sometimes not appreciated, is the benefit of stakeholder engagement during your requirements-capture programme.

- The consultation allows you to identify and escalate issues raised, such as project scope and direction.

4.9.1 The next chapter

It is necessary to document the needs, now that your requirements analysis is complete (or at least the main burst of it, since requirements are always emerging). The next chapter addresses the process of documenting the captured output. You will transform personal information from a mixed group of attendees into a statement of organisational need.

4.10 REFERENCES

Cadle, J., Paul, D. and Turner, P. (2014) *Business analysis techniques: 99 essential tools for success*, (2nd edition). BCS, The Chartered Institute for IT: Swindon.

Frese, R. and Sauter, V. (2003) 'Project success and failure: What is success, what is failure, and how can you improve your odds for success?'. UMSL, University of Missouri – St Louis. www.umsl.edu/~sauterv/analysis/6840_f03_papers/frese (10 November 2014).

IT Cortex (2014) 'Project failure statistics'. IT Cortex. www.it-cortex.com/Stat_Failure_Cause.htm (10 November 2014).

Krigsman, M (2007) 'Non-technical complexity'. ZDNet. www.zdnet.com/blog/projectfailures/non-technical-complexity/163 (10 November 2014).

Rouse, M. (2013) 'What is cloud broker?'. TechTarget, SearchCloudProvider. http://searchcloudprovider.techtarget.com/definition/cloud-broker (10 November 2014).

Shuttleworth, M. (2009) 'Hawthorne effect: Observation bias'. Explorable. https://explorable.com/hawthorne-effect (10 November 2014).

Smith, M. and Erwin, J. (2011) 'Role and responsibility charting (RACI)'. PMI, California Inland Empire Chapter, Inc. https://pmicie.org/images/downloads/raci_r_web3_1.pdf (10 November 2014).

4.11 FURTHER READING

4.11.1 Books and articles

BCS, The Chartered Institute for IT (2014) 'Related BCS books for BCS International Diploma in Business Analysis'. Available from http://certifications.bcs.org/category/15705 (10 November 2014).

Paul, D., Cadle J. and Yeates, D. (2014) *Business Analysis*, 3rd edition. BCS, The Chartered Institute for IT: Swindon. Especially chapters 'Investigation Techniques' and 'The Competencies of a Business Analyst'.

4.11.2 Useful websites

International Institute of Business Analysis (IIBA) www.iiba.org

4.11.3 Related formats by download

From http://shop.bcs.org/offtheshelfextras.asp the interview list as GDPM responsibility chart.

5 REQUIREMENTS DOCUMENT: DOCUMENTING AND AGREEING REQUIREMENTS

'The difference between the almost right word and the right word is really a large matter.'

Mark Twain (1835–1910)

5.1 WHAT YOU CAN LEARN FROM THIS CHAPTER

- Appreciate the different, relevant requirement formats.
- Recognise that requirements intended for a software product selection (rather than software construction) must be expressed in a different way.
- Understand the processes for marshalling, agreeing and refining your requirements document.
- Grasp the workshop process for establishing the importance of each requirement.

5.2 OVERVIEW

You want to create a clear statement of requirements that can be used to measure and score candidate suppliers and their software. There should only be one requirements document that addresses the following multiple audiences:

- internal reviewers;
- external partners, for example you may consult major customers or suppliers if them realising the benefits means they will connect to your new solution;
- internal IT experts, or external providers of outsourced IT;
- the candidate suppliers.

This makes the wording of your requirements document sensitive. Terms that make sense to an internal readership will baffle outsiders. Statements that might be just about diplomatic enough if only read by members of staff might damage your organisation's reputation in the eyes of external readers. Yet, your document must contain clear statements if there are internal processing difficulties that need to be solved by the new automated solution.

Ultimately, you need to define a set of requirements that are:

- specific to your organisation;
- critical without being merely 'whinging' or unhelpful;
- well-articulated so that they are understood by stakeholders;
- specific enough to be an effective yardstick to measure solutions;
- generic and non-prescriptive enough to allow candidate suppliers to apply their expertise and innovation to deliver the solution.

There are some specific wording examples in the figures showing the requirements documentation formats. There is also a wealth of supporting material with techniques in Section 5.10.

5.3 ORGANISING REQUIREMENTS (CATALOGUING)

After elucidating requirements using the techniques in the previous chapter, you should consolidate them. It is usual before documenting requirements to analyse, organise, classify and simply think about them. This thinking and processing is necessary because you are going from an extensive set of notes capturing personal (or departmental) statements into an organisation-wide document of requirements.

You need to spot duplicate requirements, although sometimes you have 'fragments' of the same requirement from different interviewees and you need to fit the jigsaw pieces together.

You may have conflicting requirements. If you articulate both, you should cross-reference them. The candidate solutions might meet one, the other or both with settings for which is supported.

Another technique when preparing to document requirements is to determine whether a piece of information from an interview should actually be one of the criteria to measure candidate solutions. People attending requirements-capture interviews and workshops often present a mixture of information about the organisation, its objectives, processes and flaws alongside its 'pure' needs for processing information. For instance, an interviewee might state that your organisation tends to under-appreciate and therefore under-resource training when introducing new software. This aspect is unlikely to favour one candidate over another. It is a generic organisational problem. Therefore, I recommend a standard section at the back of your requirements document to capture 'project notes'. These relate to the overall project and its management. They are important pieces of knowledge to capture, but they should not form part of the yardstick to measure candidates. When you release the agreed requirements document externally, for review by external partners and in due course the candidate suppliers, you can leave this back section out.

When analysing and organising requirements, it is often sensible to introduce 'mechanical' processing, such as classifying requirements by type so that you can pull them together by filtering or sorting. Example requirement types or categories might (in a commercial business) include sales, logistics or product development. In a public sector organisation, categories might include citizens, households or central government reporting. All organisations will have non-functional requirement categories that relate to the whole solution, such as finances, regulatory compliance or IT technical requirements ('solution must run on database X'). And there will be the project notes for the back section.

Some requirements approaches refer to this intermediate stage as the requirements catalogue, and the process as requirements cataloguing.

There are several options for physically processing notes, depending on your fluency with different technologies.

- Your organisation may already be familiar with tracking statements of need on a requirements database. On a large project with hundreds of requirements, one option is to enter your IT requirements into such a tool. Requirements databases then track categories, revisions and versions. They register who reported the requirement, though you may choose to hide this information if it risks the process becoming politicised. Requirements cataloguing can therefore be explicitly supported with facilities to sort, report, combine and trace the individual statements.

- You may have taken paper notes on multiple sheets for each interview or workshop. These can be organised into different piles, especially if you had ideas before your interview programme about what some of the categories might be.

- A more high-tech solution, if you make notes on an electronic tablet, is to use the note-taking application to cut or copy notes into a new compilation note set, which is organised by your categories.

- Another computer-supported approach, when titling each requirement, is to add a temporary category prefix. You can use outlining in a word processor and these leading keywords to sort the titles together by category.

5.4 REQUIREMENT FORMATS

The following are options for document formats. You would not usually use all these formats, but one (or perhaps two) to complement each other and that suit your organisation's culture and expectations.

5.4.1 Detailed requirements document

A general term for the requirements document is the Statement of Requirements (SoR).

The detailed statement of requirement should be specific enough to be understood by business users and software suppliers, without prescribing the solution (see Figure 5.1). It should include:

Figure 5.1 Format of detailed requirements document

C. Prime List: Requirements, Grouped By Function
Section: Procurement & Inventory   Colter OTS Solution – Requirements | Approved

Vendor Data Includes Approved Range   **0102**

The vendor management solution should store data on the product range that a vendor is approved to supply, and their approval status. These link certain suppliers to certain safety-critical commodities or material types. For instance, one company might be an approved vendor for low-pressure pumps but not high pressure.

- A status flag should appear if someone tries to use a vendor who is unapproved, is outside their approval parameters or has a poor performance rating. The reasons should be readily available to the user. A workflow might escalate for senior approval.

- Some parts or material classes may be marked 'approved supplier purchases'. This means Colter Civils should have an *approved* supplier to raise an order. For reasons of safety and liability, the solution should object when the requisition or purchase order attempts to invite a supplier to provide material for which they are not cleared.

Avoid Overloading Suppliers   **0103**

In addition, the solution should help Colter Civils avoid overloading suppliers. Vendors should have an order limit – for both a single order value and the total of the work in hand. Preferably, they should also have processing limits such as number of units per month. The solution should warn if an order exceeds the maximum Colter Civils can order for the whole supplier, or for that part/supplier combination.

Identify Preferred Supplier   **0104**

Colter Civils focus on a small number of preferred suppliers, with several 'single source' deals. The solution should allow the preferred supplier to be marked, from a small set of suppliers for each product.

As part of creating the preferred supplier list, the solution should cross-refer parts to suppliers, such that of course one supplier can provide many parts, but also one part can have multiple suppliers. Where this is the case, the solution should track the price, lead-time, units of measure and economic order quantity for each of the suppliers – preferably with notes.

It may be necessary to identify the preferred supplier based on *location*. The US may have a

- Long, specific titles to summarise the requirement – almost like a newspaper headline.

- Requirement numbering – this is essential to internal cross-referencing. It aids discussions, correspondence and supporting documents, such as the scoring spreadsheet. This is best automated with 'fields' within a word processor or database.

5.4.2 Scenarios

Another useful format is the Scenario (Alexander and Maiden, 2004: 3–6). The scenario shows the steps to achieve a goal as interactions between 'actor' and 'system'. It is a type of Use Case (Cadle et al., 2014). I quote this excellent example about software to control cars because most readers can identify with the application: 'The driver walks towards the car and presses his key. The car recognises the driver, unlocks the doors, and adjusts the driving seat, steering wheel, radio, and mirrors to the driver's preferred settings' (Alexander and Maiden, 2004).

Figure 5.2 gives an example of specifying requirements for an off-the-shelf solution by scenario. (Note that scenarios would usually avoid 'flashbacks' such as at 0104, but in this illustration the base requirements are consistent with Figure 5.1.)

Figure 5.2 Format of requirements as scenarios

Copyright 2014 Colter Civils	Colter OTS Solution – IT Requirements Definition

CANDIDATES DISCUSS	NOTES
Procurement & Inventory	
0102. A new buyer tries to raise a purchase order on a contractor to manufacture a safety-critical item. The screen blocks them, because the contractor's vendor rating was dropped last week. It suggests another vendor for this part.	
0103. The software checks the value of the order – it is within the other vendor's monetary limits for both the size of a single order and their cumulative outstanding work.	To avoid supplier overload.
0104. Last week, responding to a vendor rating alert, the UK Purchasing Manager had marked this contractor as the approved supplier for that part. The US Purchasing Manager was also warned to review the country-specific preferred vendor.	

The scenario format has the advantage of being briefer, and is especially useful if the transformed organisation and business processes will look very different from the current approach. If the to-be-computerised processes will diverge from the old ones, it is not worth investing everybody's time in agreeing that the as-is process descriptions are accurate.

Note the use of the present tense – effectively, the writer simply assumes the specification will be met and what is asked for actually happens. Because the description is a story, it draws on people's ability to visualise the situation. They make it real, even if the description is terse.

The clear and unemotional 'flat' statements are almost as though you are creating a documentary about a workplace that does not yet exist, but will.

5.5 GUIDELINES FOR ARTICULATING REQUIREMENTS

Documenting requirements remains a skill and there is no substitute for experience. However, the following guidelines should help you to organise your requirement statements into 'packages' that have the appropriate size and content.

PRINCIPLE WHEN RECORDING REQUIREMENTS

When articulating requirements against which you will select a solution, it is important that you only state the business need. You cannot state the solution or processing – in some organisations, the phrase is 'don't solutionise'. You simply state **what** is wanted, not **how** it is to be achieved (Price, 2010).

For instance, it is a good idea in a sales management product for an organisation with a retail branch structure to say you need, within 24 hours of month-end, statistics on sales volume, margin and profit broken down by branch, area, region and nation.

In contrast, it is a bad idea to include somebody's requested report design, or to stipulate that the output should be in hard-copy report form. It might be that the more powerful products offer online management information, with drill-down from the national summary chart through the necessary levels of detail.

Remember that the fundamental objective is a requirement that can be scored later, meaning that (during the detailed evaluation stage) your evaluation team will examine three or four candidates against that requirement and (in a later, separate scoring meeting) will allocate points for how well each solution meets each requirement. Each requirement needs to be expressed clearly enough that it flushes out any significant differences between candidate solutions.

5.5.1 Group requirements to sections by category

Never organise requirement statements by the person making the request or by department. This risks the requirements becoming political or factional. Examples of effective categories are: **Supply Chain**, because this cuts across the organisation; **Finance**, because money is a theme that permeates the organisation; **Timesheets**, because everybody completes one in your organisation.

Moreover, you should sequence the sections by rough business flow, product life cycle or project structure, depending on what makes sense to your organisation. For instance, if you were a manufacturer, you might sequence the sections as: **Sales,** because you have to sell it first; **Supply Chain**, to get the material; **Production Control**, to monitor the manufacturing; then **Logistics**, to dispatch the finished product. In addition, further down your document, you would position: **Finance**, an important but thematic topic; then **Interfaces**, such as batch load facilities. Such 'technocratic' topics are usually less interesting to the general audience, so you should present the business topics with a general readership early in the document.

5.5.2 Separating requirements

You should divide requirements so that they are not overlapping. The aim is to structure your requirement statements such that, during scoring, a candidate is rewarded in one place (against one requirement) if it presents a piece of processing that is suitable for your organisation. For instance, if there was a non-functional requirement for 'drill down and drill across', this requirement should appear in one place (as one requirement entry) so that it can be scored and rewarded there. It should not be repeated in multiple requirements, such that a candidate solution with good drill-down keeps winning points for the same feature against multiple requirements.

Keeping requirements separate requires cross-referencing, such that one requirement can cite another related requirement. For instance, there may be a sales requirement for customer information and a finance requirement for each customer to have a credit limit. These requirements are separate, because it is possible that some solutions will have extensive customer information (such as several addresses) but might lack credit limits. The customer details might appear in the sales section of your requirements document, whereas the credit limit is in the finance section. They should refer to each other, usually by requirement number and by fields in a word-processing document. This avoids people asking you to add requirements that are already tracked, but in a section that they are unlikely to read.

OPTIMUM LENGTH FOR A REQUIREMENT STATEMENT

Try to avoid large, multi-paragraph requirements that contain several statements of need, even if they are related. One requirement covering a single page (of A4 or US Letter) is probably too large for a software selection – solid real world experience indicates 2–4 requirements per page.

Your editorial decisions may sometimes seem arbitrary in breaking up requirement statements, but different levels of sophistication within the organisational need can often drive the decision to split.

For instance, if the software is expected to store timesheet hours, you might have one requirement to store the hours per day against a job code for each person. You might have a separate requirement that each person must have multiple charge-out rates, according to their role, seniority or the project on which they are working. It is entirely possible when you look at solutions that some will capture the hours, but do not have multiple rates. If these two requirements are articulated separately, it is an excellent opportunity to spot the difference between candidates. Potentially, all the candidates will score well against the (simpler) requirement for hours, whereas only a few candidates will score well by supporting the (more demanding) need for multiple rates that respond to context.

Another example is an 'escalating family' of requirements whereby successive requirements are more difficult to meet. For instance: (A) support my national standard accounting **format** for expressing profit and loss; (B) allow me to **consolidate** accounts from different companies; (C) allow different companies to have **different** base currencies; (D) allow **each** company to reflect **local,** national, generally accepted accounting principles (GAAP). Some candidates will not support C and D, so will lose points compared to more sophisticated products.

Sometimes, requirements should be kept separate because they have different risk profiles. For instance, changing the data structure of an off-the-shelf solution is high-risk. Two requirements might be to request certain data content and then to request some reporting on it. Later, during scoring, if, say, all shortlisted candidates had the data structure, but only one had the standard report 'in the box', then this would reveal a small difference between the candidates. However, if one candidate lacked the fundamental data structure, it would lose points heavily because addressing that absence is a high-risk piece of development.

Another reason to split is if two portions of your requirement have different levels of importance to your organisation. If part of the requirement is essential ('Mandatory' within this approach) and part seems far less crucial, the two parts should be expressed as separate requirements. This will facilitate giving them different weights for importance during the weighting workshop (see Section 5.7).

5.5.3 Measurable and testable requirements

Remember that you must be able to allocate points later in the process for how well each candidate meets the requirements.

Requirements that encapsulate key performance indicators (KPIs) or SLA targets are often suitably 'crunchy' (measurable). An example is the opening hours of the support or help desk. If you ask for Monday to Saturday 0800–1800 Eastern Standard Time, you will be able to give different points for the degree of fit to three different candidates offering:

1. 24x7 Follow-the-Sun;
2. Monday–Saturday 0800–1800;
3. Monday–Friday 0900–1700.

In the context of measurable requirements, some statements seen in immature documents are meaningless. For example:

- The program shall be user-friendly.
- The supplier must be reliable.
- The screen response must be fast enough for customer-facing staff.

Worse, such statements signal that you are an inexperienced customer. For many software suppliers, such statements flag you as a poor prospect. Others might be predatory and detect 'easy meat'.

5.5.4 Mutually exclusive requirements

Sometimes, you will write a pair of requirements that are deliberately mutually exclusive. One example is where a solution that is currently embedded into the organisation might be subsumed by this project and replaced by the capabilities of the new product. An alternative outcome is that it remains a part of your IT estate, but requires an interface to pass across data. In the circumstances, you would write two requirements, one to state the business needs that must be met if the old solution is decommissioned and another to state the characteristics of an effective interface. Once again, the two requirements should contain cross-references to each other to make it clear that you expect one or the other to be met.

A striking project example was the requirement to either interface to Microsoft Project, or to replace its scheduling and resource management capabilities within a larger project-orientated ERP solution. The two requirements had different weights for importance, since it was essential to interface but desirable to replace. In the scoring, most candidates interfaced, but one candidate that could do both rightly got double points. It meant that the customer had options as to which approach to use and when – including a different policy for different project plans. Against the paired requirements, these options rightly made this the superior candidate.

5.5.5 Business volumes

At least three requirements should relate to volumes – (see Figure 5.3). These will test the storage capacities of the new solution. This is a defence against candidate solutions that perform superbly on two demonstration customers, but slow to a completely unusable speed when you load your own 20,000 live customers. Note that this will also be tested during the reference site stage (see Chapter 11).

Current volumes

State the number of key entities (items, objects, records) in your current software; for example, the number of customers, suppliers, sales orders, purchase orders, accounting journal entries, households, citizens or cities tracked – whatever indicates the 'size' of your operational data. In some cases, you can actually quote gigabytes of data, for instance how much data is occupied by current CAD models.

Projected volumes

For some of the key entities itemised at the current volumes, identify the informed people and ask for their best guess at what these numbers will be in five years' time. The estimate will be imperfect, but it will at least give you some defence against a product that only has enough capacity to cope with today's volumes and no room for growth.

Figure 5.3 Examples of volumes in requirements

C. Prime List: Requirements, Grouped By Function	
Section: Critical Information & Volumes	Colter OTS Solution – Requirements | Approved

Critical Information & Volumes

Purpose Of Section

To give sample sizing metrics, to safeguard against a solution that demonstrates well on small volumes, but becomes too slow to use when the database is filled with production volumes.

Business Volumes – Current	**0001**
Metrics On Business Size & Complexity – Now	
Number of employees (snapshot mid-year, routinely expanding)	230
Number of staff in UK	c150
Number of staff in the US	c50

Business Volumes – Expansion / Future	**0002**

The volumes will grow significantly. The solution should be able to accommodate the following expansion.

Indicators Of Annual Business Growth	
Number of proposals per year	25
Number of new programmes per year	c5

Data retention

There may be policies that affect your organisation, such as statutory requirements, that require you to retain information for a set number of years. You may prefer to store this information electronically rather than be obliged to retain paper archives. In this case, the new application will need some sort of current and historical data structures or an enormous capacity in the live data such that you can store back-years without impeding daily operations. In case there are technical limits as to how many entries can be added to certain critical data tables, you might state maximum values for pivotal variables, such as the number of customers or orders. If you prefer the software not to impose archiving, you might use the phrase that storage is 'limited only by hardware'.

TEN CHARACTERISTICS OF A WELL-FORMED REQUIREMENT FOR OFF-THE-SHELF SELECTION

1. **Non-prescriptive:** concentrates on business outcomes, without mandating the IT processing method, location, medium (such as paper) or person involved (except to set context).
2. **Collected:** brings together similar requirements from different verbal notifications or project documents.
3. **Thematic:** avoids silos, is non-partisan, reflects systematic thinking.
4. **Unique:** avoids duplication to prevent double counting during scoring (duplicated rewards or penalties).
5. **Sequenced:** placed in a logical order in the document flow, preferably within requirement 'families' or categories for a coherent response by specialists.
6. **Standalone:** without concomitant peers that automatically score high/low in sympathy, so each requirement ideally measures a different dimension of the candidate.
7. **Measurable:** articulated with a contractual commitment to delivery in mind.
8. **Shrewd:** avoids vague (arguably naïve) terms such as friendly, fast, flexible, instant, immediate or 'etc'.
9. **Positive:** states future need, but avoids dictatorial vocabulary to better 'manage the talent' and motivate suppliers (see Chapter 2).
10. **Referenced:** such as a number to tie back to scoring – manageably fine-grained, with typically 2–4 discrete requirements on a page.

5.6 VALIDATE, AGREE AND REFINE REQUIREMENTS

Documenting requirements will involve several iterations of validating, agreeing and refining the statements in the requirements document. Experience shows at least four versions of the requirements document are needed if you follow the method stages.

- The first is soon after requirements capture, exclusively to the project sponsor, to remove any gross understanding errors in the writing that would otherwise erode credibility.

- The second is for general circulation, to play back requirements to all the interviewees and workshop attendees – plus wider reviewers who did not attend.

- The third is input to the weighting workshop (see Section 5.7).

- Lastly, you produce a final version to reflect discussions at the weighting workshop.

When revising, it is important to reflect comments scrupulously, creating new requirements or rewording.

Sometimes, such changes will not in fact materially affect the statement of requirement. For instance, you may have quoted a bullet list of required status values for a user-defined list when installing the new solution. It does not matter if you have missed one of the values from your requirement wording. The missing value would simply be added during implementation. However, if a reviewer points out the missing value, and they do not see it in the next version of the document, it looks as though you do not care or possibly never seriously wanted comment on the draft.

This means that some revisions 'have to be seen to be done'. They improve ownership of the document, even though the revised statement is no more likely to select the best-fitting candidate.

DOCUMENT COLLABORATION TO REVISE REQUIREMENTS

Because you need a written requirements statement against which to measure the candidates, it is inevitable that you must painstakingly invest in a definitive document with an agreed form of words.

If people are comfortable with responding via comments and tracked changes within a word-processed document, this can be highly productive. It means that people can concentrate on what they want to say, without describing where their comment applies. Reviewing, accepting or rejecting tracked changes then lifts the author's productivity.

5.7 THE WEIGHTING WORKSHOP

5.7.1 Introduction to weighting

Before you can consider the requirements document as definitive, you need a small, but knowledgeable, team to 'weight' requirements to clearly establish their importance. This allocates a number against each requirement to reflect the scale from 'must-have' through 'nice-to-have' to 'do-not-need'.

The weighting workshop is the process to establish the importance of each requirement. You typically go round the table and people 'vote' for what they believe is the appropriate weight. You discuss and settle an agreed weight. You normally use a spreadsheet to capture the votes, to analyse the pattern of votes (such as the standard deviation), the agreed weight and some control metrics (distribution of weights, estimated time to complete the workshop).

It is a democratic and mathematical approach. Rather than using only two values (must versus nice), it uses a scale of 1–5 to record the spread of importance. The high-weighted (critical and mandatory) requirements will drive your preliminary shortlisting questionnaire, the RFI (see Chapter 7). Later, the 'weighted attribute' scoring matrix will reward any candidates that are strong in the areas that are important to your organisation (see Chapter 9).

Note that requirements definition can exploit the MoSCoW (Must, Should, Could, Won't) rules for expressing the importance of each requirements entry (Morgan and Dale, 2013). However, coding the weight for importance as a number is better for later calculations on the scoring matrix. While the different levels of importance are mixed together, spreadsheet filtering will reveal the different types.

EXECUTIVE PERSPECTIVE: AN IT SUPPORT PROVIDER'S EXPERIENCE OF WEIGHTED REQUIREMENTS

We used the evaluation method to select the best-fit ERP software package in a moderately complex manufacturing environment.

The weighting meeting crystallised the requirements' relative importance and the weighting technique produced a highly useful deliverable against which to measure prospective suppliers' products.

In our case, where no package was found to have an exact fit, it had a welcome additional benefit of facilitating supplier negotiations over features and price.

The method engaged previously reticent stakeholders and its rigour instilled confidence in senior management that an objective and thorough evaluation had been conducted. As an adviser, I was comfortable in the knowledge that the decision-making process was transparent and auditable.

5.7.2 Participants

The weighting team will make critical decisions that will steer your procurement. Hence, its composition is significant both practically and politically. The team must contain the correct people to get the weighting as sound as possible, and should have representatives from all departments, divisions and nations that are in scope. It will tend to be made up of leaders in the organisation, but not just formal leaders (managers) since informal opinion leaders or project champions can have high influence without seniority. A good workshop size is 4–10 people.

The team must also be accepted as the right group by those not in the room, including those senior to the group, peers and strong influencers lower in the organisation.

- Some should be interviewees, partly because it helps to have people who understand the process from earlier meetings and partly because they have already invested in the requirements.
- A few should be new faces, because this deepens the roots of the project.
- Overall, the weighting team tends to be more senior, such as heads of departments. They have more of an overview of business needs. Moreover, the weighting meeting has real impact on the project and attending this meeting (if no other) is the most productive use of senior time.

5.7.3 Time and meeting management

A weighting workshop will usually last 1–2 days, depending on the combined number of requirements and participants. Weighting requires intensive time and meetings management, because you have a significant group of people who need to make a very large number of small decisions collectively. If the group loses its way, the time will balloon and you will not be nearly finished when the time runs out.

Some people will attend only part of the meeting. Specialists might attend only the section of the meeting that relates to their interest. The HR representative might only attend the initial briefing and then the weighting of requirements in the HR section.

You may need an address by a very senior stakeholder (preferably the sponsor) to open the meeting, as with the scoping workshop (see Chapter 3).

PART-TIME ATTENDANCE BY SPONSOR

The project sponsor might 'top and tail' the workshop. They appear at the beginning to meet and greet as host, experience the detailed briefing on the workshop process and participate to determine the first block of weights (normally a short, easy section of requirements). They re-appear at the end to help review the weighting results.

This all shows support for the project and will help their own confidence when briefing senior colleagues.

After the senior figure has spoken, you should give a short status report. Bear in mind the new faces. Include how the requirements document came together (see Chapter 4).

Explain the weighting workshop purpose and process, including showing a preview of what the finished scoring matrix will look like – when the weights for importance are combined with the candidate scores for fit (see Chapter 9).

As a group, decide who votes. For instance, public sector organisations have clear distinctions between their **advisers** and their **officers** (executives or elected officials who have decision-making authority). An external facilitator for the workshop would not be a decision-maker and would not have a vote in determining weights, even if they knew the business and its requirements.

As a group, decide in what order you will vote. Normally, to avoid confusion, it is safer to go round the table and vote in sequence. However, you should rotate the lead – meaning at each new section the first person to vote advances one place round the table. This avoids one person being consistent opinion leader.

Decide what sections you are going to process first – unless these are pre-determined by invitee availability. If you have a free choice, weight first those general categories that need the full group around the table for the process to be credible.

Weighting the less-urgent categories might involve a decision about how to finish if you run out of time. You might re-convene, finish by video or audio conference (because people will then be familiar with the process) or delegate authority to a sub-group of the weighting team. For example, the IT supplier section (considerations about the reseller, not the software product) might be handled by a smaller group led by Procurement. The IT technical section (such as database standards to observe) might be delegated to the IT representative because meeting attendees believe that they do not have enough knowledge to express an opinion about the significance of such requirements.

5.7.4 Outcome per requirement

The main aim is to agree – for every requirement – a number that expresses its importance to your organisation. However, the secondary aim is a thorough requirements review, so you must be prepared for modifications. This means that the possible outcomes per requirement are:

- **Agree** weight of 1, 2, 3, 4 or 5 (see Table 5.1).
- **Delete** requirement (Weight = 0).
- **Merge** into another requirement (because the weighting team believe two requirements are too close to keep separate).
- **Move** to a more appropriate section in the requirements document, then weight as normal.
- **Split** the requirement in order to weight different components (for instance, with one part being mandatory while the other is trivial).
- **Reword** the requirement (with the person documenting requirements making quick notes only on the agreed changes to wording), and then weight the adjusted requirement as discussed rather than as currently written.

The weight for importance to agree per requirement

The numbers in Table 5.1 represent the importance of the requirement to your organisation, in descending order of significance. For the number of occasions the values 1–5 are allocated, you will be looking for a roughly normal distribution (the bell-shaped curve, centred on 3).

Table 5.1 Values used during weighting workshop

	Class	Description	Proportion of requirements
5	Mandatory	The absolutely 'must-haves'. Solutions without explicit support for even one 5-weighted requirement will be rejected out of hand as unfit for purpose.	0–5%
4	Critical factor	Use very much by exception for items that are critical, but not quite so important that they single-handedly disqualify a candidate.	3–5%
3	Major factor	It is important for solutions to consistently score well against this type of requirement to be credible.	25–40%
2	Minor factor	Some significance. A bonus if supported.	15–25%
1	Trivial	Requirement of little importance and therefore only slight influence when selecting solutions.	5–10%
0	Not significant	Support for this requirement should not influence the choice of solution at all. Remove from requirements document. (Also used to mark requirements to merge into similar ones, or moved out of scored requirements into project notes.)	

5.7.5 Decision-making cycle within the weighting workshop

You may have noticed in meetings that people have long discussions, but then realise they agreed at the beginning of the debate. They were trying to persuade people into a view that, actually, they already held – they were 'violently in agreement'.

The weighting workshop process needs to avoid this phenomenon, because there are too many decisions to make to waste time on those where people already agree.

You only need to debate requirements where views are split on how important the requirement is. Therefore, for each requirement, always start with an instant vote cycle. Go quickly round the table so people can simply state their vote 0–5, without supporting argument. Note that people with no strong view can abstain, and allow the average to be set by those who have a clear opinion.

You should record the votes on the spreadsheet displayed to the meeting and immediately review the calculated average and distribution (see Figure 5.4). Normally, you round up or down conventionally (3.6 becomes 4). Record the agreed weight.

Figure 5.4 Weight voting spreadsheet

Colter Civils Requirement Weights Aligned To Version 4.0	Nbr @ V 4.0	Belle	Sebastian	Stuart	Alan	Avge	Count	StdDv	Agreed
Section									
Critical Information & Volumes	0001	5	5	5	5	5.000	4	0.00	5
Critical Information & Volumes	0002	5	4	4	4	4.250	4	0.50	4
Critical Information & Volumes	0003	3	3	3	4	3.250	4	0.50	3
Critical Information & Volumes	0004	3	5	4	3	3.750	4	0.96	4
Critical Information & Volumes	0005	5	5	5	5	5.000	4	0.00	5
Sales & Marketing	0006	2	3	2	2	2.250	4	0.50	2
Sales & Marketing	0007	2	4	2	2	2.500	4	1.00	3
Sales & Marketing	0008	1	2	A	1	1.333	3	0.58	1
Sales & Marketing	0009	3	2	3	3	2.750	4	0.50	3

However, if there are diverse views (mixed high and low weights) you need to educate each other by explaining the reasons for the respective weighting. To save time, I recommend that participants use the standard phrase that they want to 'talk up' (say 3 to 5) or 'talk down' (say 4 to 3). After this short discussion, hold a re-vote. Again, participants give their number without supporting argument. Record the agreed weight. Move on to the vote cycle for the next requirement.

At section breaks, you should monitor the timekeeping and review the distribution of weights. Looking for the roughly bell-shaped curve, you often have to become less free with Mandatory 5 weights. These should really be the 'show-stoppers' – entries where any candidate lacking explicit support for the requirement is not a credible contender.

If by the end of the meeting you have a large number of weight values at 4 and 5 but none at 1 and 2, you may have to transform or downscale (all at 3 to 2, and so on). Then re-vote for the top band to escalate a limited number of those with a downscaled value of 4 back up to the Mandatory 5.

5.7.6 After the weighting workshop

Final revision of requirements document

After the weighting workshop, you should create the final revision of the requirements document – Version 4 – as agreed with the workshop participants. Remove any requirements weighted at 0. Split, merge and move requirements. Revise wording from your notes.

At this point, baseline the requirements document and place it under configuration management control. The method has a mechanism for accommodating later learning about requirements as part of the scoring definitions (see Chapter 9).

The sponsor might formally authorise Version 4 for release – later – to shortlisted suppliers, but usually does not interfere with the text because the wording of requirements has been agreed as part of weighting. This means that the workshop process indirectly 'signs off' the SoR. This avoids the traditional (but usually ineffective) approach of circulating a massive document, requesting comments and saying that if you hear nothing in two weeks you will assume it is all okay.

Circulate the weights document

You need to align the spreadsheet of weights with the Version 4 requirements document; for instance, allowing for the deleted, split, merged and moved entries.

Circulate the weights, suppressing the individual votes and revealing only the agreed weight. Supply the Version 4 requirements document to anyone who wants the full detail of the requirements.

Normally, workshop participants will no longer be interested in the weights, but this circulation allows other stakeholders to contribute. By exception, they might 'appeal' an allocated weight.

5.8 CHAPTER SUMMARY

TAKE-AWAY POINTS

Documenting requirements creates a foundation for the whole project – one document that is circulated to business reviewers and eventually candidate suppliers. The concession to confidentiality is that you might have internal notes in a separate section at the back of the document, which is not included in early supplier copies.

How you articulate the requirements is crucial. They need to be unambiguous, measurable (they will be scored for fit later) and you must avoid being prescriptive as to how the requirement is met.

5.8.1 The next chapter

Now you have the requirements secure, the projects focus swings from the internal (the organisation, its requirements) to the external (the marketplace, the products available, the candidate suppliers). The next stages are to approach the marketplace to see what products are available (see Chapter 6) and to re-purpose the requirements as a shortlisting questionnaire (see Chapter 7).

5.9 REFERENCES

Alexander, I. and Maiden, N. (2004) *Scenarios, stories and use cases.* John Wiley & Sons: Chichester.

Cadle, J., Paul, D. and Turner, P. (2014) *Business analysis techniques: 99 essential tools for success*, 2nd edition. BCS, The Chartered Institute for IT: Swindon.

Morgan, J. and Dale, C. (2013) *Managing IT projects for business change: From risk to success*. BCS, The Chartered Institute for IT: Swindon.

Price, K. (2010) 'Requirements defined (in just 24 letters)'. Real World BA, WordPress. http://realworldba.com/requirements-defined-in-24-letters (10 November 2014).

5.10 FURTHER READING

5.10.1 Books and articles

Alexander, I. and Stevens, R. (2002) *Writing better requirements*. Addison Wesley: Harlow.

Paul, D., Yeates, D. and Cadle, J. (eds) *Business analysis*, 3rd edition. BCS, The Chartered Institute for IT: Swindon.

5.10.2 Related formats by download

Detailed requirements document format with table of contents and Scenario requirements format from http://shop.bcs.org/offtheshelfextras.asp.

6 TRAWLING THE MARKETPLACE: ESTABLISHING THE LONGLIST

'May the holes in your net be no larger than the fish in it.'

Irish Blessing

6.1 WHAT YOU CAN LEARN FROM THIS CHAPTER

- Understand the nature of the longlist of candidates.
- Grasp the criteria for longlisting and maintaining the balance of risk such that your evaluation team do not waste time on unsuitable candidates, but, at the same time, do not miss opportunities.
- Identify techniques for trawling the marketplace, including sources of information and risks when researching.

6.2 OVERVIEW

SPECIAL NOTE ABOUT EARLIER CHAPTER

If you skipped Chapter 2 about talent management and supplier psychology because you were not contacting suppliers at the start of your project, you should read that chapter now.

The method uses the term **candidate** to encapsulate one software **product** from one **supplier**.

Because of reseller networks, the supplier that you will eventually select is not necessarily the software author. Within the evaluation, you would track two candidates if, for instance, one supplier has two suitable products or if two different resellers put forward the same author's software.

You will look at a large number of candidates at first, intending to detect efficiently those candidates that should not be taken forward into the next round.

You find out only enough at each stage to decide whether to take a candidate forward or 'park' them. This keeps work to a minimum, for the evaluation team and for unsuitable suppliers.

As you go on, knowledge about each candidate improves and the detail you seek increases, while the number of candidates declines. Of course, this means that you will invest most time in the very strongest contenders.

The progressive shortlisting has very clear decision gates, with a set of explicit stop-go decision points. These decisions relate not only to each candidate, but also whether the project itself should continue.

It is conceivable (although improbable) that you reach a 'shortlist of zero', meaning that you have eliminated all feasible off-the-shelf solutions. In this case, you will either need to abandon your search (switching to bespoke software development re-using the requirement statements marshalled so far) or you will need to adjust your criteria (because they are too ambitious or applied too stringently).

EXECUTIVE PERSPECTIVE: AN ARCHITECTURAL PARTNER'S EXPERIENCE OF PREMATURE SHORTLISTING

When our business needed to invest in a new CAD system we looked into the options. This involved identifying the market leaders from the architectural press, and management then deciding on the basis of opinions (and prejudices) garnered from other practitioners. In due course, 'the system we selected' left us with some unexpected problems, not least recruitment, and resulted in two offices running different systems during a busy period.

Having later encountered the methodical approach it is clear we could have made a more reasoned judgement that would have, at the least, highlighted the issues we would face. It would also have given management the confidence to consult the technical team more fully.

6.3 CREATING THE LONGLIST

When you seek candidates, there is a large range of sources and techniques that you can use. Your research must cast a wide net because you do not know where the answer lies (see Figure 6.1). The sources and techniques to use include the following.

6.3.1 Researching published information

For sector-specific software, trade journals can be a rich source of information, especially if you ask subject matter experts to suggest titles. Scan for adverts and look for articles – industry-specific articles, such as case studies, often mention software products.

Figure 6.1 Spreadsheet for collating the longlist

Status	Referred By	Company	Product(s)	Web S	Contact Name	Job Title	Email	Mobile Ph	Phone	Address 1	Last Results
RFIout	Incumbent	Candidate A	Product A		Contact A	Job Title A	Email A	Mobile A		See hidden col	2015-08-25 Emailed RFI
RFIout	Top Vendors Repc	Candidate B	Product B		Contact B	Job Title B	Email B	Mobile B		See hidden col	2015-08-25 Emailed RFI
RFIout	Expert Recommer	Candidate C	Product C		Contact C	Job Title C	Email C	Mobile C		See hidden col	2015-08-25 Emailed RFI
RFIout	Email Belle	Candidate D	Product D		Contact D	Job Title D	Email D	Mobile D		See hidden col	2015-08-25 Emailed RFI
DNR	Former candidate	Candidate E	Product E		Contact E	Job Title E	Email E	Mobile E		See hidden col	Did not respond to call & email
RFIout	Feasibility Costing	Candidate F	Product F		Contact F	Job Title F	Email F	Mobile F		See hidden col	2015-08-25 Emailed RFI FS vn
Withdrew	Email Sebastian	Candidate G	Product G		Contact G	Job Title G	Email G	Mobile G		See hidden col	Withdrew - not sector
RFIout	Trade Show	Candidate H	Product H		Contact H	Job Title H	Email H	Mobile H		See hidden col	2015-08-25 Emailed RFI
RFIout	Top Vendors Repc	Candidate I	Product I		Contact I	Job Title I	Email I	Mobile I		See hidden col	2015-08-25 Emailed RFI
RFIout	Former Candidate	Candidate J	Product J		Contact J	Job Title J	Email J	Mobile J		See hidden col	2015-08-25 Emailed RFI

Trawling the marketplace necessarily involves web searches. The nature of web information makes it particularly suitable in a field where products are regularly superseded and the companies supplying them might merge. Software companies normally have a strong web presence. Think carefully about the search terms you use. I experienced one sponsor who was convinced no off-the-shelf solutions existed because software companies used a different term for their niche. Sometimes you can look up one product (found by a different research path) and use its web pages to inform future searches.

6.3.2 Knowledge of colleagues and other contacts

Time-honoured 'asking around' has multiple benefits. Your industry or public sector area may have some prominent offerings, and it would discredit your project process if you overlooked the products that have 'mind-share' in your field. Moreover, engaging people partly involves examining products they believe in.

You might also ask your major customers and suppliers what solutions they use, and the good or bad products they have heard of. Again, this is good stakeholder management, especially if you hope your customers and suppliers will connect to your new solution. In some fields, the industry bond is strong enough to even ask competitors if someone in your organisation has a good enough relationship with somebody in the rival.

In the public sector, many organisations expect to collaborate and share experiences. For one fire service project, a senior officer rang comparable services to ask what they used for fire crew rostering. This was partly to see if in-house or off-the-shelf software prevailed as well as to collect product names.

6.3.3 Previous research and lists

Sometimes you can further exploit research that has already been done. You may already have internal lists within your organisation of suppliers and solutions that might fit. These might be from an early iteration of your project, or a related project that threw up products unsuitable for use at that time, but more suited to your project scope now.

Internal staff – such as requirements definition interviewees – may have lists of products from their own research. Search your email if you have been working on the project for a while and might have forgotten some snippets about software products. Remember to review your browser bookmarks.

6.3.4 Sales exhibitions

Sales exhibitions aim to marshal a concentration of suitable software products and suppliers, especially those shows that occupy a niche.

TRADE SHOW TECHNIQUE

- Personal management is required at shows.
- Remember the suppliers are there to sell.

- You must know what you want to see.
- You should have your 'script' ready to rapidly describe your needs.
- Do not spend so much time with one supplier that you overlook other candidates.

Because the largest or most specialist exhibitions occur annually, the exhibition date may not be right for your project. However, you might be able to buy the previous show catalogue after the event. Even with a high cover price, they pay for themselves in saved time and reduced risk. They combine significant quantities of educational material with product listings and often-helpful product comparison, such as summary feature tables.

While trade shows constantly change their name, venues and locations, they are usually easy to find via web searches and magazine adverts.

6.3.5 Industry bodies, special interest groups and portals

You may also be able to contact trade associations or professional bodies that relate to your sector.

For instance, if you are an accountancy practice, or if you are looking for dedicated financial software, check the ICAEW.

If you seek manufacturing software, portals such as The Manufacturer often list products by specialist areas, such as production control or job costing. Websites such as ERP Connect often list by specific product area.

6.3.6 Listings services, IT reports and market analysts

Several services manage lists, study software and sometimes 'match make' products to your high-level statement of requirement. Stay alert to their business model: some take a commission, so may have a sales-driven approach; some charge the supplier for listing (or evaluating) their product, so their lists will be incomplete since some suppliers will not pay the fee.

Notwithstanding, IT analysts such as Bloor or Gartner can certainly be a source of product names and frequently of preliminary product information.

6.3.7 Role models

You should compare yourself to organisations in your field – or other fields if you are more adventurous – that are perceived as successful adopters of IT. Sometimes, you can 'copycat' to get similar levels of benefit, while saving the higher cost and risk of 'bleeding edge' adoptions.

Some of the information about successful exploitations of IT might come from your best practice research (see Chapter 4).

ENSURE EMAIL ADDRESSES ARE PERSONAL

Email is the standard way to confirm contact details (now) or to contact candidates (later). You should never use generic email addresses (sales@, enquiries@), but always secure a named individual with a personal email address. Make sure that they are expecting to receive your RFI (the shortlisting questionnaire) by a specific backstop date. Ensure they know how to contact you if it does not arrive by the deadline.

6.4 RISKS WHEN ENGAGING WITH THE MARKETPLACE

Sometimes, organisations selecting software regard supplier information and sales executive time as an educational resource, but free help usually comes at a price:

- Part of selling software is to influence the 'basis of decision' such that the supplier's product is the only one that fits.

- This will distort your later product scoring, because the criteria favour their product.

- If a supplier can 'load' your requirements with entries where they are strong or even unique, they know that their particular product will be the best fit, that you will be happy and loyal (because of managed expectations) and the initial sale (with the support cash cow) will not be price sensitive.

Remember that stakes are high. Selling software is superficially about providing features and benefits, but can be about accumulating wealth and power. Remember that two of the top five richest people in the world in 2014, Larry Ellison and Bill Gates, made their fortune in a single generation by creating successful software products (Forbes, 2014).

6.5 LONGLIST LENGTH AND WHEN TO INCLUDE CANDIDATES

The length of your longlist always depends on the context, not an arbitrary number. On prior IT selection projects, 10–40 candidates have proved effective. However, one project had only two candidates. This was for specialised public administration where there were only two credible off-the-shelf solutions available. The highest was 200 candidates. A peculiar requirement disqualified all the original candidates, and we had to do a second, wider sweep informed by this knowledge. We did find more candidates, and one from the second sweep proved highly suitable and won the evaluation.

As a rule, you need a longlist that is short enough to be manageable, but long enough to be credible. This means that:

- People reviewing your list must see the candidates they expect – or an explanation why they are not listed.

- You must be confident that you have cast the net widely enough so your winner is not merely 'the best of a bad bunch'.

The nightmare scenario late in a selection is to find what you believe to be the best one only to have a clearly superior candidate come out of nowhere.

If in doubt, include rather than exclude. Moving from longlist to shortlist involves the overhead of writing your preliminary shortlisting questionnaire, the RFI (see Chapter 7). This takes the same amount of time to create for any number of candidates.

When looking at the replies, an effective RFI assessment process can average as little as 40–60 minutes for the preliminary evaluation of each candidate response. With so little time per candidate, it is better to include any doubtful candidates as insurance. You are trading a small amount of time for the confidence that you have been exhaustive and there are no surprises out there in the marketplace.

As with most deliverables within the method, you need to iterate to create a credible document. The longlist will generally have, at the very least, one draft listing, with a circulation inviting comment on omissions or inappropriate entries.

You will revise it, with research as necessary, before releasing your definitive longlist of candidates to be explored.

6.5.1 Reasons to include a candidate

You should be clear that your longlist is not a list of winners. It is not even a list of credible candidates. It is the list of possible solutions where you do not yet know enough about their capabilities to reject them. You simply need information to decide if they are a contender.

Putting a candidate on to your longlist means you need to look at it with your qualifying questionnaire to gather information about the capability.

Another reason to add a candidate to your longlist is that an internal stakeholder suggested it, or even favours it. Do this even if you fear it is not suitable. As part of managing the organisational dynamic, it is acceptable to include the 'pet product' of a senior manager (Axelos, 2012). It will be taken forward (or parked) on its own merit. If it is a poor fit, it will not matter where the suggestion came from. If it proves to be a good fit, you have gained a strong contender. Whatever the outcome, the stakeholder has had a voice and an influence within your process.

6.5.2 Reasons to exclude a candidate

As your longlist contains candidates to examine in order to assess suitability, you can avoid an entry if a candidate is known to be unsuitable. You may have enough information now.

For instance, an exhibition catalogue may have a high-level feature list. The comparison table may have a heading for 'job costing module', say. If your scope and requirements are such that job costing is a critical piece of processing, a product that lacks the tick in the feature table will prove unsuitable in your evaluation. It is a waste of time putting it on your longlist. You might make a project note in your decision log as to why it has been excluded.

Sometimes, the information comes internally. For instance, a trusted insider within the organisation may argue that there is a deal-breaking cultural rift between you and a potential supplier. Provided that their advice is informed and you trust that their interests are aligned with your organisational goals, you might use this soft information to exclude a candidate that otherwise might need investigation. Again, your project decision log should have a corresponding entry.

6.6 THE INCUMBENT SOLUTION AS A CANDIDATE

Optionally, another entry on your longlist might be the current or incumbent solution. Listing the incumbent does not mean that you are revisiting the strategy to replace it because it no longer fits the organisational strategy, or re-making that decision. You are formally checking whether the incumbent meets that strategy, and at the same time validating the strategic decision in case it was misled by poor understanding of the current solution.

You need to check as a customer that you understand the current solution fully and that you are exploiting it to its limits. Software can get a bad name and replacing it may be an ill-considered decision or 'knee-jerk reaction'. Sometimes, your organisation will not have a software capability problem, but an understanding and training problem, whereby the incumbent solution is far better than presently perceived.

You should also decide whether to treat the internal staff experts as the candidate supplier, or to go back to the original reseller or author. There may be a later version, unfamiliar to your own people, which is more capable and better suited to your needs today.

If you decide to list it, the incumbent software should go through the same process as other candidates. If you place it on your longlist, you will formally measure it against requirements. You will score it at longlist and (potentially) shortlist stages. This allows you to compare the fit of the incumbent solution to the best available off-the-shelf replacements.

The incumbent might be the best solution, and your best option might be to invest in it. This would probably involve some combination of adopting the latest version, taking more optional modules to extend the processing capability, licensing more seats to make it more widely available and laying on more training.

6.6.1 Benefits of assessing the incumbent

Listing and formally evaluating the incumbent solution is also part of change management. Measuring your old one can clearly illustrate the benefits of replacement. If the current software is a poor fit, it will score low, or fail mandatory requirements, or both. The scoring matrix at longlist and shortlist stages will demonstrate clearly whether there are significantly stronger, yet affordable, offerings available off-the-shelf.

Formally evaluating the incumbent is also part of managing stakeholders. People who like it are simultaneously shown that it got fair treatment and how weak it is. Moreover, your incumbent supplier is important to your organisation. For instance, you might need their help to migrate your data into the new solution. It is civil, professional and in your interests to treat them fairly and allow them to put the latest version of their product in the best light. If they are unable to answer the majority of the questions on the questionnaire sent to the longlist candidates, they will have proved to themselves that their solution no longer meets your need and that replacing it is appropriate.

6.7 CHAPTER SUMMARY

TAKE-AWAY POINTS

The solution that you eventually install can only be as good as the best entry on your longlist. This means that you must ensure that you have effective, broad shortlisting with redundancy in your search. The consultation while you are compiling the agreed longlist is also another opportunity to manage change and stakeholders.

6.7.1 The next chapter

Now you have established your longlist, you are in a position to use the RFI shortlisting questionnaire to process this longlist of candidates effectively and efficiently to identify your shortlist. The next chapter shows how this paper-based exercise will eliminate unsuitable candidates quickly and will allow you to invest in the most likely candidates.

6.8 REFERENCES

Axelos (2012) 'Common glossary'. Global Best Practice Portfolio, AXELOS. www.axelos.com/glossaries-of-terms.aspx (10 November 2014).

Forbes (2014) 'The world's billionaires list'. www.forbes.com/billionaires/list (10 November 2014).

6.9 FURTHER READING

6.9.1 Books and articles

CIPS (2007) 'Jargon buster'. The Chartered Institute of Purchasing and Supply. http://cips.studyserve.com/skins/cips/customfiles/content/jargonbuster.asp (10 November 2014).

Easterby-Smith, M., Thorpe R. and Jackson, P. (2012) *Management research*, 4th edition. SAGE Publications: London.

6.9.2 Useful websites

Listing of exhibitions, including software trade shows: www.tradefairdates.com.

Reference and educational information for finance software from The Institute of Chartered Accountants in England and Wales: www.icaew.com.

Manufacturing software information from EEF, the Manufacturers' Organisation: www.eef.org.uk.

ERP Connect show and matchmaking service from The Manufacturer portal: www.themanufacturer.com and www.whicherp.net.

Matchmaking of UK small and medium size enterprises with solution providers: www.intelligencenetworking.com.

Vendor-supplied technical content, including free IT white papers and technical articles: www.techrepublic.com.

6.9.3 Related formats by download

Spreadsheet to assemble longlist from: http://shop.bcs.org/offtheshelfextras.asp.

7 ASSESSING LONGLIST CANDIDATES: SELECTING THE SHORTLIST USING THE RFI

'I'll give you a definite maybe.'

Sam Goldwyn (1879–1974)

7.1 WHAT YOU CAN LEARN FROM THIS CHAPTER

- Understand how to evaluate your longlist of candidates to create a shortlist confidently – by ensuring that your process for the Request For Information (RFI) is both effective and efficient.

- Understand the nature, purpose and format of the RFI.

- Appreciate the nature of effective RFI questions, to help select and write them.

- Grasp the approaches to assessing the candidate supplier responses.

- Recognise ways to summarise and present your findings from the assessment meeting.

- Be aware of ways to make efficient use of supplier and assessor time.

7.2 OVERVIEW

Requirements, with their weights, are crucial to the RFI process. The weights allow you to build a shortlisting basis of decision using those criteria that are most important to your organisation.

This then feeds into your shortlisting questionnaire (RFI), which extracts the most important requirements – those with the highest weights – and turns requirement statements into closed questions.

The RFI is the first major document your candidate suppliers will receive from you. It is designed to create a good impression on them, while being both efficient and effective at cutting down your list of candidates to evaluate. Its objectives are:

- to convince suppliers that your organisation is an attractive prospect and an IT purchaser who is both informed and organised;

- to give suppliers enough information to either 'qualify out' or to commit the resources necessary for a serious opportunity. Your approach must prove you are not a 'tyre kicker', since IT procurement is partly talent management (see Chapter 2);

- to eliminate unsuitable candidates early, before either you or the candidate supplier invests time wastefully;

- to evaluate and score the longlisted candidates and therefore select a shortlist.

The RFI is all about consistency of approach – because consistency in approach is the best way to spot diversity in candidates. Your objective is to compare candidates efficiently against selected requirements in order to spot the differences, and then use your findings on difference to establish the minority – the shortlist of candidates to evaluate in detail.

The RFI gives the candidate suppliers the same project briefing and allows you to put a standard response ladder against questions to encapsulate the degree of fit. You also provide space for supplier explanations. Before marking the RFI responses from candidates – and preferably even before sending it out – best practice is to agree the model answers to create a marking scheme. This means you have formalised the basis of decision before applying it, which makes assessing responses quicker, less controversial and more reliable.

7.3 APPROACH TO EVALUATION AT RFI STAGE

- **Desk-based:** RFI assessments are 'desk-based' – documentation is sent and received. There are no long supplier meetings or demonstrations yet, although there will probably be conversations – from candidate suppliers to clarify your needs, and to suppliers during the assessment process to clarify their responses.

- **Consistent comparison:** Throughout the entire evaluation process it is essential to avoid comparing software products to each other. This approach usually breaks down in confusion and disagreement because it is impossibly complex and distorted by evaluator 'experience' (meaning assumption, misunderstanding or prejudice). The only effective way to manage the assessment of multiple, complex software solutions is to measure them all against the same yardstick or benchmark. In this case, the yardstick is your preliminary shortlisting questionnaire – the RFI. This tests those attributes of the software and its supplier that are most important to you as a potential customer, concentrating on those aspects that can be tested in a 'paper-based' exercise.

- **Limited ambition:** Keep in mind that this is a staged decision-making process, with multiple gates. At this stage, you are not aiming to pick the winner. You are dividing the pool of candidates who respond into those who are held (or 'parked') for the meantime and the minority who are taken forward for the more detailed evaluation against the full requirements. 'When it is not necessary to make a decision, it is necessary not to make a decision' (Lord Falkland, 1610–1643).

- **Quick no:** One of the basic rules of quality control is that you do not invest in 'the rejects'. For instance, a garment manufacturer will inspect the roll of cloth on delivery to ensure that there are no dye or weaving flaws before investing the effort to cut, sew and finish. The assessments at this stage are quick ones. An efficient RFI can process many candidates without the assessment being prohibitively labour-intensive.

- **Blind responses:** Candidates do not know the weightings when they receive your RFI (apart from the general point that RFIs concentrate on the most important aspects). To avoid distortion, it is best they respond to a point without knowing how significant it is. The statement of capability should not be influenced by them thinking that lacking that facility is (in sales terms) a 'deal breaker'. This approach – whose austerity is deliberately rigorous and sometimes unpopular – is also applied later in the method during the scoring of candidates by your internal evaluation team (see Chapter 9).

- **Current version:** The basis of evaluation must be the current shipping version that is demonstrable today and can be seen in client reference sites. Evaluating future facilities is extremely dangerous and usually means a selection project underperforms. This is because all software is malleable. If you have enough time, money, expertise and organisational will, you **could** perfect software. However, if you assume the software **will** be improved, this means all the candidates are perfect – and indistinguishable.

7.4 PRIOR PLANNING

7.4.1 Your effort

By this stage, the RFI process assumes that not only are the requirements collected, documented and agreed, but that they are also weighted for importance (see Chapter 5). This helps you to identify a sub-set, concentrating on those requirements that are most important to your organisation. These will reward those candidates that are strong in important areas.

It should generally take you (and probably one colleague) two to five days to derive your RFI from the combination of the full requirements document and the weights that encapsulate the importance of each requirement. This allows time for you to extract the sub-set of requirements with higher weights for importance (see section 7.5), formulate your special RFI questions (see section 7.5.3) and circulate a draft for comment. You must also allow for one or two days' effort during the RFI response period to field supplier questions.

7.4.2 Scheduling others

When setting the supplier response deadline, or giving your assessors forward notice of the dates for your internal assessment meeting, the following figures, for both effort and duration, should be useful.

External candidate suppliers who fill in RFI

The sales executive at candidate suppliers will normally need to enlist some implementation consultants to prepare their response to your RFI. Assuming they know their own product, it will take them typically one or two days' effort to complete your questionnaire. (This is for each solution; sometimes resellers choose to put forward two candidate products, filling in two separate questionnaires.)

You should allow suppliers about 10 days, although you will give them advance notice of the date to expect your RFI as well as your response deadline. Personally, I aim for dates that span two weekends. While it is not fair to demand that supplier responses cut into their weekends, you have at least given them the option to put in some work over a weekend if they are slipping against schedule and are motivated to do so.

Internal customer assessors who mark responses

You should allow one to three days to conduct your assessment of responses and to present the findings. This represents a substantial time saving over conventional evaluation processes. Note that, in practice, an effective assessment process can average as little as 40–60 minutes for the evaluation of each candidate's RFI response. This is because you have asked closed questions, have a 'marking scheme' and can eliminate the least suitable candidates before you have even fully marked their response. Contrast this to some evaluations that allow multiple weeks to establish the shortlist. This time would even include some candidate supplier meetings. However, by using this method that is unnecessary – a premature commitment or 'over-investment' in candidates who have not yet established that they are worthy of in-depth evaluation.

7.5 FORMULATING EFFECTIVE QUESTIONS

7.5.1 Selecting good questions

As a guiding principle, each question on the RFI should earn its place. Remember that by including a question you are committing resources, since the question will require a commitment from multiple individuals or indeed multiple teams. You should be conscious of the multiplier effect on labour content when deciding whether to include a requirement.

Every question has to be set, agreed, revised and distributed. It then needs to be responded to by suppliers – and you should treat supplier time as a precious resource (see Chapter 2). Finally, it needs to be marked when the response comes back and the outcome of the assessment included in the summary and the presentation to the decision-making body that will approve taking the shortlist into the next phase of detailed evaluation.

The following aspects can help you to establish which questions to include.

Support important areas

To focus on important requirements, you should include most requirements weighted 5 and many weighted 4, subject to the qualifications in the rest of this section.

Occasionally you should include a few requirements with weights lower than 4. Some requirements, while of moderate importance, are a good 'litmus test' of the sophistication and capabilities of a solution. Meeting your requirement might require features that are only seen in a software product that is extremely well designed and skilfully constructed.

Likely to differentiate candidates

Questions should be 'discriminatory' in the purest sense, in that they should discriminate between candidates by discerning the differences between them. A question where there is a high probability that all candidates are equally capable does not really earn its place. When trying to identify the candidate that fits best for a financial solution aimed at large corporations, it is probably a waste of time to ask if the product is multi-currency. A smarter question may be to establish how many currencies the software supports in case there is an upper limit.

Defend project reputation

Some questions are to protect the project reputation. Some processing is so fundamental that failing to express a requirement might look as though you have failed to understand organisational need.

Suitable for desk enquiry

Sometimes an investigation of fit – say, one intended to test the cultural match between supplier and customer – can only be progressed effectively by conversation. The RFI concentrates on those areas where the need can be expressed as a written prompt and the capability can be expressed in a written response. There should be a limited need for second-level questions to clarify your needs or the supplier response, and no need for resource-intensive face-to-face meetings at this stage.

Representative sample

Another factor is balance. If your requirements document has 10 sections with 15 requirements each, you should have at least two questions from each of the sections. This ensures that the different areas are checked, and safeguards process integrity. Nobody can later accuse the evaluation team of selecting a winner without considering 'their area'.

Optimistic working assumptions with back-check

When identifying suitable questions at RFI stage, you may make a limited number of optimistic working assumptions. The fact that the candidate actually meets the requirement – which is initially assumed from their response – can be tested later during the detailed evaluation of shortlisted candidates. There is a calculated risk that a candidate slips through to the shortlist even though it lacks a crucial requirement, forcing rework of the shortlist. This is a trade-off against economy of effort.

7.5.2 Avoid premature evidence

Preliminary questionnaires can be unnecessarily long and involve wasted effort to write, complete and assess because they seek information that could better be managed by exception.

You should only ask the questions that you need to ask – the questions that are going to elicit information that distinguishes between candidates. At this stage you should also only ask for substantiation if necessary. For instance, your organisational procurement standards might stipulate that the supplier must have public liability insurance to $5 million. You should not stipulate that the RFI response must incorporate a certified photocopy of their insurance certificate. For most candidates, apart from the three or four you are going to shortlist, this will be an irrelevance – they will miss the shortlist for other reasons.

It is better to handle such stipulations by exception. In the briefing document (or in one 'super-requirement' giving future conditions of customer order), give a schedule of all the assurances you will need if a prospective supplier is successful – such as insurance covers, health and safety policy, service level agreements or employee vetting procedure. State clearly that they will be conditions of your eventual order and that you will be seeking proof just before the negotiation stage.

This means that only the minority of suppliers have to compile this material, and assessors do not need to look at multiple certificates. More importantly, seeking a gradual commitment is in your interest. Later, when the shortlist is two, a prospective supplier will not lose a major contract if it proves one certificate is the sole omission from their capability. For instance, they may well extend their public liability insurance if it is currently inadequate, since the additional insurance premium is trivial compared to your contract value. At RFI stage, the commitment you want from the supplier is not that they have all of these essential attributes now, but that they are prepared to get them if they become a final hurdle.

7.5.3 Ensure wording is specific

A well-formed RFI question can be described as 'crunchy' – meaning measurable.

Many individuals who work for software suppliers are in love with their product, and hate to acknowledge it has shortcomings. Therefore, they will be reluctant to say, 'No, it does not do that'. The wording of your RFI question must push them to take a position – so that it is at least clear later if they in fact have been unhelpful or misleading. This is one of the reasons for asking closed questions: it makes it harder to 'talk around' the question without answering it.

HOW NOT TO DO IT: EXAMPLES OF WEAK RFI QUESTIONS

Is your solution future proof? This phrase is meaningless in practice. There are much better ways to define the characteristics of a flexible software product and its ability to 'roll with the punches' as new requirements emerge.

Is the solution user-friendly? This is impossible to test by a closed question on a survey document. Every supplier will respond, 'Yes'. Additionally, it is not readily measurable as usability is based on perception.

Are your helpdesk staff customer-focused? Good luck to your negotiators trying to nail down a binding contractual commitment to the answer!

Always remember the fundamental objective when writing your RFI – to create a set of questions that allow you to detect the spread of capability amongst the candidates.

The questions can sometimes be open in that they allow for more detail than a yes-no answer, but they need to be focused enough to require specifics.

7.5.4 Strong questions

Table 7.1 illustrates strong RFI entries to reinforce the principles of formulating effective questions. In the left-hand column, in some cases, the software type was the entire project type; in other cases, it was a large project where solutions had modules addressing different areas, in which case 'type' reflects one of the major sections of a larger RFI. In the right-hand column are notes to you as reader, not the candidates.

Table 7.1 Strong RFI questions

Software type	Example RFI question for candidate supplier	Note to reader
Customer relationship management (CRM)	Does the software integrate sales management (suspects, prospects) with service management (after-sales care) such that customer service calls are raised and progress-chased from a common customer database?	This specific wording safeguards against a loose interpretation of one of the software industry's favourite words – integration.
Financial	Does the software provide a history of cost price changes – so the latest price is shown, but the user can drill down to a **history** of prices (each with the date, login of the person who entered it and a note for the specific price)?	Many financial solutions necessarily cover statutory reports and accounts – so, to find differences, this question explores a more unusual requirement.
Product lifecycle man-agement (PLM)	Does the software support production models – bills of material with added **operations** (like inspections) and **resources** (like plant or an amount of skilled engineering time)?	Searches out more modern PLM solutions that support much more than just 'the bill'.
Computer aided design (CAD)	Does the modelling of moving assemblies detect clashes such that simulating a vehicle bogie turning will highlight that it will foul the underframe?	Another clash detection question might go further to stipulate a degree of precision.

(Continued)

Table 7.1 Continued

Software type	Example RFI question for candidate supplier	Note to reader
Human resource management (HRM)	Does the software explicitly support the skills database with skills, qualifications and the expiry dates for certificates?	Note the distinction between a skill and a qualification – and the more demanding requirement of dates.
Time recording and charging	Does the software record time booking with hours charged at multiple rates, based on the client, the programme, the person and the skill or role?	Requires a rich data structure to support this many options – a litmus test question.
Procurement and inventory	Does the software hold supplier details including turnover and credit rating, scope of supply, approvals, accreditations and exchange rate agreements?	Asking for 'supplier information' is too vague – all procurement solutions hold some – so this seeks specifics that are important and less usual.
Manufacturing resource planning (MRP)	Does the software support styles (finished goods) by a product-variant matrix or family such that one style in five sizes and four colours is **not** 20 stock codes, but one with variants presented as a matrix or as 'child' sub-products?	Style-colour-size processing is critical to MRP for apparel, making it hard to use 'generic' products rather than 'niche' or industry-specific products.
Asset management (AM)	Do existing customers use the solution to monitor multiple measures (e.g. volts, amps) on power-generating devices?	Another RFI question would explore technical limits on the number of devices and signals (measures) per device.
Demand and supply chain management (SCM)	Does the solution upload data from multiple MRP systems into SCM, such that it integrates multiple MRP datasets – one being the in-house solution, but others being outside our control at joint ventures or contract manufacturers?	Given the volumes of data on the intended application, manually loading stock data would have been unfeasible.

(Continued)

Table 7.1 Continued

Software type	Example RFI question for candidate supplier	Note to reader
Technical IT needs	Does the software run under a single sign-on (or 'one-login') system that recognises Microsoft's Active Directory?	The IT department are stakeholders and some 'technical' requirements become RFI entries.
IT supplier assessment	Do you offer reference sites that are pro-ject-based companies rather than batch manufacturing or high-volume distribution flow lines?	Some requirements, and therefore RFI sections, relate to the supplier rather than the software.

Do not let these examples mislead you into thinking that RFIs are all about artificial authoring techniques to create 'clever' questions. Many questions will be rather mundane. The most important aspects are that, in all cases, the requirement is important to that particular evaluation, can be turned into an RFI question and is likely to reveal differences between candidates.

7.6 PREPARING THE RFI

7.6.1 Background or briefing section for candidates

Give basic details of your company such as market segment, geographic distribution and size. You should provide links to published information, such as your company accounts or website. In the original material you create, concentrate on those aspects of your company that are not widely known but are more likely to attract a software supplier, such as your track record for intelligent capital investments.

Explain your project, especially the opportunities it presents to both parties, and any constraints such as statutory compliance, budgets, deadlines or other IT systems that cannot be moved.

Explain the RFI process, including the progressive shortlisting and some detail about your assessment process at RFI stage. Say how many candidates are on the longlist at this stage, but do not normally give names.

Cover the supplier response required. For instance, stipulate that candidate suppliers should answer all questions even if – especially if – their answer is essentially 'No'. As a minimum, the supplier response to each question should select one of the levels of fit on the predetermined ladders that you offer (see Figure 7.1).

Stress that it is to their advantage to add at least one or two sentences to substantiate their responses. Stress that, while supporting material is welcome, any appendix material should be tied back to the original RFI question number. For suppliers, an effective response is partly a matter of 'exam technique'. It is their job to understand their own product, then marshal that knowledge and put the answer 'under your nose'. They must answer the question with the correct capability or feature in the software matched to the appropriate requirement.

Make it plain that after negotiation you intend three attachments to contract – your requirements document, the scores after detailed evaluation and the scoring definitions document. Since the RFI is derived from the requirements document, this means that supplier responses during detailed evaluation will in due course 'have contractual significance'. (Subtext: any aggressive misrepresentation now will be 'found out'.)

Make clear your response deadline and the format of response required. To safeguard against diary mistakes, stipulate your deadline in unambiguous terms, such as Monday 23 November 2015 by 5 p.m.

Cover the RFI assessment schedule, including meeting dates and when you will notify the outcome. Request a single point of contact for queries during the assessment period.

7.6.2 Basis of costing

It is not feasible to seek a fixed cost at this stage. However, it is possible to establish if there are substantial differences in cost profile for some candidates. For instance, some software is known for the expense of the supporting service providers and one supplier might have a day-rate for their implementation consultants that is 50 per cent higher than another.

The objective when providing costing parameters is to gain an outline, indicative and non-binding estimate of those project elements that are predictable early on. It is more important for costings to be comparable between candidates than entirely accurate. The philosophy of costing metrics is that all the estimates will be somewhat wrong, but your aim is to make them at least consistently so. In practice, by controlling as many input metrics as you reasonably can, you aim to make the cost spread more likely to reflect the real price differences. You do not want the cost spread merely to reflect the suppliers making different costing assumptions.

Examples of costing metrics statements in the RFI include the following:

- 'Suppliers should include the cost of any optional software modules (with their additional licences and annual support fees) necessary to meet the requirements.'

- 'Assume "seat" licence numbers at 300 named users, or 200 concurrent users, whichever is the more cost effective. Stipulate which method you are using, or which you recommend if there is a customer choice.'

- 'In case these need to be factored into your pricing, we believe the number of servers will be two (in USA and Germany), country jurisdictions will be 10, trading currencies at five but languages at only one.'

7.7 TECHNOLOGY USED FOR RFI QUESTIONS AND RESPONSES

You will process a high volume of detailed information. The only practical way to manage this volume is to be heavily electronic. For example, it would be prohibitively expensive for you and suppliers to post a bulky RFI then accept handwritten responses that would need transcription into some sort of document during marking.

Your organisation might be sophisticated enough to set up a web-based questionnaire, perhaps using one of the hosted surveying tools with user-defined forms driven by templates. Survey tools are an effective means of collecting information, especially if you use one that updates a response database. It will be essential for people to be able to save drafts and then submit when their response is finalised.

The medium-technology approach (one which is normally good enough) is to send out a briefing document and a separate 'turnaround' spreadsheet. Invite its return with the candidate supplier name built into the updated spreadsheet. (An alternative might be a cloud-based document-sharing platform – provided you can keep the different candidate responses separate.) The spreadsheet is a good container for work by you and candidates because you can hide supporting columns while working on content, or use filtering to concentrate on, say, the 5-weight requirements. You should add validation to standardise responses via drop-down lists.

You should have section headings, because the supplier response team (and later the internal assessment team) will specialise and tackle different sections according to their expertise.

For each entry or requirement, there should be a question number, the question itself, the original requirement number for traceability and two columns for reply.

- The first reply column uses validation so that the supplier response must pick from a stipulated list of values. These define rungs on an escalating ladder of fit (see Figure 7.1).

- The final column should be a wider free-text format for supporting notes, including cross-references to any substantiating material supplied in appendices.

Figure 7.1 Candidate response with drop-down values

Ref	Category	Questions [Vn 2.0]	RDD	Response Notes
108	Interfaces	Similarly, does the system support EDI with the XML standard/specification?	0314	Standard
109	Interfaces	Does EDI processing support high volumes of serial numbers? Such that EDI 856 Advance Shipping Notice (ASN, packing slip) for a container full of small products might have 25,000 S/Nos.	0318	✓ Standard User-defined Partial Mod Outside scope
110	Interfaces	Many smart manufacturing machines collect statistical information about production throughput, with exceptions, and capture locally the batch/serial number of materials used in a build. CC need to be able to trace failures at a machine, with associated parts. Does the system accept output from manufacturing and assembly machines?	0332	

7.8 MARKING SCHEME

Standardised or coded responses structure supplier replies to help you spot the differences between products and organisations. The wording is also deliberately intended to make it easy for suppliers to drop themselves onto an attractive rung on the ladder. For each question, they should be able to identify one of the phrases and think, 'that's us'. It also recognises the fact that suppliers do not like to say no. The explanation of the values follows.

7.8.1 Outside scope

Not supported by the current solution. The supplier does not envisage this processing in the foreseeable future. They do not expect it to be available as a paid modification. In other words, it is 'not what they do'.

7.8.2 Modification

This would require a program code modification of the software. The supplier would expect this to be chargeable.

7.8.3 Partial

The software offers some support for this requirement, but not as outlined in the requirement. Such a response will generally need a supporting description so that the assessors can understand the level of fit. Note that this category does not involve **future** facilities unless they will be:

- free in the sense of included in the standard product;
- available in the standard software and subject to the normal support and upgrade mechanisms;
- available in the version of the product that will ship before the expected contract date.

7.8.4 User-defined

The desired processing is achieved by exploiting user-defined features to meet the requirement as expressed, meaning the need can be met by configuration and not by code customisation. This assumes an educated user with the training and authority to apply the relevant settings, probably with standard implementation consultancy at the beginning of the project.

7.8.5 Standard

The desired processing is achieved using standard, in-built logic and data in the current, shipping version of the software.

7.9 PREPARING IDEAL ANSWERS

At the very least, you should design the 'model answers' before you start to mark the responses. However, ideally you should create the marking scheme or ideal answers before you finalise the RFI and send it out. If you (or your test volunteer) cannot answer a question, you cannot expect the suppliers to answer since they are people external to your organisation and do not have your tacit knowledge about your business and project.

The model or ideal answers can be expressed briefly. Against one question, you might simply have MBY – standing for 'must be yes'. Or against the question for the number of people staffing the helpdesk, your ideal answer might read: minimum 10.

You would normally put the marking scheme in an extra column at the right-hand edge of your spreadsheet. Of course, when you have finalised the RFI questionnaire, you must remember to delete this column. Unless you are sufficiently sophisticated to have hidden columns that are protected with a password, this means that you will need to have two versions of the RFI – the external public version and the internal marking version. However, the public version is derived from the full version (the one with ideal answers) at the very last minute – simply by saving it under a different name and deleting the dangerous columns.

7.10 DISTRIBUTING THE RFI

You should email the RFI out to suppliers. Each should go to the named individual that you found earlier during your burst of telephone calls to get contact names, numbers and email addresses. You should never send RFIs to generic email addresses such as enquiries@example.com in case it is not passed on.

As the documents will be bulky and will be distributed internally amongst multiple team members at suppliers, avoid attached documents if you can. It is better if the email contains links to documents the candidates can download from a company website, a procurement portal or one of the cloud storage services. As well as the benefits to project administration, effective use of tools during the project process is another way of establishing your organisation's image as a 'savvy' potential customer – the sophisticated buyer who will also exploit the successful supplier's software successfully.

Make sure that your covering email repeats the response deadline. Make it clear that you want only the spreadsheet to be returned, and that it should be renamed to reflect the supplier and product so that you can distinguish the material. Remind candidates that they should answer all questions.

Expect follow-up questions and keep track of the additional information provided. Consider distributing clarifications to all RFI candidates to avoid additional briefings giving one of the candidates an unfair advantage. Tracking also records the supplier ability to understand information, which is especially relevant if they claim sector expertise.

7.11 WHO – ROLES ON THE ASSESSMENT TEAM

Assessment team members might have multiple roles. The team roles you should cover are:

7.11.1 Core member

For consistency, it is important that a core team mark all responses for all candidate suppliers. The minimum 'core' team size is two people, who must be dedicated to the assessment days and sufficiently IT literate to understand the supplier responses. To avoid deadlock, a third person can be important so that there is an opportunity to augment your core team with 'rotating specialist guest assessors'.

7.11.2 Rotating assessor

The guest assessor (or perhaps a pair of guests) joins your meeting for particular sections of the RFI that relate to their expertise and department. The guest assessors give your project deeper roots and enhance the credibility of the assessment results. Engaging them also creates a larger pool of people who have a good experience of the project and who therefore might be prepared to join future phases, especially the highly labour-intensive detailed evaluation.

7.11.3 Recorder

Appoint a meeting 'scribe' who maintains the master list of actions, such as follow-up calls to clarify a response and confirm the mark awarded. However, all the assessment team will mark up the responses, so the scribe is not the only person writing.

7.11.4 Facilitator

Appoint a timekeeper and host. It is best to have an outline schedule of the sequence (by section) in which you will mark the RFI so that you can give the guest assessors an indication of the timeslot when they will join the meeting. The facilitator then gives people shorter-term notice and pulls them into the meeting for 'their' section.

7.12 ASSESSING THE RFI RESPONSES

7.12.1 Agreeing the detailed method

Agree the rules of engagement for assessing with your co-assessor (or the core team if it is larger than two people).

- Agree how you are going to treat withdrawals or 'did not respond' (DNR). Agree whether they will be listed on your master matrix of candidates. Some people prefer all the candidates that receive the RFI to be listed for completeness, and then mark zero those that did not respond. Simply giving them a total score of zero makes it easy to filter them out.

- Agree how you are going to handle non-compliant responses, for instance incomplete submissions, late submissions or ones that are so obviously deficient (say, the majority of requirements not supported) as to be not worth marking. Decide whether you put such a response to the meeting or do not even assess it.

- Agree the sequence in which you will be marking submissions at the section level. You will have a preliminary view based on constrained availability of guest assessors. This will need to be adjusted on the day to reflect people's actual availability.

7.12.2 Briefing the meeting

To save time and misunderstanding, prepare short notes on these agreements and the process for a standard briefing. It will be delivered multiple times. Explain the process in the fewest possible words to your co-assessor(s). Get feedback, then adjust your notes and deliver the briefing to each guest assessor as they join the meeting.

7.13 HOW – THE MAIN RFI ASSESSMENT MEETING

At the start of the meeting, create a reference or baseline copy of all the material submitted – such as by burning a DVD or using a cloud-based archive. The protection of an evidence trail is all part of process integrity. Whichever candidate you eventually choose, there will be some critic ready to say the people who ran the selection were incompetent or corrupt. Sometimes, you need the audit trail to show that you have been thorough, professional and even-handed.

7.13.1 Marking values

Overall, you must beware responses that talk around but do not directly address the RFI question. You safeguard against this by imposing a structured response 'ladder'. Your marking slots the answer onto the correct rung. You already have the basis of this and can award points according to the ladder at Table 7.2.

Table 7.2 Standard RFI marking scheme

Points	Response	Meaning
8	Standard	Standard processing in current shipping version of system.
6	User-defined	Processing achieved by exploiting user-defined features to meet requirement as expressed.
4	Partial	Some support, but not as outlined in requirement. For instance, lacks capacity (e.g. three required, two available).
2	Mod	Would require a code modification of system, probably chargeable.
0	Outside scope	Not supported by current system; not envisaged; not available as paid modification; not what we do.

You should also consider introducing extra values to the assessment.

You might award one point less for an **unsubstantiated** answer. For instance, if you award eight points for a standard feature where you are confident of fit because it has been adequately described, you might award only **seven** points if the supplier response selected standard, but has not written a single word describing the way their standard facility fits your requirement.

On some projects, the assessors have also very selectively used the **bonus nine**. If a candidate clearly sets the standard for perfection (meeting the requirement with consummate ease, with plenty of headroom to the requirement as stated and with multiple options) they may deserve more points than just standard. For instance, there may be not one but two or three facilities that all meet the requirement, each of them credible and each useful in a different context. One example was a PLM requirement to hold multiple variants of the bill of material. The most capable software not only did this, but also responded to login ID and showed the default variant to each user based on their role in the project. The trigger for awarding bonus nine is often when assessors say, 'wow' when reading the high-end response. Introducing the extra values gives the extended marking scheme at Table 7.3.

Table 7.3 Extended RFI marking scheme

Points	Response	Meaning
9	Bonus	Exceeds requirement with usable extra facilities. Sets standard of excellence.
8	Standard	Standard processing in current shipping version of system.
7	Standard – unsub	Standard, but no substantiation given.
6	User-defined	Processing achieved by exploiting user-defined features to meet requirement as expressed.
5	User-defined – unsub	User-defined, but no substantiation given.
4	Partial	Some support, but not as outlined in requirement. For instance, lacks capacity (e.g. three required, two available).
3	Partial – unsub	Partial, but no substantiation given.
2	Mod	Would require a code modification of system, probably chargeable.
1	Mod – unsub	Mod, but no substantiation given.
0	Outside scope	Not supported by current system; not envisaged; not available as paid modification; not what we do.

7.13.2 Sequence of marking

It is crucial to mark **all of the different candidate responses for a single question** and then move to your next question.

- First, this is the only practical way to manage your time, especially if you have guest assessors attending the meeting for their specialist block of RFI responses.

- Second, and more subtly, such an approach improves process integrity, because the scores awarded are less likely to be distorted by favourable impressions of one candidate. If an assessor marks all responses for a single candidate in a batch and is favourably inclined towards that candidate, they tend to give more points than justified. However, if at every question they are comparing the capability of their unconsciously preferred candidate to the other candidates, they receive a 'reality check' at every single question.

- Third, in practice, it is easier to identify the difference in capability between packages if you deliberately forget about the big picture and just make small or 'atomic' assessments of each candidate against each requirement. This is another very real demonstration of the practicality of comparing all candidates to the same yardstick or benchmark, rather than comparing them to each other.

In terms of document management, it is usually better to print all submissions (certainly all of the core response spreadsheets). If you lay them out around a large boardroom table, it allows the assessors to walk literally round the job. The physicality of this approach makes for higher energy levels. It also makes it easier to apply parallel processing, because the assessors can walk round the table one behind the other in a train, marking up the responses.

As the group starts to assess, they will develop a feel for which questions tend to tease out the difference between candidates. In a section of 25 RFI questions, there might be two 'killer questions' that tend to knock out candidates because they fail mandatory requirements.

In these circumstances, on the grounds of economy of effort, your assessing team may mark all candidates against these two questions first. If a candidate is rejected, one method to make this clear is to turn their response document upside down. These various techniques of management by exception explain why the average length of time to assess each response using this process is so low. The meeting continues, with guest assessors arriving and leaving, until eventually all the questions have been assessed for all the candidates remaining.

You will need to follow up some responses after the meeting or even during the meeting if you are held up. There is always the risk that a perceived difference of fit is actually explained by different amounts of information and understanding. Let us assume that you have agreed that the shortlist will have three entries. You might clarify some responses for the candidate that is emerging as rank fourth. You would not for one ranked eighteenth – it is not the margin of error that is keeping them out of your shortlist. If the cut-off to shortlist is rank three, you need to be confident in the scores for the third, fourth and possibly fifth ranks, especially if the points are close.

Alternative full marking

Note an alternative, more labour-intensive, approach. Some assessment teams feel it is fairer to mark all responses for all candidates, even though it means certain candidates have failed multiple mandatory requirements. The reason for this might be that some assessing teams want to give comprehensive feedback to either the project board or to the candidate suppliers. Therefore, this includes the full score and the number of mandatory requirements that the candidate failed.

This approach can be an important defence against an aggressive, litigious supplier who objects if not shortlisted, or in the situation where the decision-making body have heard of (and may be inclined towards) a high-profile candidate that is actually provably unfit for purpose.

7.14 SUMMARISING THE ASSESSMENT OUTCOME

Compile the marks onto a detailed RFI assessment spreadsheet. This summarises the RFI yardstick, optionally with a short 'keyword' summary of the questions and an audit trail back to the original requirement number. Columns for each candidate show the marks awarded, preferably with totals and ranking. See Figure 7.2 for a small extract from an RFI assessment: the candidates would be named in your project.

7.14.1 Treatment of estimated costs

As they can only be at list price, before negotiation, the cost details collected can only be indicative and cannot be used for budget costs. However, they should allow you to compare candidates. Large software packages are usually procured with a mix of the following main cost categories. You should seek and compile the costs under these headings.

- **Software or initial licence costs.** Software is usually a combination of **modules** (the extent of capability, especially where there are optional components) and **seats** (the number of users with access). This should be a consistent number, given that your requirement will state the maximum number envisaged for the lifetime use of the product.

- **Support and maintenance charges.** These are based on a percentage of the software cost and charged annually. If you calculate a 10-year costing, a 20 per cent maintenance charge means that you buy the software twice more in the period.

- **Services costs.** These are usually for training and implementation consultancy hours. During implementation they are generally invoiced monthly in arrears after consuming the hours. However, for your costing you may either ask for an estimated number of hours to implementation – an unreliable number – or simply ask for the day-rate for implementation consultants and project manager.

- **Hardware.** Sometimes excluded on a large project that runs on standard corporate infrastructure (which is treated as a general overhead), but if extra hardware will be needed, given expected volumes, some capacity planning is necessary. You would only cost hardware if it is a distinguishing factor – for instance, if some candidates are likely to have higher lifetime cost of ownership because they require massively more hardware to run.

Figure 7.2 Fragment of RFI assessment results

Colter Civils
RFI Assessments
To Version 2.0

Ref	Category	Questions [Vn 2.0]	Sub Sys	RDD	Short	Candidate A	Candidate B	Candidate C	Candidate D	Candidate E
LS	International Count	7		7						
75	International	Does the software support IFRS, with reference sites of international companies listed on a major stock exchange.	ERPfin	0214	IFRS	7	0	8	0	7
76	International	Does the software explicitly support multi-currency including budget currency exchange rate? Such that overseas subsidiaries have, per currency per year, at least one planned exchange rate to the Group home currency (Sterling/GBP).	ERPfin	0215	Multi-currency exchange rate	7	4	8	0	7
77	International	Does the software explicitly support currency gains and losses (ForEx variance)? Such that when an actual invoice is paid, any difference between the budget and actual exchange rates should be posted to an exchange rate gain or loss account.	ERPfin	0216	Currency variation	7	0	8	0	7
78	International	Does the software explicitly support pricing, accounting and budgeting in multiple currencies per operating company? Such that each subsidiary within the CC group can have its own ledger system and the functional currency will be the local currency.	ERPfin	0217	Currency per company	7	0	8	0	7
79	International	Does the software consolidate accounts with currency conversions? Such that, where JV companies are part owned by CC, the software should be able to consolidate accounts taking say 50% of profits from another currency.	ERPfin	0223	Currency conversion	7	0	8	0	7
80	International	Does the software allow statutory accounts compliant with different local national regulations? Such that the same solution installation (possibly with multiple companies on the system) generates multiple sets of national accounts, each reflecting local national accounting standards	ERPfin	0224	Local statutory accounts.	7	0	8	0	7
81	International	Does the software compliance with export and import controls? Such that it supports a matrix to recognise the limitations, stipulations and embargoes of such rules as ITAR.	ERPfin	0225	Export/import control	4	4	4	0	7

7.15 PRESENTATION TO THE PROJECT BOARD

The best presentation is a summary matrix with rankings (see Figure 7.3).

Give some highlights from your shortlisting process, such as requirements (RFI questions) that were particularly potent in knocking out candidates or a candidate where the 'gut feel' was positive but it fell astonishingly short in important areas. This means that candidates stand on their merits even if they were previously viewed favourably, or

Figure 7.3 RFI assessment summary

Summary Of Scores & Costs

Candidate	Status	Rank (Respects Filters)	RFI Capability Points	Cost £K - Low	Cost £K - High	Software Cost For PPI £k	PP Index - Points/£K	PP Index - Rank	General Note	Note For PB	Chart	10-Year Software	10-Year S/w+Services Ratio	Services Est
Candidate A	Hold - Benchmark	5	902	£ 555	£ 775	£ 775	1.2	5			Unified	£ 2,324	2	£ 4,648
Candidate B	Hold	8	793	£ 9,999	£ 9,999	£ 9,999	0.1	12						
Candidate C	Shortlist	3	1047	£ 734	£ 825	£ 825	1.3	3	Points gap to 4 of 110		Unified	£ 2,475	2	£ 4,950
Candidate D	Hold - Benchmark	16	430	£ 150	£ 300	£ 300	1.4	1						
Candidate E	Hold - Reserve	4	937	£ 900	£ 1,250	£ 1,250	0.7	7			Unified	£ 3,750	2	£ 7,500
Candidate F	Hold	6	867	£ 9,999	£ 9,999	£ 9,999	0.1	11						
Candidate G	Hold	14	591	£ 9,999	£ 9,999	£ 9,999	0.1	15		Offered mods 52pt				
Candidate H	Hold - Benchmark	11	649	£ 700	£ 900	£ 900	0.7	8	Points gap to 1 of 430					
Candidate I	Shortlist	2	1076	£ 675	£ 862	£ 862	1.2	4			Unified	£ 2,586	2	£ 5,172
Candidate J	Shortlist	1	1079	£ 750	£ 1,100	£ 1,100	1.0	6			Unified	£ 3,300	2	£ 6,600
Candidate K	Hold - Benchmark	13	594	£ 1,240	£ 1,877	£ 1,877	0.3	10						
Candidate L	Hold	7	848	£ 600	£ 600	£ 600	1.4	2						
Candidate M	Hold - Benchmark	10	673	£ 272	£ 1,443	£ 1,443	0.5	9						
Candidate N	Hold	15	465	£ 9,999	£ 9,999	£ 9,999	0.0	16						
Candidate O	Hold	12	624	£ 9,999	£ 9,999	£ 9,999	0.1	14						
Candidate P	Hold	9	762	£ 9,999	£ 9,999	£ 9,999	0.1	13						
Integrate I+K	Hold - Benchmark	1	1102	£ 1,915	£ 2,739	£ 2,739	0.4	11			Paired	£ 8,216	3	£ 24,647
Integrate A+M	Hold - Benchmark	6	1013	£ 827	£ 2,218	£ 2,218	0.5	10			Paired	£ 6,653	3	£19,960
Integrate C+K	Hold - Benchmark	4	1072	£ 1,974	£ 2,702	£ 2,702	0.4	12			Paired			
Bubble Chart	Chart Variables		X-axis				Y-axis	Size						

might be a 'pet product' (Axelos, 2012). This commentary with highlights is especially important if there are unexpected or controversial results – it is your chance to pre-empt challenges during the project board meeting.

One of the most powerful graphics is a value-for-money bubble chart (see Figure 7.4). This tracks the capability (points won) of each candidate on the X-axis versus the projected software-only cost on the Y-axis.

The power of the bubble chart is to track a third variable, in this case the value-for-money or price-performance index. While this is essentially a restatement of the other two variables, it is visually persuasive to show circles where increasing diameter reflects increasing 'bang for buck'. It is one of many defences necessary to counter the 'buy the cheapest' argument.

Figure 7.4 Bubble chart for strongest candidates - RFI points, cost and price-performance

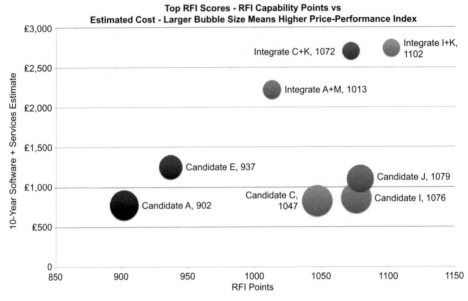

Figure 7.4 illustrates a project bubble chart after assessing the RFI responses.

Note that in this project the RFI was more sophisticated since it needed to address two questions – not only who to shortlist, but also whether it would be necessary to take two major products (of software classes ERP and PLM) and integrate them.

Hence, there are the three unusual, exploratory candidates at top right. These were **hypothetical** integrations with pairs of the best-in-class products, with higher capability but higher 10-year cost. The higher points (capability measured to RFI) did not justify the higher cost.

The three unified, out-of-the-box candidates C, I and J had capability nearly as good (or better) for significantly lower capital cost (let alone the internal labour effort of operating two huge solutions). These three went forward to detailed evaluation, with one of them procured at the end of the evaluation.

7.15.1 Defensible, evidence-based decisions

If the agreement is to shortlist, say, three candidates, you need to be sure that you can justify the boundary between those included and those excluded from the shortlist. Using the RFI process as outlined here, the shortlist is usually self-explanatory. It is based on the scores and consequent ranking after some candidates are excluded for failing to meet one or more mandatory requirements.

The advantage of 'running the shortlisting by the numbers' is that it gives a robust, clear and defensible outcome to the decision-making group, even though they were not personally involved in the assessment.

Remember, at RFI stage you are asking to proceed to the next stage of your project with two agreed lists. One of the candidates shortlisted for detailed evaluation. The other of candidates held or parked (at least for now).

7.15.2 Notifying candidates

Notifying suppliers who are held or parked

You should 'never say never' and you leave your options open. Do not describe an unsuccessful candidate as rejected or failed. Simply use the more neutral term that they are held or parked. When letting them know that they have not been shortlisted, make it clear that you may need to get back to them. It may emerge that one of the shortlisted candidates was misunderstood (or misrepresented) and proves unsuitable on later inspection.

While suppliers will naturally seek feedback on the areas where they missed out, it is generally best to give this much later in the process. You do not want to get into a debate with multiple suppliers at this stage.

Notifying suppliers who are shortlisted

For the shortlisted candidates, consider offering them a tour of your most impressive premises if this will help prove you are a strategic sale (see Chapter 2); for instance, if your investment in equipment or premises shows you are better funded than published information like annual accounts might suggest, or if you have heavy capital investors and innovative technology you can show off. These site visits suggest that you are an organisation that can invest in capital equipment – including IT – if the business case is right.

7.16 CHAPTER SUMMARY

TAKE-AWAY POINTS

The RFI is not trying to pick the winner. It seeks to gather just enough information to proceed through a gate. It creates an understanding of which candidates are strong enough to merit the more detailed, labour-intensive, in-depth evaluation deserved by those on the shortlist.

As such, the RFI stage is another example of decision-making that is deliberately 'good enough' without being more detailed or labour-intensive than necessary.

There is always the risk that, with high-level and brief evaluations, the gap between candidates is smaller than the margin of error. However, at this stage the margin of error between, say, the candidate in pole position and the candidate at runner-up is irrelevant. If you are taking three candidates forward into detailed evaluation, the significant gap is that between the third-ranked supplier and the 'also-rans'. This is why you clarify those candidates just inside or just outside the shortlist, especially if the difference in points is small.

The shortlisted candidates will be assessed afresh at the next stage. They will be treated the same and will take their chances when they are scored (again) after your detailed evaluation meetings. The rank order at RFI stage is no advantage or disadvantage to those candidates that are shortlisted.

7.16.1 The next chapter

The next chapter will move on to the detailed evaluation. This evaluation is more labour-intensive, although by now you are on safe ground. You will not be wasting time on unsuitable candidates, and you will have confidence in strong shortlisted candidates. It will therefore be worthwhile investing the effort and time into detailed evaluation meetings – these now consider all your requirements, not just the sub-set used in your RFI.

EXECUTIVE PERSPECTIVE: A DIRECTOR'S EXPERIENCE OF FORMALLY MEASURING FIT

My organisation used this process to select and procure an ERP and PLM system while I was Engineering Director. This was a strategically significant decision for the business because of its purchase price and its criticality to the success of our operations.

The method is powerful because it made us focus on our requirements – enabling us to develop a clear understanding across the user group of what we really needed from our system, and helping us to focus on those in the selection and shortlisting process. In the course of this, we gained insights into the strengths and weaknesses of our own business and we were able to deal confidently and decisively with our prospective suppliers.

The methodical approach quickly gained acceptance within our business because it was coherent, structured and transparent. It had clear milestones and deliverables so that the team, management and sponsors could see progress. It brought specialists, functional managers and operational managers together and enabled them to contribute in a structured and equitable way. It enabled the team to make solid decisions based on visible evidence. The decisions that we made using project deliverables such as price-fit charts were respected.

To make this process work, it is important to allocate a good cross-section of subject matter experts, project staff and a finance rep to the team, and give them the time and space to do their task diligently.

7.17 REFERENCES

Axelos (2012) 'Common glossary'. Global Best Practice Portfolio, AXELOS. www.axelos. com/glossaries-of-terms.aspx (10 November 2014).

7.18 FURTHER READING

7.18.1 Books and articles

CIPS (2007) 'Jargon buster'. The Chartered Institute of Purchasing and Supply. http://cips.studyserve.com/skins/cips/customfiles/content/jargonbuster.asp (10 November 2014).

Gillham, B. (2008) *Developing a questionnaire*, 2nd edition (Real World Research). Continnuum-3PL: London.

7.18.2 Related formats by download

RFI supplier briefing document with headings; RFI questionnaire spreadsheet; RFI assessment summary spreadsheet. From http://shop.bcs.org/offtheshelfextras.asp.

8 DETAILED EVALUATION: ASSESSING THE SHORTLISTED CANDIDATES

'On an important decision one rarely has 100% of the information needed for a good decision no matter how much one spends or how long one waits. And, if one waits too long, he has a different problem and has to start all over. This is the terrible dilemma of the hesitant decision maker.'

Robert K. Greenleaf (1904–1990)

8.1 WHAT YOU CAN LEARN FROM THIS CHAPTER

- Understanding the objectives, process and outcomes of the detailed evaluation meetings.
- Being aware of the main risks and pitfalls, so that you have a successful set of evaluation meetings.

8.2 OVERVIEW

IT systems automate detailed rules and the people obliged to use their organisation's software often love it or hate it on the basis of a few of these details. Software is inherently inflexible, and it can be difficult and expensive to change the processing of an application that does not fit your needs. The job of the evaluation team is to understand the large and small differences between candidate products before you commit to buy one.

TERMS DURING DETAILED EVALUATIONS

Evaluation team: your group, representing the customer.

Response team: group from one candidate supplier.

Supplier, response or evaluation meeting: different terms for same meeting (with multiple sessions) where one response team goes through requirements and explains the fit of their software and services to the evaluation team.

Scoring meeting: subsequent meeting where the evaluation team (without any suppliers present) consider fit and score all candidates (see Chapter 9).

Evaluation meetings are the main vehicle for assessing the suitability or fit of the software to your needs. You experience detailed verbal responses from each candidate to each requirement. You gather facts about the fit of software and services to your organisational requirements as follows:

- hold separate evaluation meetings with each candidate – typically three or four suppliers;
- review, for each supplier, all those requirements that will be scored for fit;
- clarify and discuss specific capabilities and best fit with suppliers;
- take notes from the supplier responses by annotating copy requirements documents;
- review and confirm, in cycles, both verbally and through later documentation.

Bear in mind that you are definitely not picking a winner at this stage. Neither are you scoring the candidates against one another – you do this in the later scoring meeting. Instead, at this stage in the method, your main objectives are as follows:

- To meet the need for due diligence, given that an IT selection is a high-risk decision, which will have a long-term impact on your organisation.
- To experience the candidate credibility, honesty and chemistry. Previous responses have been written in the highly constrained format of the RFI. Face-to-face meetings are now important to verify the potential relationship.

You must ensure that your evaluation team adequately comprehend each candidate. You can now afford to invest further in understanding the software and building a relationship with its supplier. You are looking for the best amongst a small group of strong contenders. Usually there will be three or four candidates by this stage.

As you are now working with the strongest candidates, you can ethically expect the suppliers to invest also. They will study your documentation in advance, prepare answers and handouts and respond during labour-intensive meetings.

You should let suppliers know the number of candidates on your shortlist. However, you should not normally give the names of rivals yet. You are still in 'anti-collusion mode' (see Chapter 12, Section 12.4.3).

8.3 WHO – THE ROLES, TEAMS AND SKILLS

8.3.1 New internal stakeholders

This stage is the next opportunity to engage new stakeholders. The newly active role on your project is the evaluation team member. Normally, you will enlist a select group from the interviewees, workshop attendees, weighting workshop participants and RFI assessors. However, you can have entirely new faces on the evaluation team at this stage, especially since some contributions are only a few hours and can be done remotely. For instance, this may be an opportunity to involve an overseas colleague.

8.3.2 Your evaluation team

Advantages of evaluation teams over individuals

Having an evaluation team (rather than an individual person) on a major IT selection project has the following advantages:

- It spreads the workload and reduces the risk of a single point of failure.
- Groups make better decisions, provided the group dynamic is sound, and especially when participants see organisations as communities (Heller, 2001).
- It deflects complaints that an internal stakeholder group were not consulted or represented during the decision-making process.
- It can be easier to schedule meetings and participants since it allows for division of labour and specialism, with some of the subject matter experts attending only portions of the evaluation meetings.

Standing evaluation team

You will normally have a smaller 'core' evaluation team, who should be available to attend all the evaluation meetings. This is a demanding commitment and you will need the cooperation of their manager to have them released for a substantial block of work involving many days and several trips away from the office. The standing evaluation team provide continuity. One of their roles is to ensure that at least two assessors are available for every section of the requirements document.

Visiting or 'rotating' guest evaluators

Visiting or guest evaluators cover specialist topics. They are usually departmental staff. For instance, sales and marketing staff would view the CRM section of a large ERP evaluation.

They may 'visit' by video conference, if travelling to the meeting is not justified when only attending for a few hours. This is provided that they can not only see the demonstrations and slides, but also ask questions of the presenter and their colleagues via audio conferencing. (Such data and video conferencing must also meet your organisation's security policies.)

Consistent attendance is essential

Each evaluation team member – standing or visiting – must be able to attend 'their bit' of all the evaluation meetings with candidate suppliers and then 'their bit' of the subsequent scoring meeting.

If you are assessing four candidates at shortlist stage, it invalidates the process if the same assessors do not see, say, the CRM section for all four candidates. This process is about detecting (now) and scoring (later) the differences between candidates. It is nonsense to score without seeing all the candidate responses to the relevant set of requirements. Likewise, it is completely wasteful to attend the supplier meetings, but then not score.

Chair

As so often happens, the chair is one of the key roles for the meetings, because you rely on them for group management. This is emphatically a group activity and a poor group dynamic will spoil the effectiveness of your evaluation. It is best if the chair works for the customer, your organisation. Their job is to maintain engagement, to ensure that everybody contributes without one voice dominating and to manage both timekeeping and questions. You might be the chair if you are driving the process. If not, possibly the member of the evaluation team who is most senior or most adept at facilitation is the best candidate (Thomas et al., 2012).

Tracking roles and contributions

The sophisticated assignment of roles might be the impetus to use a responsibility assignment matrix (RAM), also called the RACI matrix – Responsible, Accountable, Consulted and Informed (Smith and Erwin, 2011). The matrix records the participant involvement in tasks or deliverables, especially in cross-functional projects. You can use it to map people to requirement document sections and to register session-specific roles such as chair or scribe.

8.3.3 Response team from candidate suppliers

For a major opportunity, the candidate supplier will assemble a response team. Their team members will be of three main types:

- The sales executive allocated to your opportunity, who will normally stay throughout the process, marshal the people, manage the hospitality and probably organise the copious handouts.

- A senior management representative, who will normally drop in occasionally, to act as ambassador and to show that the software supplier is taking your opportunity seriously.

- Subject matter experts, who will be specialists in particular modules of a large software product, for instance the expert in the Resource Management module. With large software products, there is rarely one person who knows enough about every module to give a good response, including coping with the unforeseen questions.

8.3.4 Skill set of customer and supplier attendees

In most organisations, there is competition for resource and everybody wants the best people. For your project, you must fight for an accomplished evaluation team, because their understanding of the software in the next few meetings will have a massive impact on the welfare of their colleagues who will use whichever solution is eventually selected. The skills you require in an evaluation team member are as follows:

- Understanding of the organisation, and therefore its requirements.

- Objectivity, especially when absorbing new or challenging information.

- Being effective in meetings.

- Effectiveness at recording, in this case the information about how features support requirements.
- Being good in teams and especially accomplished at cross-organisation collaboration – which is not the same thing (Archer and Cameron, 2013).

While it is out of your direct control, you seek similar personal attributes in the members of the supplier response team. In their case, understanding of your business is less important, but they must understand (their bit of) the software, digest your requirements and be able to map facilities to requirements.

EXECUTIVE PERSPECTIVE: A DIRECTOR'S EXPERIENCE OF DELEGATED EVALUATION PROCESS

We were at a high-risk crossroads as a business and extremely time-pressed as directors. We needed to replace our single national distributor by creating our own customer database, sales force and logistics, then building up internal functions like customer service, accounts receivable and IT. Lost sales during the handover might never be recovered because the departing distributor was looking for a competitor brand to maintain their product portfolio.

The business transformation impacted all aspects of our national operation. We needed all-encompassing new software and related hardware within 12 months, but had no experience of selecting off-the-shelf solutions.

By adopting the pre-existing selection method, it made it easier for us to subcontract the management of the selection process. Formally defining the requirements covered many internal business areas and also involved identifying customer and supplier processes. This was especially revealing, as most of the senior management team had worked for the company for at least 15 years. The act of discussing and defining the requirements provided an important insight into current best practice.

8.4 WHERE AND WHEN – THE MEETING ADMINISTRATION

8.4.1 Venue

You should hold each evaluation meeting at the respective candidate premises. This gives the supplier the maximum opportunity to shine. They are on their home turf with extensive, familiar resources. It is also important that they can bring in specialists for the relevant parts of their response.

Visiting the candidates also means the evaluation team can assess additional dimensions. One traditional dimension is 'substance'. The supplier's office can represent financial solidity, although you should be cautious of 'flashy office syndrome' (a reflection of style rather than substance). The evaluation team can also much more easily assess intangibles like staff attitudes (see Section 8.5.5).

8.4.2 Material

You should normally allow candidates to use standard sales demonstration data and handouts such as brochures. Their familiarity with the material reduces their preparation time and allows the supplier staff to give you the best, quickest response. Later, at demonstrations, you will insist on using your own sample data, but this is more labour-intensive so is better deferred until your shortlist is even shorter (see Chapter 10).

8.4.3 Time management

Time allowed

You should allow between one and three days per response meeting. Of course, this depends on the length of your requirements document, and to a lesser extent on the size of your evaluation team.

You must allow the same amount of time per candidate supplier. Partly, this is on the grounds of fairness. Mostly, it is necessary because each set of meetings covers the same ground – all the scored requirements in your requirements document.

Importance of finishing

It is essential to finish the meeting, meaning you go through every requirement. The meeting management must be conscious of 'exam technique'. This means the supplier must answer the question. If they give broader context, it must be done quickly. Their specific response must directly address how the requirement is supported by the software, or state clearly if there is no explicit support.

All the meeting participants, especially the presenter of the solution, must stick to topic and strenuously avoid digression. Responses need to be disciplined to avoid answers 'spilling over' and accidentally, say, anticipating requirement 0124 as part of discussing 0121.

However, it is legitimate to deliberately explain a common feature and then give 'block' answers – for instance having shown a reporting tool, the presenter might say that you would use the same reporting tool to address requirements 0121–0124 and 0252–0256.

Take breaks but stay on site

Of course, meeting breaks are important. These will be intense meetings, requiring great concentration – both by the presenters to pass across the information efficiently, and by the evaluation team to absorb and note the information effectively.

This means you should, for example, take advantage of the break points at the end of every section in your requirements document (see Chapter 5, Section 5.5.1).

You will also need refreshment and meal breaks – usually it is best to organise a working buffet on site to reduce travel time. Do not view evaluation meeting lunchtimes as opportunities for long, luxurious, heavy meals at company expense – think sandwiches, strong coffee and a brisk walk round the car park.

Mingling over a working lunch is also an excellent opportunity for informal conversations that give an insight into culture and some idea about the likelihood of a strong relationship.

Create evaluation meeting schedule

The agenda is your requirements document and you know how many requirements there are in each section. You can calculate roughly how much time to allow for each section and therefore each session of your evaluation meetings.

A timed agenda with slots per section is a very important discipline on the meeting. It shapes your performance and timekeeping (see Figure 8.1).

It is also handy to support part-time contributions. Subject experts from customer and supplier know roughly when they will be needed during the day. It also allows you to show separately the physical and video attendees – this orientates the group and means you know when facilities are needed. You might combine the scheduling function with the role tracking of your RACI matrix (see Section 8.3.2).

Follow up outside the meeting

To discipline timekeeping, you need to be clear how to handle explorations, clarifications and fact checking. Of course, the ideal situation is that the requirement was so clear and the presenter preparation so thorough that you get a perfect answer first time; your evaluation team immediately understand the capability of the software against that requirement. However, with questions, there may be new or subtler issues revealed. There are various ways of handling such exceptions:

- You should mark the requirement in your notes 'return' or 'come back to finish'.

- Be clear who is taking away that point, and agree a time limit on the response. It may be that the presenter is going to check immediately once they finish their session, and get back before the end of the day.

- They may need more time, in which case their response might be covered in the wash-up session before you leave the premises the next day. They may need to email you something, in which case they should be aware when your scoring meeting will be, since that is the deadline for response.

8.5 HOW – THE EVALUATION PROCESS AND MINDSET

8.5.1 Preparing your evaluation team

You must brief the team before the first evaluation meeting so that they understand the process. Although you should stress the importance of running to time and avoiding unnecessary digression, the evaluation team members must also feel empowered to ask pertinent questions, including follow-up questions if the initial answer does not make sense.

Figure 8.1 Timed agenda slots and attendance plan on spreadsheet

Evaluation Team from Colter Civlis
Response Team from Candidate A
Types of attendance at evaluation meetings
P - Physical meeting
V - Video attendance

Candidate A	Sess	Date	Start Time	RDD Seq	RDD Section/Category	Count	Start Nbr	End Nbr	Section Mins	Breaks	Total Mins	Total HH:MM	Evaluator A	Evaluator B	Evaluator C	Evaluator D	Evaluator E	Evaluator F	Evaluator G	Reponder A	Reponder B	Reponder C	Reponder D	Reponder E	Reponder F
A	1	Wed	13:30	0	Supplier Intro / Look & Feel [Not Scored]				60	5	65	01:05	P	P						P	P				
A	2	Wed	14:35	13	Environment	23	0270	0292	62	5	67	01:07	P	P						P	P				
A	3	Wed	15:42	6	Procurement & Inventory	57	0097	0153	154	10	164	02:44	P	P						P	P				
A	4	Thu	09:30	12	Management Information	11	0259	0269	30	5	35	00:35	P	P	P					P			P		
A	5	Thu	10:05	9	Demand & Supply Chain Planning	12	0202	0213	32	5	37	00:37	P	P	P					P	P				
A	6	Thu	10:42	11	Financials	32	0227	0258	86	5	91	01:31	P	P	P					P			P		
A	7	Thu	12:13	10	International Considerations / Lunch	13	0214	0226	35	35	70	01:10	P	P	P					P			P		
A	8	Thu	13:23	3	Managing Customer/ Design Requirements	12	0028	0039	32	5	37	00:37	P	P	P					P		P		P	P
A	9	Thu	14:00	5	Product Lifecycle	42	0055	0096	113	10	123	02:03	P	P	P				P	P	P	P			
A	10	Thu	16:03	16	IT Supplier Considerations	34	0354	0387	92	10	102	01:42	P	P	P	V		V	P	P	P	P			
A	11	Fri	09:30	0	Supplier Intro/Feel (Precis) [with vid]				15	5	20	00:20	P	P	P	V	V	V	V	P	P?				
A	12	Fri	09:50	2	Sales & Marketing [with vid]	22	0006	0027	59	5	64	01:04	P	P	P				V	P		P			
A	13	Fri	10:54	7	Time Recording & Charging [with vid]	14	0154	0167	38	5	43	00:43	P	P	P		V		V	P			P		
A	14	Fri	11:37	8	Programme Mgt & Acctg (PMA) [with vid] / Lunch	34	0168	0201	92	35	127	02:07	P	P	P		V		V	P			P		
A	15	Fri	13:44	4	Resource Management [with vid]	15	0040	0054	41	5	46	00:46	P	P	P		V		V	P				P	
A	16	Fri	14:30	14	Interfaces [with vid]	45	0293	0337	122	10	132	02:12	P	P	P	V				P		P		P	
A	17	Fri	16:42	15	IT Technical [with vid]	16	0338	0353	43	5	48	00:48	P	P	P	V				P		P			P
A	18	Fri	17:30	1	Critical Information & Volumes [with vid]	5	0001	0005	14	5	19	00:19	P	P	P	V				P		P			
A	19	Fri	17:49	99	Finish & extra handouts								P	P											
						387																			

8.5.2 Evaluate current shipping version of product

The basis of evaluation must be the current shipping version that is demonstrable today and can be seen in client reference sites. Your mindset is the same as during the RFI assessment (see Chapter 7, Section 7.3).

8.5.3 Philosophy of the evaluation

Evaluation meetings are all about information gathering. The main content of the evaluation meeting is for the relevant evaluation team members to experience the response to each requirement on 'their section' of the requirements document. They want to hear how the candidate solution will support those requirements they are allocated to evaluate.

The philosophy during evaluation is broadly positive. You make two optimistic working assumptions. First, you presume that the software will work for your organisation. This makes for a more constructive meeting. You have parked the unsuitable candidates from the RFI responses. You are nowhere near to making a commitment to buy, because you have not scored yet and there are further project gates. (However, note it is ethical to warn the supplier team not to read too many 'buying signals' into your positive reactions.)

Second, you presume that the suppliers understand their software, have thought about how to apply it to your requirements and are giving a fair representation of the capabilities of their product. You should make the evaluation meeting a type of early implementation and configuration planning. Again, it makes for a more constructive meeting. Also, you are not heavily exposed to risk of deliberate misrepresentation. In a requirements-driven evaluation, you will soon find out if and where the software does not fit.

8.5.4 Evaluation team mindset and vocabulary

Meetings management is one of the skills expected of evaluation team members. As part of their behaviour, it is best not to unduly criticise the software, its presenter or indeed your colleagues during the meeting. It is counter-productive because it suppresses debate.

Software people are normally enthusiastic about their product, and can take it personally when you criticise 'their baby'. For instance, they sometimes cannot understand why somebody would even want a feature that their product lacks.

Verbal attack is not useful. Avoid these phrases, since the vocabulary is unhelpful:

- 'Well, that doesn't work!'
- 'There must be a bug!'
- 'That's a showstopper!'
- 'That's a deal breaker!'

Since you are there to elicit information and not to pass judgement, you should use more neutral phrases when clarifying a feature, especially one that you think is off-target for your needs.

- 'Is it a design feature?'
- 'Is it by design?'
- 'Is there a characteristic that...?'
- Possibly even, 'Is there a limitation that...?'

8.5.5 Overt and covert techniques

You will use mostly overt evaluation techniques, with a couple of covert ones. The main techniques are absolutely overt. There is no hidden agenda, because the agenda is your requirements document. The objective at the meeting is to go through all the requirements.

As part of getting a reaction to every requirement, you must allow for follow-up questions: candidate suppliers ask them to clarify your requirement; you as prospective customer ask them to clarify the response and software facility. You must ensure that the mutual understanding is as great as possible in the time available.

The covert techniques are not sophisticated:

- Occasionally you ask a few questions where you already know the answers from previous research or responses. You are looking for consistency, such as consistency to the RFI response related to that requirement.

- When walking around the supplier's office, keep your ears open. If you overhear conversations by the staff, it may reflect the supplier culture and their attitudes to customers or customer service.

- If you are waved towards a vending machine on arrival and expected to buy your own welcoming coffees, the behaviours tell you something about the host's customer culture and maybe the social skills of its employees.

8.5.6 Review sessions

End of day

You should run a group catch-up at the end of day, usually away from the evaluation meeting and often back in your hotel. Check if you missed any points, and discuss questions or requirements to follow up the following day.

After your final evaluation session

When closing the meeting on the final day, check the availability of your contact at the supplier. Let them know your scoring meeting dates and establish how to contact them in case follow-up queries emerge from scoring. Get details for a deputy if your main contact is not available on a scoring day.

EXECUTIVE PERSPECTIVE: A FINANCIAL REPRESENTATIVE ON EVALUATION TEAM'S EXPERIENCE

After realising our four-year-old system had been eclipsed by business growth, we adopted this selection methodology that brought with it the following benefits.

- It had logical evaluation steps that helped the evaluation team better assess their area of responsibility, but also helped them understand how their area interacted and integrated with other related system modules.

- Communication between the selection team members was very efficient as we all had a better understanding of each other's area.

- The evaluation document that was produced at the end of the evaluation process was very exhaustive and, as such, helped enormously when we came to decide on the winner.

- The weighting methodology clearly identified the final contenders and identified the strengths and weaknesses of each solution.

- When reporting back to the Finance team, I found it easier to explain the pros and cons of each system and the benefits that the selected system would bring to our area and to the business as a whole.

8.6 DEFENCE MECHANISMS IN THE EVALUATION

8.6.1 Unsupported statements, with check and balance

Some candidate responses will be purely verbal – unsupported statements – but some will be substantiated. For instance, there may be quick demonstrations for selected requirements, often because it is quicker to show the software feature than to explain it. Also, there may be handouts, such as printed reports from the solution, or selected sales material.

Your colleagues responsible for 'traditional' procurements will probably be nervous about suppliers providing information that is verbal, rather than documented. They may even criticise your approach as naïve and overly trusting. However, there is a crucial check and balance in the method.

- The responses during the evaluation meetings will shape the resulting scores awarded by your evaluation team for each combination of requirement and candidate.

- The strongest contenders (normally the top two candidates) will have an opportunity to verify their own scores. They can apply for adjustments (to take the score up or down) as appropriate if the evaluation team have misunderstood the capabilities of the software.

- These scores will be one of the attachments to contract. What this means is that the verbal responses still 'have contractual significance' in the jargon of procurement (see Chapter 9 for scoring and Chapter 12 for contracts).

8.6.2 Routine defences

Evaluation meetings are pivotal in the process. They have intense content, they can be long and everybody is human. For those reasons, there are various defence mechanisms built in against accidental misunderstanding or even deliberate supplier misrepresentation.

- Clarification during and after the meeting is important, with standard mechanisms such as briefly 'playing back' so you verify your understanding and the presenter knows that you followed them. It is especially useful to volunteer linkages between points that you saw earlier.

- Some of the answers are of course substantiated. This is particularly useful where a general feature, such as a reporting tool, will be the answer to several requirements. A quick demonstration of the reporting tool will allow 'policy' answers to multiple requirements (such as, 'That's another reporting job').

- There will be the follow-ups to your questions. Some will be emailed and therefore documented.

- Later in the method, at their demonstration, candidate suppliers will illustrate many more of the points they made in the evaluation meetings. Moreover, the demonstrations will test their data structure because you will load some of your own example data (see Chapter 10).

- Ultimately, the responses from the suppliers shape scores, which will be verified and attached to the contract for the successful supplier (see Chapter 9 for scoring and Chapter 12 for contracts).

8.6.3 Emergency ejection and substitution

It is possible (although highly improbable) that one product proves badly flawed during the evaluation meetings. Perhaps the sample requirements in your RFI did not test its weak spots, or the supplier misunderstood your requirement, or even gave misleading answers. (Note that in 50 projects this has never happened because unsuitable products were discovered by the RFI.)

In the unlikely event that your evaluation team find a candidate that fails several mandatory requirements, you must go into a private huddle and decide whether to abort the rest of your evaluation visit. You may need to reactivate one of the candidates that was previously parked.

This means that you might need to reschedule and extend your evaluation tour to accommodate the reactivated candidate.

8.7 NOTE-TAKING BY THE EVALUATION TEAM

Note-taking is crucial to the later usefulness of the evaluation meetings and it is almost impossible to take too many notes. If you end the day with writer's cramp, you are probably getting it about right. On previous projects, during scoring meetings (see Chapter 9), evaluation team members have sometimes said they thought they took enough notes but wished they had taken even more. This means that your evaluation colleagues must keep extensive notes to crystallise their understanding as it builds.

Bear in mind that not every evaluation team member attends every session – meaning, in practice, not every section of the requirements document. However, if somebody does attend a session, it is virtually guaranteed to be a waste of time if they do not make notes.

Evaluation notes are all about ensuring that you do not go 'snow blind'. The main danger during software evaluation is that the candidates blur. Either you cannot see the difference between them (even though there was one), or you remember the processing but not which software provided it. Worst of all, next week, you might 'cross-over' and associate some distinctive processing with the wrong software.

8.7.1 Relating notes to specific requirements

Since your evaluation meetings must get a response to every requirement, your notes must be related to each requirement. During the scoring meeting (see Chapter 9), evaluation team members will compare notes for each requirement for each candidate.

Keeping notes about each requirement for each candidate, usually by annotation, is consistent with the philosophy that it is impossible to compare several candidates to each other, but feasible to compare them all to the same yardstick of requirements.

Evaluation meetings are rarely the occasion to make an aggressive statement about the paperless office. You will normally write evaluation notes onto multiple copies of the requirements document.

In practice, you print one copy of the requirements document for every supplier for each evaluation team member – four candidates with an evaluation team of five means you are obliged to pre-print 20 copies before your evaluation tour.

- It is best to print the 'core' requirements section of your document, skipping the introduction and all appendices since they will not be scored.
- I recommend adding a watermark or header to reflect the candidate for each meeting set.
- If you print off at 70 per cent scale, the substantial margins are perfect for your annotations.

8.7.2 Relating samples to requirements

As you collect samples, illustrations, handouts or screenshots, use simple two-way tagging to link them to your requirements document.

- Write the requirement number on the sample, plus an index letter such as A.
- In your requirements document note, include 'See sample A'.

8.7.3 Following your subject leader

Sometimes, your notes will simply read against one requirement 'Joan was happy', where Joan is the subject matter expert.

If the team member who specialises in the area is visibly satisfied with the response, it matters less if you did not fully understand it. You can fall back to looking for the reaction of the relevant colleague and questioning them later.

8.7.4 Feasibility of note-taking by digital mark-up

It might be possible to exploit electronic note-taking using an application, such as a pen-driven portable writing on top of an image of the requirements document. However, your technology must not slow down the meeting. You must already be familiar with it – if you are not fluent, it will be difficult to be fast enough.

8.8 CHAPTER SUMMARY

TAKE-AWAY POINTS

Despite the temptation to form premature opinions, remember that evaluation meetings are never to pick the winner, but to establish an understanding of the software against the framework of the requirements document.

Evaluate the current, live version of the software, not futures.

You must explore enough to solidify your understanding of the product under review and build confidence in your own knowledge.

You absolutely must make comprehensive notes to aid your memory – you will score the candidates later.

8.8.1 The next chapter

Having gathered understanding and notes, you are now going to score candidates in order to crystallise all this information into a single, simple percentage fit score.

8.9 REFERENCES

Archer, D. and Cameron, A. (2013) *Collaborative leadership: Building relationships, handling conflict and sharing control.* Routledge: New York.

Heller, R. (2001) *Charles Handy (Business Masterminds).* Dorling Kindersley: London.

Smith, M. and Erwin, J. (2011) 'Role and responsibility charting (RACI)'. PMI, California Inland Empire Chapter, Inc. https://pmicie.org/images/downloads/raci_r_web3_1.pdf (10 November 2014).

Thomas, P., Paul, D. and James, C. (2012) *The human touch: Personal skills for professional success.* BCS, The Chartered Institute for IT: Swindon.

8.10 FURTHER READING

8.10.1 Books and articles

Cooper, R. and Sawaf, A. (2000) *Executive EQ: Emotional intelligence in business.* Texere Publishing: Knutsford.

Highmore Sims, N. (2006) *How to run a great workshop: The complete guide to designing and running brilliant workshops and meetings.* Pearson Business: Harlow.

8.10.2 Related formats by download

Evaluation tour itinerary format; timed meeting schedule format from http://shop.bcs.org/offtheshelfextras.asp.

9 SCORING: ESTABLISHING DEGREE OF FIT AND RANKING

'A great many people think they are thinking when they are merely rearranging their prejudices.'

William James (1842–1910)

9.1 WHAT YOU CAN LEARN FROM THIS CHAPTER

- Understand the scoring matrix. This is one of the most valuable and important project deliverables.
- Realise that your scoring matrix must be credible when presented to senior decision-makers and, indeed, the candidate suppliers.
- Recognise the process necessary to create this reliable scoring matrix.

9.2 OVERVIEW

Scoring involves a set of three crucial documents.

- The **requirements document**. This was created earlier in your project, authorised and then baselined (see Chapter 5).
- The completed **scoring matrix**. This records the level of fit against each requirement for each candidate. The mathematics then builds upon the previously determined weights for importance (also see Chapter 5).
- The scoring **definitions document**. This links the other two. It is a bulky document with one page per requirement. Each page records the issues that affect your scoring and the level of capability associated with any level of score you award.

The scoring matrix is the best expression of the principle that with IT selections you should not compare options to each other. Each candidate has a million 'moving parts' and the complexity is impossible if you cross-compare. Instead, you must measure all candidates against the same yardstick or benchmark – your requirements.

9.3 CRUCIAL ROLE OF SCORING

Scoring has multiple roles in the method, all of them critical.

The bulk of detailed fact gathering about the different solutions is during your evaluation meetings (see Chapter 8). The scoring meeting brings all this information together and reflects your particular combination of requirements and shortlisted candidates. Creating your scoring matrix to reflect this body of knowledge generates a project deliverable that is unique, entirely new and extraordinarily useful.

The matrix produced by scoring identifies and articulates any differences between the candidate suppliers or their software. More importantly, it helps you reach a balanced overall view, despite facing an array of wins, losses and trade-offs.

Scoring is important to reduce confidently your shortlist to (normally) two candidates for demonstration. Unless there is compelling reason to override the decision (there never has been in over 20 years of these projects), you call to demonstration the two candidates that score the highest.

You might have come across a supplier who is so driven by sales that they do not actually have the capability to meet all their promises. As scoring encapsulates your evaluation team's appreciation of the software and the supplier, this understanding can be validated. The top candidates, normally two, will verify their own scores. When suppliers do this, they are also committing to a specific and clearly stated level of promised capability.

Scoring provides consistency, transparency and audit. It is one of the most important safeguards to ensure that products and suppliers are treated fairly, without undue bias or prejudice.

The scoring matrix provides inherent protection from disappointed expectations. This technique, with your related documentation set (requirements, scores and definitions), is tremendously specific about the level of customer expectation. This expectation will be clearly associated with the eventual contract price you pay, because these documents are attached to your contract.

EXECUTIVE PERSPECTIVE: A PUBLIC SECTOR TRAINING MANAGER'S EXPERIENCE OF SPONSORING THE SELECTION

It's a truth in business that worrying about making the wrong decision often leads to inertia. When the decision involves a high value purchase with lots of evidence in the media of how hard it is to make the right choice, it's easy to become completely stalled. Nowhere is this more true than in IT selection. If the NHS, HMRC and MoD waste huge sums on projects that end up being scrapped, what chance have I?

As is often the case, the answer is out there. Find a clearly structured process that allows frequent exit options and take the journey one step at a time.

Some of the key benefits:

- Clearly defined deliverables give the project sponsor the tools to get funding and buy-in for the project.

- Structured workshops ensure staff use their knowledge to build a comprehensive set of requirements.
- Involvement in weighting builds staff understanding of the need for changes or priorities.
- Staff confidence and commitment to the outcome grows as they see the clarity of the process.
- Involving staff builds their understanding of their own business and the potential to do things better.
- Supporting staff to do the maximum amount of the work internally is cost-effective and maintains ownership.
- Understanding what you want, and what you can compromise on, changes the relationship with the vendor out of all recognition.

9.4 STAGE OUTPUTS – SCORING MATRIX

Before the remainder of this chapter gives more detail about scoring, this section and Section 9.5 'jump to the end' of the process by describing the **outputs**. Have a quick preview of Figure 9.1.

The scoring matrix encapsulates huge knowledge. It brings together an enormous amount of information, marshalling and presenting it clearly. In summary, scoring means you will:

- clarify the degree of fit to each requirement of software features and supplier service offerings;
- establish the differences of fit as they affect your organisation;
- reflect these differences in the scores for fit.

Note, the scoring matrix is a well-established decision-support technique that can be found under many different names, including weighted attribute matrix, analytic hierarchy process (AHP), weighted criteria matrix, Kepner–Tregoe analysis or rating grid (Rebernik and Bradač, 2008).

The left-hand side of your matrix contains your requirements, with their weights for importance. This crystallises the hundreds of staff hours spent during the project process to capture requirements, to agree them and then to weight them for their importance (see Chapters 4 and 5).

The requirements-capture interviews were in turn informed by many decades of collective staff experience in understanding your business, its problems and its requirements for better information.

The right-hand side of your matrix is the scoring for fit. This also crystallises hundreds of staff hours from your evaluation meetings (see Chapter 8) and scoring. It also contains decades of collective experience at the suppliers when they drew on their understanding of the software and responded to your requirements document. Moreover, the supplier

Figure 9.1 Simplified example of scoring matrix

Scores To RDD-IntegratedPES-45-Approved-ColterCivils.pdf

Categ (A)	Requirement Title	Nbr	Wgt (B)	Perfect Max (C)	Candidate I Match I (D)	Candidate I Fit Xtd I (D)	Candidate J Match J (D)	Candidate J Fit Xtd J (E)
Product Lifecyc	Partners Access Designs	0081	5	15	3	15	2	10
Product Lifecyc	Formal Processes For Design & Programme R	0083	3	9	2	6	2	6
Product Lifecyc	Design Flexibility Means Approvals At Element	0084	4	12	3	12	3	12
Product Lifecyc	Traceability	0086	3	9	3	9	2	6
Product Lifecyc	Monitor & Control Concessions	0087	3	9	2	6	1	3
Product Lifecyc	System Codes Or Uniform Station Numbering	0089	4	12	3	12	2	8
Product Lifecyc	Fault Codes & Correlations	0090	4	12	3	12	3	12
Product Lifecyc	Total Waste Management Including Tracking, R	0095	5	15	3	15	2	10
Product Lifecycle		**8**	**3.9**	**93**	**94%**	**87**	**72%**	**67**
Procurement an	Integrated Ledger For Projects/Programmes	0097	5	15	3	15	3	15
Procurement an	Supplier Details - Effective Dates	0101	5	15	3	15	2	10
Procurement an	Vendor Data Includes Approved Range	0102	5	15	3	15	3	15
Procurement an	Avoid Overloading Suppliers	0103	3	9	2	6	1	3
Procurement an	Identify Preferred Supplier	0104	4	12	3	12	2	8
Procurement an	Standard Supplier Ts & Cs (Terms Of Supply)	0106	3	9	3	9	3	9
Procurement and Inventory		**6**	**4.2**	**75**	**96%**	**72**	**80%**	**60**
Time Recording	Time Booking - Capture Hours	0154	5	15	3	15	3	15
Time Recording	Time Booking - Charge Hours At Multiple Rate	0155	5	15	2	10	3	15
Time Recording	Overhead Costing & Charging	0158	4	12	3	12	3	12
Time Recording	Facility To Convert & Round Bookings	0159	3	9	2	6	2	6
Time Recording	Re-Allocate Time After Booking	0165	5	15	1	5	3	15
Time Recording	Generate Customer Invoice For Time Booked	0166	2	6	2	4	3	6
Time Recording and Charging		**6**	**4.0**	**72**	**72%**	**52**	**96%**	**69**
Management In	Analysis Dimensions	0260	5	15	3	15	3	15
Management In	The Board Pack & Key Performance Indicators	0261	4	12	3	12	2	8
Management In	Specific KPIs - Required Graphs Or Charts	0262	4	12	3	12	1	4
Management In	Specific KPIs - Scorecards With Traffic Lights	0263	4	12	2	8	2	8
Management In	Executive Information System (EIS)	0267	4	12	3	12	3	12
Management In	User-Defined Personal Dashboards	0268	3	9	2	6	3	9
Management Information		**6**	**4.0**	**72**	**90%**	**65**	**78%**	**56**
IT Supplier Con	Sound Company - Developer	0356	4	12	3	12	3	12
IT Supplier Con	Documentation - Levels & Customisation	0359	3	9	2	6	3	9
IT Supplier Con	Global Reach	0361	3	9	3	9	3	9
IT Supplier Con	Training Availa	0366	4	12	2	8	3	12
IT Supplier Con	Standard Warranty, Contract & Negotiated SLA	0376	5	15	3	15	3	15
IT Supplier Con	Indicative Prices	0383	4	12	3	12	3	12
IT Supplier Con	Flexible Licensing Arrangements	0385	4	12	3	12	2	8
IT Supplier Con	Changes In Pricing Models	0386	1	3	1	1	2	2
IT Supplier Con	Termination Costs	0387	2	6	3	6	3	6
IT Supplier Considerations (F)		**9**	**3.3**	**90**	**90%**	**81**	**94%**	**85**
Grand		**35**	**3.8**	**402**	**89%**	**357**	**84%**	**337**
Rank out of: 3						**1**		**2**

response teams are representing large pieces of software which themselves often crystallise staff centuries of development effort.

Your decision-makers benefit from vast amounts of experience that they themselves could never personally hold. You will be encouraging them to 'go with the numbers' because your scores mean so much.

9.4.1 Format of the scoring matrix

The scoring might be implemented in a requirements database, provided you already have one, that has an inbuilt facility to use formulae to extend (multiply) and create totals and sub-totals and for which you are a proficient user. However, most organisations are unfamiliar with requirements databases and so will use a spreadsheet.

In the simplified example at Figure 9.1, to fit on one sheet, there are deliberately fewer requirements, categories and candidates than a typical selection. (A typical matrix will have three to four candidates and 100–350 requirements.) Observe the following in the illustration:

A. Note the use of a category for all requirements, with each one featuring its descriptive title and reference number.

B. The column for weights reflects the importance of the requirement: these were decided during the weighting workshop. (Note that requirement category, title, number and weight usually come from the 'weight voting' spreadsheet, which itself extracted the list of requirements from your requirements document (see Chapter 5).)

C. In the scoring scheme of 0, 1, 2 and 3, the top mark is 3. The perfect candidate would score maximum points at every requirement. Extending each weight by 3 creates your benchmark 'pool' of points such that all candidates can be compared to perfection (in this case, 402 points).

D. In this simplified example, there are only two candidates at **Match I** and **Match J**. These columns express the degree of fit, with scores established during your scoring meetings, as explained in this chapter. In this example, at requirement 0081, **Candidate I** scored 3 (top points), while **Candidate J** scored a point less.

E. For each requirement, the score for fit is multiplied by the weight for importance. You can see this extension process has opened up the gap between the candidates. The single point difference in fit score has become a 5-point difference at the extended fit, because requirement 0081 was weighted 5.

F. You can see the grand totals, with sub-totals per category (meaning per requirements document section).

G. At sub-total and total level, the mathematics compares the points each candidate has actually scored to the maximum points available – the theoretically perfect candidate. This allows you to express the fit as a 'percentage of perfection', 'percentage degree of fit' or simply 'percentage fit'.

The figures for percentage fit are the most important tangible deliverables from the fact gathering in your lengthy evaluation meetings. Assuming four candidates, decision-makers can afford to ignore enormous amounts of detail and concentrate on the four summary numbers – the four values for percentage fit. Naturally, this is provided that you have delivered process integrity and your decision-makers believe they can trust your fit scores. That is why this chapter places great emphasis on process integrity during scoring – especially see Section 9.12.4.

9.4.2 Analysis from the summary scores

The matrix now encapsulates huge amounts of experience and effort, articulated as simple numbers. It is easy to improve the decision-making by extracting intelligence with simple analysis (see Section 9.13.2), statistics or charts. For instance, by adding (perhaps later on) expected cost, you can calculate for each candidate a price performance index (PPI) to reflect 'bang for buck'.

You can also easily create charts that are immensely powerful in making the fit explicit. An extremely useful one is to contrast, at category level, the top two candidates with the 'perfect' candidate (see Figure 9.2). Note that the back line **Max** shows the 'shape' of the perfect solution. In front of it are the two strongest contenders, **I** and **J**.

Figure 9.2 Illustration of fit at category level – top two versus perfect

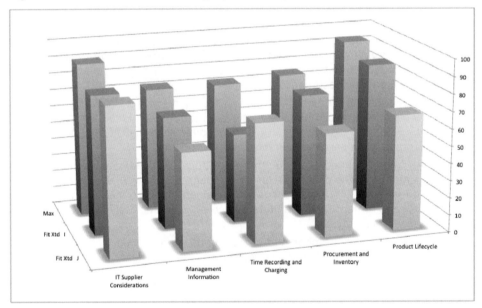

While this illustration has a simplified sub-set of requirements categories to match Figure 9.1, this format with more content is powerful at decision-making meetings. Attendees are usually engaged by the idea that the evaluation can actually visualise something as intangible and elusive as the fit between multiple complex requirements and sophisticated software products.

9.5 DEFINITIONS DOCUMENT WITH LANGUAGE LADDERS

This section continues the 'jump to the end' of the process by describing the outputs.

The third document in the trio contains scoring definitions, with their language ladders. The scores both use and update the 'marking scheme' recorded in your definitions. This means that the role of the definitions document is to articulate precisely the basis of decision, whenever it needs clarifying, then state the level of fit or capability that was required for a candidate to achieve a given level of score. Both aspects are vital to explain why a candidate was awarded a given number of points against a requirement.

There will be one page per requirement, and each definitions sheet has three main areas as shown in Figure 9.3.

Figure 9.3 Sections of a definitions sheet

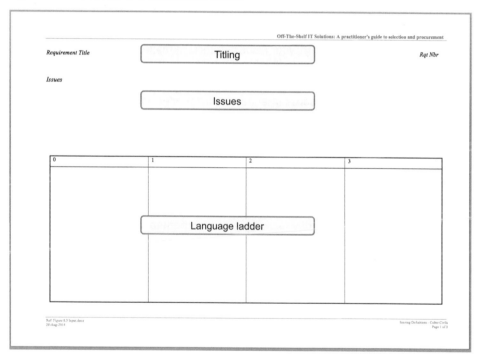

9.5.1 Titling

Since there is one page per requirement, to make the document self-indexing, the sheet title is the requirement name and number.

To speed up this process, you can set up a template page with a standard format, with a small table for the language ladders and standard definition text for 0 and 3. You will add fields for the requirement title and requirement number. You will then use mail merge processing to combine this template with a separate list containing all of your requirement titles and numbers.

This will generate a lengthy document with one page per requirement. The requirement title and reference number will head each page. It will then have the spaces for the scoring issues and the language ladders with your default definitions.

9.5.2 Issues section

The top section allows you to state – as usual, by exception – any issues that were revealed during your evaluation meetings or your scoring meeting.

- Sometimes, you need a statement of common themes, for instance which parts of the requirement made a difference to your scoring.

- Perhaps your evaluation team realise that the requirement – or a portion of the requirement – should come out of the basis of evaluation. Occasionally, an entry has slipped through every review of your requirements document. It is only exposed as inappropriate by the intense scrutiny of detailed evaluation meetings. Perhaps one portion of the requirement might be better covered (and scored) elsewhere. Therefore, your issues statement makes clear which portion of your requirement **is** rewarded in this score.

- Sometimes you add an entry that is anonymously addressed to one of the candidates. For example, some intended future processing was not rewarded with additional points because it would not be available before the anticipated contract date.

- Your requirement may have been revealed during supplier meetings as not ambitious enough. It is appropriate to raise the bar and award 'top points' **above** your original statement. This usually happens if one candidate exceeded your requirement **and** the excess was so useful to your organisation that the evaluation team re-baselined your requirement. Top points will now be awarded to candidates that exceed your original documented requirement. Those candidates that 'merely' meet your requirement will get fewer points.

9.5.3 Language ladder for capability

The lower section contains a table to define the relevant levels of capability necessary to achieve a given score for fit. Initially, regard the fit in the very general terms shown at Table 9.1.

Table 9.1 Conceptual values for fit during scoring

General score for fit	Represents
0	Up to 25% fit
1	Up to 50% fit
2	Up to 75% fit
3	Up to 100% fit

However, by exception, you can adapt each language ladder to be more specific to your requirement. This reflects a combination of the demands of each requirement and the distilled capabilities of each candidate.

You can see at Table 9.1 that the set of values available to you is 0, 1, 2 and 3. The vital outcome is to define any score that you allocate. As input to scoring, the extremes of 0 and 3 can start with default bi-polar definitions (see Figure 9.4).

Figure 9.4 Default language ladder entries for 0 and 3

0	1	2	3
No explicit support in current version without program code modification.			Facility in current version meets or exceeds requirement in RDD-IntegratedPES-45-Approved-ColterCivils.pdf without program code modification.

To save time, your definitions process heavily exploits management by exception:

- at Issues, you only complete the section if there is something to say;
- at the language ladders, you do not always need the full set, only definitions for the points that you award (say 0, 2 and 3);
- at the language ladder entries for 0 and 3, you only reword the standard phrases if you need to be more precise.

The illustration at Figure 9.5 is adapted from a project where there were three candidates, but two candidates were scored the same (2 points) at requirement 0103. Remember that you only put in the level of investment to your definitions that is needed

Figure 9.5 One completed definitions sheet as output by scoring

Requirement Title
Avoid Overloading Suppliers

Rqt Nbr
0103

Issues

No points for minimum order quantity.
Needs to be maximum number of items, not monetary value.
User-defined facilities accepted, provided they do not rely on customisation.
NB Definition revised at Version 0.7.

0	1	2	3
No explicit support in current version without program code modification.		Only by order value limits. Or By user-defined fields and an event – then event itself can exploit variables so it always acts on orders this current month.	Supplier capacity at item level, expressed as a quantity – pieces per user-defined unit time, such as day.

to distinguish candidates. For this requirement, tracking the spread of capability required defining three levels of capability, one with default wording.

The peculiar layout of language ladder text (not quite sentences but not quite bullets) is to emphasise the difference between two definitions. The 'delta' may come down to the word 'but' for a 2 score as opposed to 'and' for a 3. Positioning these distinguishing words side-by-side helps. It also accelerates the creation of your text during scoring sessions – you often paste the most wordy language ladder into the next cell and cut out or change a few words.

USING DEFINITIONS DURING THE SCORING MEETING

You do not print the definitions document, but update it on-screen during your scoring meeting. If you 'leap around' your requirements document (scoring the requirement categories out of sequence) the three-digit or four-digit requirement number is an important search term. It allows you to jump to the relevant page.

Do not give in to the temptation during your scoring sessions to scribble definitions onto a paper copy of the format. Everybody must see the same wording, by projection. You should appoint a fluent scribe who does not slow down your meeting.

9.5.4 Scores reflect the absolute level of fit

You should be clear that your scoring of candidates against one requirement is not a ranking. More than one candidate can get any given level of score for fit. Indeed, for many requirements, all candidates will get top points of 3 because they easily meet your requirement. Alternatively, they may exceed your requirement, but any differences in the excess are not specifically helpful to your organisation.

Imagine a deliberately simple example of capacity. Suppose you needed a solution capable of tracking 5,000 live purchase orders. Two candidates quoted existing customer sites with 100,000 purchase orders; one candidate quoted 250,000; the fourth candidate quoted 500,000. All the candidates comfortably meet your requirement. Within your planning horizon, there is no conceivable circumstance where you will need even 100,000 purchase orders. So all candidates have sufficient capacity and indeed lavish over-capacity. The difference between, say, the uppermost values of 250,000 and 500,000 will never come into play within your planning horizon. In these circumstances, for your specific project and organisation, 500,000 is actually no better than 250,000. All candidates easily meet your requirement and they should all get 3 points. You have disregarded a 'golden feature' that looks impressive and might add cost, but does not add value for you.

It is, of course, also conceivable that all candidates get 0 points for fit against a requirement, because not one of them had any explicit support for your requirement. In this case, at your language ladder description of 0, you might leave the default wording. You can justify this by economy of effort – you will concentrate your energy into wording ladders where you need to communicate a difference between candidates.

9.5.5 Opportunities to elevate the requirement

The original requirements document was baselined at version 4, having been revised after your weighting meeting and authorised by your sponsor (see Chapter 5). However, while the document that is used to measure candidates may be static, your learning process is not.

As the evaluation team become aware of the sophisticated processing available off-the-shelf, they may choose to 'raise the bar' such that one product sets the gold standard or high benchmark. They award full points to the candidate that exceeds requirements, provided it does so in a way that is genuinely useful to your organisation.

This means you have made your requirement more demanding, based on the opportunities you now realise are presented by the new technology. During your scoring meeting, this might be referred to by short slang phrases such as 'sets the bar'.

This means that candidates now score below full points if they 'merely' meet the original requirement. The team completes the **Issues** section for this requirement to document the fact your requirement has been made more demanding. This will also allow the other candidates to establish whether their offering meets the revised, more sophisticated requirement.

When scoring is complete, your completed definitions document, with its issues and ladders, records your evaluation team's expectation against every requirement. This is crucial to process integrity and therefore project reputation.

Definitions are crucial reference items during later meetings, for instance if one decision-maker challenges your scores and needs clarification or reassurance. They may want to know why Candidate A was awarded three points, while Candidate B (which they favour) was given only a single point. You can go back to your definitions document, look up that requirement and show the level of capability associated with three and one points respectively. (You could then go further back, to your handouts, to illustrate capability for both candidates.)

Just as important is creating a document to play back to the candidate suppliers as a comprehensive register of expectations. Selected suppliers (normally the top two) will be asked to verify their scores. They can only do so by using the information contained in your language ladders.

9.5.6 Protecting suppliers with explicit concessions

As a general philosophy, the selection process recognises that no off-the-shelf solution can be expected to be perfect. The language ladders are the pragmatic upshot of this philosophy and deliver protection to suppliers.

Each score that is less than 3 points is effectively granting that candidate a 'contractual concession'. This means you are declaring that you understand the solution is less than perfect here.

Let us assume that the candidate that scored the highest overall is the successful candidate and that you contract with them. Even though they had the highest overall score, this supplier still has a comprehensive statement to record the areas where their software provides weaker support. The statement is explicit, expressed at the requirement level and part of your contract.

9.6 WHO – THE SCORING TEAM

The scoring process is inherently about identifying any differences between the candidates, so it is crucial that those scoring a category or section of requirements have witnessed all the candidates (see Chapter 8, Section 8.3.2).

Attending their allocated sessions is the minimum contribution. But allow an evaluation team member to attend more sessions, if they can spare the time. Even if they cannot score unfamiliar requirements, they still act as a witness to process integrity and can report to their department that the evaluation team put in the work.

The entire evaluation team must 'top and tail' by attending your initial briefing (see Section 9.8.1) and your concluding review (see Section 9.10).

Depending on the word processing skills of your meeting facilitator, you may enlist an additional participant – a dedicated scribe who has no responsibility to score, but updates the scoring matrix and definitions document as the decisions are made.

9.7 WHERE AND WHEN – THE MEETING ADMINISTRATION

For managing your scoring meeting, some suggested best approaches follow.

- **Time allowed**: You should allow the same amount of time for your scoring meeting as for one of the supplier response meetings. This works as an estimating metric because you are processing the same number of requirements – all of them – during your scoring sessions as during one response meeting. This means scoring sessions usually last between one and three days – depending on the combined number of requirements, candidates and participants.

- **Booking your scoring meeting**: As part of originally engaging your evaluation team, you will have briefed them to expect your scoring meetings and roughly when. Once you have your scheduled dates for your evaluation 'tour' you will firm up the subsequent scoring dates with your evaluation team. This is an internal meeting, so your group should be easier to schedule. You should aim to start your scoring sessions within 1–3 working days of your final evaluation meeting with suppliers. This keeps memories fresh.

- **Venue for scoring sessions**: You should hold your scoring meeting somewhere the participants can easily reach and where you will not be interrupted. If your central office is the home base for most members of your evaluation team, you might hold your scoring meeting there. Alternatively, you may take it to a nearby conference venue to avoid interruptions and provide a working environment that is more spacious and airy. Maintaining concentration is important during the intense scoring sessions.

9.8 HOW – THE SCORING MEETING PROCESS AND MINDSET

9.8.1 Brief your evaluation team before the scoring

You do not expect new faces, but must still brief your team before the first scoring session so that they understand the scoring process and so that you have seeded the appropriate mindset. Use the points from this chapter and show an example of the scoring matrix so that your evaluation team understand the destination.

Stress the need to be scrupulously and self-consciously fair. Explain that your process and scores will be scrutinised. Define the fundamental terms: golden features; definitions document; scoring issues; language ladders; scoring blind; score verification (see the Glossary and this chapter for help).

9.8.2 Decide if all candidates are scored

Verify at the start of your meeting if you will score all the candidates from your evaluation meetings. You nearly always do. However, in extreme circumstances, the detailed responses in the meeting may have revealed that the responses at the RFI questionnaire were inaccurate or misleading. A shortlisted candidate may have failed several mandatory requirements. If these failures had been known at your RFI shortlisting stage, the candidate would never have been shortlisted. In this situation, the candidate is not credible and should not be scored.

Of course, this is a disturbing discovery at this stage in your project, but it is best to face it rather than invest effort in scoring a candidate known to be unsuitable. (Also see Chapter 8 about re-activating a candidate that was previously parked.)

9.8.3 Capture gut feel for later calibration

At the start of your meeting, hold a secret ballot. Ask all evaluation team members to write down their perception of the rank order of the candidates without thinking it through in detail. They should fold the impromptu ballot papers. The most senior person in the room acts as a returning officer, but simply collects and stashes away these voting slips. You will examine and discuss them at the end of your meeting to calibrate and reflect on your scoring process.

9.8.4 Philosophy of scoring

Scoring identifies and rewards the differences between candidates for each requirement.

The scoring matrix is a 'bottom up' technique. Each requirement is scored individually, for each candidate.

The evaluation team do not themselves determine the strongest candidate overall. The mathematics of extension and summation finds the overall best fit by ranking candidates on their total scores.

9.8.5 Score without sight of weights

Hide columns in your scoring spreadsheet so the weight column is not shown, and neither are the figures for fit that have been extended by the weights. Figure 9.6 illustrates the spreadsheet state at the start of scoring and the format displayed throughout the scoring sessions. Note the following:

- The visible focus on bare scores for fit.

- The use of -1 as the place marker value for 'not yet scored'. You should never use 0 before scoring, because that is one of the valid output values, while the alternative of space can throw out spreadsheet formulae.

- The Notes column for work-in-progress and flags to follow up.

Figure 9.6 Matrix configured for scoring meeting

Scores To RDD-IntegratedPES-45-Approved-ColterCivils		Candidate C	Candidate I	Candidate J	
Categ Requirement Title	Nbr	Match C	Match I	Match J	Notes
IT Supplier Cor Sound Company – Developer	0356	-1	-1	-1	
IT Supplier Cor Documentation – Levels & Customisation	0359	-1	-1	-1	
IT Supplier Cor Global Reach	0361	-1	-1	-1	
IT Supplier Cor Training Available	0366	-1	-1	-1	
IT Supplier Cor Standard Warranty, Contract & Negotiated SLA	0376	-1	-1	-1	
IT Supplier Cor Indicative Prices	0383	-1	-1	-1	
IT Supplier Cor Flexible Licensing Arrangements	0385	-1	-1	-1	
IT Supplier Cor Changes In Pricing Models	0386	-1	-1	-1	
IT Supplier Cor Termination Costs	0387	-1	-1	-1	

Scoring blind (without sight of your weights) is another measure to defend against bias. Whether candidates scored well or badly to a given requirement should not be influenced by its significance. At this stage, your evaluation team are assessing **fit** to requirement – not **importance** of requirement, which was fixed during your weighting workshop (see Chapter 5).

For example, during a scoring session, if a requirement were known to be mandatory, there would be a temptation to shy away from awarding 0 points for the candidate that is perceived as strongest (it is an embarrassment) and perhaps more inclination to award 0 for the candidate that is perceived as weakest (it is easier to eliminate them).

This is another example of a process that is self-consciously transparent and fair. It is analogous to classical orchestras selecting a new musician – the applicants who audition often play behind a screen so that the ears of the selectors are not influenced by recognition and reputation.

9.8.6 Score current shipping version

Remember you should not 'evaluate futures'. You should not give credit for software facilities that are not in the current version, but in distant, proposed releases (see Chapter 8, Section 8.5.2).

9.8.7 Treatment of costs

You need to strike a balance when processing cost figures. At one extreme, it is pointless allowing a low-price solution to set cost expectations when it is simply unfit for your purpose. At the other, the perfect candidate may prove unaffordable. In practice, the impact of costs is more fluid. A candidate proven to have superb fit improves the organisational appetite to allocate budget.

- If you used indicative costs as shortlisting criteria at RFI stage (see Chapter 7), you might treat all shortlisted candidates as affordable – at least for now. If early estimates are unreliable, you may defer full costing until the negotiation stage (see Chapter 12).
- You can list a batch of cost-of-ownership requirements, and then score them in bands with reverse scale (less money, more points).
- You can score product and supplier capability in isolation, but then use fit and cost as two dimensions when calculating and charting price performance (see Figure 9.1).

9.8.8 Sequence of scoring

It is important in your meeting to score all **candidates** for a given **requirement**, and then move on to your next requirement. This is the best way to find the differences between candidates. Scoring by 'requirement rows' rather than 'candidate columns' so that you 'march down' the matrix is fundamental to the process.

If, at the end of your investigations, you were to end up with a vague impression that all candidates were roughly the same, your evaluation process would not have worked. Given the complexity within off-the-shelf solutions, studying the facilities of the software at the atomic level of each requirement is the only effective way to expose accurately and reward the differences between candidates.

Scoring all candidates by each requirement is far more robust against preconception. If one or more members of your evaluation team believe one candidate is the strongest, they are likely to consistently give it more points if they allocate all the points (for all the requirements) for that candidate in one burst. The resulting high total score is likely to be a self-fulfilling prophecy that reinforces their prejudice – confirmation bias.

Instead, participants look at the requirement, study their notes for all the candidates and then score that one requirement. The debate inherently validates their understanding of the products. Simultaneously, such reliance on evidence cuts preconceptions.

9.9 TIME MANAGEMENT DURING THE MEETING

A timed agenda that roughly schedules your scoring sessions is constructive. The schedule format for the earlier evaluation meetings had the same arguments, benefits and formats (see Chapter 8, Figure 8.1). As with the evaluation meetings with suppliers, breaks are important to maintain concentration during scoring.

9.9.1 Work in categories

Although there is a mental picture (see Section 9.8.8) of 'marching down' the matrix, you do not necessarily work sequentially from requirement 0001 onward. You typically work in the blocks that are the sections in your requirements document – your requirement **Categories**. It is sensible to score all requirements in one section of your requirements document in one scoring session. However, you can do your sections in any order.

This means that you can organise the sequence of scoring categories to reflect the availability of your specialist scorers. Subject matter experts, such as your evaluation team representative from the finance department, might join your meeting in order to score those requirements that relate to Finance and possibly to Reporting or Compliance.

9.9.2 Check facts outside the meeting

You will need to be disciplined with fact checking. The ideal (and usual) situation is that your collective understanding and notes as a group are good enough to score the requirement for all candidates. Sometimes, you realise you do not have enough information to compare candidates. For such situations, you have options.

- If you realise that you do not understand all candidate processing across this requirement, you are not in a position to 'carve up' the spread of capability and allocate your points for fit. You need extra input. Skip this requirement for now.

- You can give provisional scores after making working assumptions, although there is enough doubt that you will want to seek clarification.

If unable to complete one or more requirements, follow up by telephone or email outside this scoring session. For the meantime, flag the requirement in your Follow Up column (see Figure 9.6). If you prefer to follow up by email, remember to give a deadline for response, normally before your review of scores.

In due course, the supplier should answer verbally or by email. Ideally, they will refer you to clarification in the existing handouts or send new material as substantiation, such as a new screenshot, report sample or slide.

Bear in mind that protection is built into the method anywhere that you allocate a provisional candidate score with a working assumption. There is an inherent check, even if you do not explicitly clarify specific doubts, because the suppliers will verify their own scores. If you have allocated points for fit that were too high or too low, the supplier should spot this (see Section 9.11). Consequently, you might simply take notes to 'steer' each candidate to especially scrutinise a few of their scores.

Accordingly, a good tagging mechanism for one doubtful score is unusual formatting such as bold italic with a different colour. This will stand out when you cut down your spreadsheet and pass the respective column of scores to each supplier.

9.10 STEPS TO COMPLETE THE SCORING

It is essential to finish your scoring meeting, meaning you go through every scored requirement. The nature of the matrix is such that candidates are not accurately assessed or properly ranked until you have scored your very last requirement.

When you have run all the main scoring sessions (completing all requirements categories), you should reunite the full group for a final session. Bring back the specialist participants, who only attended the scoring sessions relevant to their subject matter expertise, to guarantee that the correct people are present.

1. **Finalise provisional scores with new information**. You will have followed up on specific scores that were flagged as queries (see Section 9.9.2). There will normally be a small number of such clarifications, so present any new information to the full group.

    Use the answers to complete any missing scores or review any provisional ones, and revise them as necessary. As normal, complete or adjust your related definitions sheet accordingly.

2. **Reveal extended scores and rank order**. At the end of scoring, whoever is managing your matrix would normally reveal the full calculations – the extended fit scores, with their sub-totals, grand totals and candidate rankings.

    You will then retrieve your gut feel ballot papers (see Section 9.8.3). Put up the perceived ranks for each member, related to the calculated rank on your matrix. If they are different, it does not mean either the instinctive or the mechanical ranking is invalid. However, where there are differences, it is sensible to discuss and attempt to explain them. For instance, what has the person who reckoned Candidate A was ranked third (when in fact it scored as pole position) learned about the product capabilities or the supplier's sales approach – and does that learning change their perception?

3. **Agree your recommendation to the project board**. The rank order from scoring is almost certainly reliable now. Verifying your scores after this scoring meeting ends (see Section 9.11) will usually change a limited number of points and is extremely unlikely to change rank order. Provided the gap between the runner up and third candidate has a safe margin (see Section 9.12.3), review your scores and discuss your recommendation to your project board. It is more important to hold your discussion while all evaluation team members are present and memories are fresh. (You can always reconvene to change your recommendation if events turn dramatic.)

Consider and agree as an evaluation team the critical aspects of your recommendations to your project board, including:

- whether it is safe to proceed to the next stage, of demonstration;
- whether the rank order is safe;
- whether you recommend demonstrating two candidates or just one;
- whether your rankings determine the two for demonstration, or whether there are compelling arguments to disregard the ranks from scores;

- how to explain the candidates 'parked';
- how to investigate any significant shortcomings revealed by detailed evaluation, including nominating the person to lead your enquiries with candidates.

9.11 VERIFYING SCORES WITH SUPPLIERS

Sharing your basis of decision and evaluation criteria with suppliers is good practice and is required within many procurement models. You now go further with the principle, by verifying your understanding of the strongest candidates.

After your scoring meeting, you contact the top two scoring candidates (usually) and play back their scores. If the gap between the candidates ranked second and third is very close, you might play back your scores for verification by the top three contenders.

Playing back your scores to each relevant supplier is an important part of the checks and balances in the method. It is a defence against misunderstanding, misinterpretation and even the possibility of deliberate misrepresentation.

9.11.1 Material for verification

Candidate suppliers need three documents to help you.

1. Candidates already have the first, your requirements document.
2. The second is your newly created definitions document. This is of course universal – meaning common across all candidates.
3. You also provide an edition of your scoring matrix that is **specific** to each candidate, as follows.

Format of the supplier-specific scores spreadsheet

You need to create copies and then cut down your scoring matrix to adapt it to each candidate.

- You remove the column for weights, because you are not yet revealing the importance of requirements. You also need to remove the extended score column.
- Most important, you remove **all** the columns for **all** the other candidates.
- To structure responses, you add three columns for use by candidates – Score Requested, Difference and Supplier Comment.

9.11.2 Supplier verification process

Each supplier examines their score for each requirement and then checks your definition of that score on the language ladder. They validate that their product or service is positioned on the correct rung of the definitions ladder. If there is doubt, they check your definitions that apply to the points above and below. Your email sending the material invited them to 'bid up' (say 2 to 3) if there is a higher definition that actually matches or to 'play down' (say 2 to 1).

Hypothetically, assume for Candidate C and requirement number 0123 that you awarded 2 points for fit. The supplier would look at your definitions sheet for 0123, digest any scoring issues and look at your definition for 2 points. If they had any doubt, they might also look at the 1 to make sure they were better than that, and also the 3 to verify that they were not quite that good.

9.11.3 Applications to adjust scores

By exception, the supplier applies to have their score moved up or down. The terms 'bidding up' or 'playing down' are appropriate because the supplier does not set their own revised score. They **apply** to your evaluation team, who remain responsible for the scores and definitions.

This is almost certainly the last chance to change rank order. Notice that it leaves the customer in control of the basis of decision. You, as an evaluation team, have stipulated the performance characteristics associated with any given level of fit score. However, to verify your understanding of capability, you draw on supplier expertise about product capabilities, product configuration and the services they offer. The supplier positions their own solution on the correct rung of the language ladder that you have pre-determined.

You will generally get back a sub-set of scores that are challenged by suppliers, typically 2–5 per cent of your scores for each of the candidates. Since the challenges are independent and will affect different requirements, you may end up needing to review 4–10 per cent of your scores. Your review (see Section 9.11.4) will be worthwhile for the additional confidence, and indeed commitment, you gain from all stakeholders.

9.11.4 Reviewing bids

Usually, a sub-group of your evaluation team will make the decision whether or not to adjust your scores, keeping brief notes as an audit trail. If your original scoring awarded a candidate, say for requirement 0009, a score of 2 but they bid up to 3, you would usually award them this. They are committing that they can comply with your expectations of the higher level, because they have read in 0009's language ladder your wording against that level of fit. Ideally, when the candidate bids up they might refer you to a previously supplied screenshot or slide to substantiate their claim for the higher points.

Occasionally, suppliers will play down. They will reveal or remind you that their processing lacks feature X and ask if it makes enough difference to drop a point. They may only be entitled to the fit score (performance characteristics) that are **below** the one you have awarded. The sub-group reviewing the applications will take a view. Even if they do not change your score, they will form a favourable impression of the candidate's honesty.

9.11.5 Benefits of disciplined verification

Benefits for customer evaluation team and candidate response teams

The mechanism of having scores and definitions with supplier verification is an important process in keeping both your evaluation team and the candidate response teams scrupulously accurate. Remember that your scores and definitions (with your original requirements document) will become part of your contract.

The supplier's interests lie in having accurate scores that are high enough for them to be the successful candidate. However, if they have 'over-promised' and painted a picture of their product that is systematically more capable than reality, they will have to deliver this level of performance for the contracted value. Any software enhancements necessary to meet this performance level, even if feasible and possible before your implementation deadline, would need to be delivered within the contracted cost. The reduction of profit margin creates a strong incentive for precision.

Benefits for your decision-makers

Verified scores significantly improve the confidence of your evaluation team when presenting their recommendation to your decision-making body at the next project board.

Your project board will be greatly reassured that the scores you present are not 'merely' the opinion of your internal evaluation team. The top suppliers have agreed them as accurate and indeed worthy of attaching to contract.

The credibility of your project deliverable – the scoring matrix – is crucial at this stage. The decision-makers (unless they were evaluation team members, which is unusual) have not seen any of the candidate solutions so far. Moreover, senior people who are on your decision-making body may not understand your requirement statements because they reflect a huge body of operational detail. Therefore, your ability to achieve a clean decision depends entirely on the credibility of your process. This manifests itself in a reliable scoring matrix.

9.12 THRESHOLDS, ERROR AND DEFENCES

9.12.1 Manage just enough information to proceed to next round

At all stages of the method, you find out just enough to separate those candidates you will take forward from those you will park. This principle also applies to your detailed evaluation. Even though you have gathered large volumes of information, this information and the scoring process you execute should be 'only just good enough' to give a safe margin between the successful and unsuccessful next-round candidates. In the case of scoring, assuming both first and second go forward to demonstration, this means ensuring that the gap between your **second** and **third** candidates is sound (see Section 9.12.3). The process aims to put in enough effort for the decision about demonstrations to be a safe one, but no more. The detailed evaluation stage is demanding enough without wasting work on information that goes beyond delivering a sound decision.

9.12.2 Guideline on threshold for feasible candidates

Your scoring is ultimately self-referential, because it 'carves up' the processing capability into the different buckets – the different rungs on the language ladder – that make sense to your evaluation team in the context of your project and requirements. Therefore, it is unrealistic to expect absolute rules.

Nevertheless, consistently in over 20 years of using this method, organisations that have selected a candidate with a fit higher than 70 per cent have been able to implement it successfully. This is a reasonable threshold to apply generally for a candidate to be considered a strong contender and a feasible off-the-shelf solution. Of course, if you have four candidates all scoring more than, say, 80 per cent fit, you are in a wonderfully strong position and almost spoilt for choice.

9.12.3 Guideline on safe gaps between candidates

If the gap between two candidates is more than 3 per cent, you will generally have a safe understanding of the superior and the inferior candidate. The closest on a prior project was 1 per cent after scores verification, with the two strongest candidates at 90 per cent and 91 per cent fit. This put us in a strong negotiation position, although it was tough to pick the ultimate winner.

Essentially, your margin of error (strictly speaking bias, because the error has to be consistently one-way) needs to be less than the gap between those candidates taken forward and those candidates left behind.

If you complete scoring and seek two candidates for demonstration, you are likely to have a non-controversial decision if the four candidates scored 92 per cent, 90 per cent, 80 per cent and 78 per cent. You may have to do more work to verify your scores if the fit has a close pattern, such as 82 per cent, 81 per cent, 80 per cent and 78 per cent.

9.12.4 Defence mechanisms in the scoring

As with your evaluation meetings, your scoring sessions are pivotal in the process, so you need multiple defence mechanisms. These defences protect your organisation, the suppliers and your evaluation team. Somebody who is unhappy with your results might accuse your evaluation team of flawed judgment or stark injustice. Consequently, this section recaps the scoring process – not in order of execution, but from the specific perspective of its defence mechanisms.

1. You work as a group. No individual determines your scores. You challenge each other to improve understanding and to reduce bias (see Section 9.6).
2. You are guided by organisational requirements, not by the software products or their suppliers (see Section 9.2).
3. You could not structure these requirements to favour one candidate (even if you wanted to). The requirements are a yardstick that was created during earlier stages, before anybody knew which candidates would be shortlisted; the requirements document was provided to your evaluation team; the weights were determined by a different team; the agreed and weighted requirements therefore embody gigantic amounts of organisational experience and authority (see Section 9.4).
4. You avoid bias to a consciously or unconsciously favoured candidate by scoring each candidate to an individual requirement, completing your matrix by rows, not by candidate columns (see Section 9.8.8).
5. You constantly refer to the evidence accumulated in your notes and the supplier handouts. This is another case of evidence-based decision-making. All the people scoring refer to the combined body of evidence (see Section 9.8.8).

6. Features that do not yet exist do not seduce you, so you do not expose your organisation to risks of 'vapourware' (see Section 9.8.6).

7. You seek information to plug your understanding gap whenever you realise you do not have enough evidence across all candidates for a particular requirement (see Section 9.9.2).

8. You score without seeing the weights for importance. This circumvents one of the most significant pressures that might otherwise distort scoring (see Section 9.8.5).

9. You have a repetitive process with a short scoring cycle that concentrates on slotting any difference of capability between candidates into an uncomplicated marking scheme (see Section 9.5.4).

10. You faithfully record the basis for allocating the points for fit in your definitions document. While these sheets are managed by exception, they are nonetheless clear, explicit whenever they need to be, and can be audited (see Section 9.5).

11. You show (by projection) participants the same scores and definitions as they build up. They can verify that they have been accurately recorded (see Sections 9.4 and 9.5).

12. You validate the feasibility of your requirements and learn from exposure to suppliers and products. Specifically, if a requirement is not sufficiently stretching, you make it more demanding when you realise that there is some desirable processing that is currently available off-the-shelf (see Section 9.5.5).

13. You sharpen the accuracy of scoring in a self-directing process. If certain scores are uncomfortably close (such as the gap between the two groups of demonstration and parked candidates) you do more verification (see Section 9.12.3).

14. The evaluation team do not explicitly decide the strongest overall candidate, which would be unsafe in the face of so much complexity and so many trade-offs. The mathematics puts forward the winners (see Sections 9.4.1 and 9.8.4).

15. You investigate sensitivities by running analyses such as 'flat weighting' and 'failed mandatory requirement' (see Sections 9.13.1 and 9.13.2).

16. You have a pre-determined threshold value that suggests an off-the-shelf solution is not feasible. This prevents a delinquent project – one that crashes ahead without high-level review when all the candidates are weak (see Section 9.12.2).

17. You include the supplier in verifying their own scores and therefore your understanding. They check them to your definitions. They have a compelling interest in accurate scores because they will be attachments to contract (see Sections 9.5.6 and 9.11, and Chapter 12).

18. You calibrate your initial perception to the calculated ranking from scoring. You account for differences between your initial perceptions and your final matrix results (see Sections 9.8.3 and 9.10).

19. You use your scores to reduce the shortlist, not to pick the ultimate winner. The next stage of demonstration verifies your scores, albeit from a different angle. You expect illustrations of those facilities that are most important to your organisation (see Chapter 10).

9.13 SELECTING DEMONSTRATION CANDIDATES

9.13.1 Sensitivity analysis

In a copy of your spreadsheet, temporarily set all weights to 1. This can be called 'flat weights' because it neutralises the extension (fit by weight) that exaggerates differences. Examine rank order for changes – specifically, whether the pole position or top scorer changed.

If the pole position does not change, this means the top rank did not just happen to 'hit sweet spots'. It is simply stronger overall (a closer fit to need) and your weights for requirement importance do not really matter in determining ranking. This can be reassuring if the earlier process of setting weights proved controversial.

9.13.2 Gap analysis

Gaps to requirements

Examine your scoring matrix – if you are familiar with spreadsheet filtering, you can exploit this now. One of the main analyses of gaps is to see if any candidate failed mandatory requirements (FMR). This means the weight was 5 (mandatory) but the score for fit was 0. Technically, 0 means fit less than 25 per cent (rather than no support at all for the requirement) but it is certainly a weak fit.

With effective RFI shortlisting (see Chapter 7) you would hope that this does not happen. However, your RFI was a sample – a sub-set of requirements – and an exchange of documents rather than a conversation. New information gleaned during the detailed face-to-face responses over several evaluation meetings may have changed your understanding.

Gaps between top two candidates

As well as looking for gaps to requirements, you can usefully analyse gaps between candidates. You are still not comparing candidates with each other, but measuring them against requirements. However, if you have a two-horse race, you can usefully create three listings to help your project board.

1. Those requirements where the two candidates scored the same – if you have two strong contenders, this will often be more than half the requirements.

Then two statements of difference, using the extended scores (after applying weight). It is best to sort your lists to descending order of difference in points.

2. The list where the overall runner up outscored the pole position.
3. The (longer) list of requirements where the superior candidate outscored the inferior.

This can be helpful now, and especially later on when your project board have to make the final choice. If the runner up is cheaper and the decision-makers are tempted to buy on price, the third list shows them the better processing they will lose. This listing alone has previously tipped the balance at a project board in favour of the higher-scoring candidate, despite the extra expense.

9.13.3 Handling a candidate that failed mandatory requirements

If you have four candidates, with the top two recommended for demonstration, and one of the bottom two has failed mandatory requirements, it reinforces the argument not to take them forward. However, if one of the recommended top two overall has failed any mandatory requirements, you will need to do some investigation and review.

- It might be that the importance of the requirement had been overstated, and it was never truly mandatory. Reduce the weight – with checks, permission and an audit trail.

- You may need to go back to the candidate supplier for further information. See if there is a workaround and discuss its suitability.

- The solution may be very strong overall, but carry an Achilles heel. Investigate ways to plug the gap (see Section 9.14).

9.14 ADDRESSING SIGNIFICANT GAPS IN CAPABILITY

Remember that the basis of your current evaluation and eventual installation is to **configure** and not to **customise**. This means that all possible facilities will be exploited to set up the product to meet your requirements. However, your project will not plan to commission customisation – bespoke 'tailoring' by the supplier that involves modifying the programs.

In the long-standing discussion of the relative benefits of custom-made versus off-the-shelf software, the hybrid of tailoring an off-the-shelf product can be seen as the best of both worlds (Bray, 2014). Unfortunately, it is difficult to realise the anticipated benefits. Off-the-shelf software implementations that hit problems often find that the cost and risk of modifying the product becomes unmanageable, with more spent on modifications than the original purchase (Solentive, 2014).

Tailored or customised off-the-shelf products can actually deliver the worst of both worlds. They have the off-the-shelf solution's relative inflexibility and tendency to demand heavyweight data content to work. Customisation combines these disadvantages with all the inevitable risks of system development, including poorly defined requirements, cost over-runs and the risk of complete non-delivery. The adapted product is then unique, only understood by a small number of people and may not be compatible with the standard version in future. Therefore, during your selection project, customisation must be regarded as the absolute last resort, rather than the first.

9.14.1 Contrasting approaches to gaps

If you find significant gaps in capability – especially cases of failed mandatory requirements in the highest scoring two for demonstration – you still have options apart from customisation.

To prepare thoroughly for your project board, you may have think through which will be the best option if you implement the successful candidate's software despite a small number of specific, known weaknesses. You may need to hold some early exploratory discussions to understand the implications and possible remedies (see the remainder of this section).

Close the gaps during negotiation

Probably the best way to close the gap is by negotiation. As a condition of order, the next version of the standard product will be contracted to contain improved processing that suits your need. If your negotiation is successful, enhancements will be at the supplier's cost, from their R&D development budget (see Chapter 12, Section 12.9).

Close the gaps at your own cost

When you implement your new solution, you can keep control if you accept responsibility for the costs of addressing the gap. The progression or escalation of the issue should be as follows – after you implement the standard product.

- Verify you have understood your business need, plus the software facilities and constraints.

- Use experts to configure your newly installed standard product to its maximum capabilities.

- Adapt your business processes to match these capabilities more closely.

- Identify any remaining gaps, and close them with 'in-fill' or 'bolt-on' software products. Examples include additional utility software, or perhaps a specialist off-the-shelf solution – one that is dedicated to a niche application and exchanges data with the main software (see Section 9.14.2).

- Address the remaining shortfall with extra clerical effort, and even temporary workers, until your system becomes second nature and people's processing speed is more representative.

- Hold out for the wails to subside. Perhaps 2–3 months after implementation verify understanding once again – your understanding and that of your users and the appropriate implementation consultant. Estimate, over 3–5 years, the relevant internal labour and software development costs. As the last resort, and only if it is clearly justified, finally specify modifications to the standard product.

9.14.2 Project example: closing the gap with a supplemental product

One clear illustration of the benefits of gap analysis before negotiation (and implementation) was a large enterprise software project that covered multiple organisational silos, including the procurement department. The strongest candidate overall had a healthy lead after scoring, with fit 7 per cent higher than the runner up. This product featured a mature purchasing module, but a noteworthy weakness to requirements emerged during scoring. The purchasing module lacked vendor rating – the ability to automatically calculate the ABC rating by applying user-defined rules on delivery date performance, quality reject rates and invoicing price accuracy. (The runner up offered inbuilt vendor-rating calculations, and was therefore more attractive to the head of procurement.)

We expected to implement purchasing within six months, but the candidate in pole position was clear about their road map. An automatic vendor-rating calculation was simply not on the development horizon for years.

The current procedure to calculate vendor ratings involved considerable number crunching, but it was an infrequent activity (roughly every three months) and the responsibility of one member of the procurement team.

We established the feasibility and proposed a supplemental vendor-rating product that ran on a PC. We only needed one copy of this extra product and it was not expensive – especially when compared to the capital budget for the enterprise project. The preferred solution was easily capable of generating a download file with the necessary details from the delivery and invoice transactions. The standalone vendor-rating product was specifically designed to import such details and it offered suitable calculation rules. The resulting ABC ratings would be transferred back to the 'mother ship' into an allocated user-defined field on the corresponding vendor records.

The member of the procurement team responsible for vendor rating was satisfied with this proposal. It looked perfectly feasible and as a personal bonus gave him experience of a sophisticated PC product that was well regarded in procurement circles. The proposal reassured the head of procurement during the project board. He withdrew his objection to the corporate solution that was in pole position.

9.15 PRESENTING TO YOUR PROJECT BOARD

9.15.1 Review scoring and prepare briefing

If your investigation has overthrown or seriously challenged the evaluation team recommendations from the end of your scoring meeting, you might need to reconvene your scoring team. However, if your analysis has instead preserved or even strengthened your position, prepare your project board briefing notes.

- You should chiefly review the contenders recommended for demonstration.
- Prepare to talk briefly but confidently on the remedies to close gaps.
- One of the candidates might be a 'pet product' – software championed by a senior manager based on impressions rather than a detailed evaluation of capability. If so, and it is now outside the top two, prepare to explain why it should be left behind. Of course, your explanation must refer to the scores – these reveal its weak points and possibly some fatal flaws.

9.15.2 Your presentation to the project board

Give a summary of progress, concentrating on the large volume of due diligence work done since the last decision gate.

- Stress how much effort and experience has gone into creating your scores. Show the full extent of the scores, perhaps by revealing a lengthy print of your spreadsheet as a 'performance prop'. Guide the discussion on to the summary fit.

- Answer the questions from your decision-makers.

- Volunteer reasons to park any pet product, if you believe it is best to tackle the issue.

- Seek permission at this gate to go ahead to demonstration – the one major piece of project governance at this stage.

- Agree it is appropriate to demonstrate two candidates. Occasionally, you **might** now shortlist down to a single candidate, if its scores were so far in front that you would be wasting everybody's time to demonstrate the runner up. (But this means you can only actively negotiate with a single candidate, keeping the runner up as backup – see Chapter 12.)

- Agree which two candidates should demonstrate. Normally, it is the top two scoring candidates. Your decision-makers might ignore the evaluation team's scoring, but would need a convincing reason to do so.

Given the rigorous evaluation and body of evidence, your mindset at the project board can reasonably be to go ahead as planned if nobody objects.

9.16 CHAPTER SUMMARY

TAKE-AWAY POINTS

The matrix that results from scoring is a huge asset and probably the major project deliverable. The rationale for the matrix is that it is impossible to hold enough understanding about the facilities of multiple candidates within the brain's limited-capacity working memory (Explorable, 2011).

However, you **can** measure candidates against the same yardstick. The bottom-line percentage fit is a summary of enormous quantities of work, experience and complexity, yet provides a small number of figures that are easy to retain and understand.

You may refer to the scoring documentation for years to come. It provides traceability and solid evidence in your project. It means project decisions can be audited.

The candidate scores are a record of the scope of supply and a reminder of commitments, such as what is included in the price. They are included in your eventual contract. In the worst case, they could even be presented during a court case. However, note that in 50 projects not one has ever gone that awry – this method is about damage avoidance.

Producing your matrix is hard work for many people, but your due diligence will be repaid many-fold. It generates clarity and clean decisions by raising confidence amongst your evaluation team, your decision-makers and the shortlisted suppliers.

9.16.1 The next chapter

Having established your scores, and therefore the top two candidates, you are going to use all the project information (especially your scores) to organise the demonstrations. These provide multiple opportunities: the suppliers can prove claims not yet substantiated; you can root your project more deeply in the business; you can evaluate more subjective aspects, such as usability, with a wider audience; you can reinforce everyone's confidence in your process.

9.17 REFERENCES

Bray, M. (2014) 'Bespoke vs. off-the-shelf software'. BCS, The Chartered Institute for IT. www.bcs.org/bespoke-shelf (10 November 2014).

Explorable (2011) 'The working memory model by Baddeley and Hitch'. Explorable.com. https://explorable.com/working-memory-model (10 November 2014).

Rebernik, M. and Bradač, B. (2008) 'Module 4: Idea evaluation methods and techniques'. Creative Trainer II, SFG. www.creative-trainer.eu/fileadmin/template/download/module_idea_evaluation_final.pdf (10 November 2014).

Solentive (2014) 'Part II: Why 70% of software projects fail and how you can ensure success'. Solentive Software. www.solentivesoftware.com.au/Portals/0/Documents/Whitepapers/why-software-projects-fail-part-2-whitepaper.pdf (10 November 2014).

9.18 FURTHER READING

9.18.1 Books and articles

Decide Guide (2014) 'Kepner-Tregoe'. Firefli Media. www.decide-guide.com/kepner-tregoe (10 November 2014).

9.18.2 Useful websites

Kepner-Tregoe – consultancy and training in structured problem analysis and decision-making: www.kepner-tregoe.com.

9.18.3 Related formats by download

Session allocation spreadsheet; weighted attribute scoring spreadsheet; definitions document format: http://shop.bcs.org/offtheshelfextras.asp.

10 DEMONSTRATIONS: PROVING THE FIT

'Who are you going to believe, me or your own eyes?'

Chico Marx (1887–1961)

10.1 WHAT YOU CAN LEARN FROM THIS CHAPTER

- Understand the vital role that demonstrations play in building confidence in the suppliers, the software products, the project process and indeed your evaluation team.
- Grasp that the people make more difference than the technology, by this stage.
- Recognise the risks with demonstrations, including appreciating some mitigating actions.
- Identify a selection of techniques for managing the demonstrations.

10.2 OVERVIEW

If you have a free choice, two is a good number of demonstrations (although there may be guidelines on the number of candidates from your procurement standards). Allow two to four hours for each. They are normally held locally, probably at your site, with a large, mixed audience to represent your user community and your decision-makers. You will supply to each candidate supplier some sample data and an outline of the main aspects that each demonstration should show.

You have now successfully reduced the shortlist to the final two candidates. This means that your evaluation team has done a significant portion of the fact gathering on your project – from the supplier responses during the evaluation meetings.

The prospect of the demonstration later in the process has been an important check and balance during your earlier evaluation stages. The fact that you advised candidates that demonstrations were part of your process has had the effect of 'policing' your earlier stages.

If a candidate supplier's sales process relies on 'vapourware' or perhaps aims to mislead the prospective customer until it is too late (and they have signed the contract), they will know that it is likely they will be found out during their demonstration. In practice, the 'implied threat' of having to substantiate claims is likely to drive away an unscrupulous supplier, and they will simply qualify themselves out at the earlier RFI stage (see Chapter 7).

While your demonstration and its audience feedback are genuinely part of the evaluation process, your demonstrations also have a critical role in 'selling' the solutions to your organisation. You have three main types of audience members.

- **Staff** who attend because they will become users of the new solution. They need to see strong software.

- **Influencers or advisors** such as representatives of your human resources department. Even if the solution does not have HR processing, adopting a software product usually means organisational change.

- **Decision-makers** from your project board. When (some of) your decision-making body attend the demonstration, they have the opportunity to verify the information that they have been given. So far, they only have second-hand information from the evaluation team about the suitability of the candidates. This will be the first time they have actually seen the software (unless you have had the unusual situation of a project board member on the evaluation team). The demonstration is the first opportunity to match the solution to the information provided. Therefore, project board members are effectively evaluating both the candidates and their own team.

This advanced stage means that you are definitely not trying to 'trip up' one or both of the suppliers. If you have any serious doubts about the capability of one of the software products, you need to handle these doubts both outside the meeting and before it. The demonstration is not the place to be 'washing dirty laundry in public'. You should concentrate on endorsement. This is one reason why you make a conscious decision after scoring whether to demonstrate one or two candidates (see Chapter 9).

Since the purpose is to reassure people, you want two strong demonstrations, not one strong and one weak to open up the gap. Often, the candidates are close; they are probably both viable; it is likely that you could implement either of the solutions and have a successful project. The remaining threats to the future success of your project are not technical – the capability of the software – rather, the human dimension will make the difference. A user community that is love-struck by 'inferior' software will make it work; software that is technically superior but faces a hostile user base will usually fail. After both demonstrations, if your audience has a strong preference for the software with a slightly weaker fit to requirements this may give you problems later in selecting the winner. Notwithstanding, this inconvenient preference is still an asset. You are in a strong position if at least one of the candidates would be warmly welcomed.

Remember, your demonstrations also reveal the credibility of your process so far. They show two strong candidates, who by now are serious contenders. (The demonstration can also present, as necessary, the justifications for the candidates that have been parked.)

YOUR ROLE WHEN ARRANGING THE DEMONSTRATIONS

You have a very unusual role when you organise the demonstrations. Given your objectives, you temporarily switch from 'gatekeeper' to 'impresario' – you want the audience to have a good time.

The demonstration is perhaps 20 per cent evaluation and 80 per cent 'selling in' the candidate systems to your organisation. Moreover, the 20 per cent evaluation is done before the audience arrives. Once suppliers agree that they can cover all the points in your outline and your data is loaded, then that 20 per cent is essentially complete. You can switch from 'policing' to 'show running'.

10.3 OBJECTIVES AND RISKS OF DEMONSTRATIONS

10.3.1 Why – objectives

Test candidates' earlier commitments

One objective of the demonstration is to ensure that earlier commitments and promises are kept.

Before the demonstrations, you will arrange for the candidates to load some representative data. If it does not fit their data structure, they probably do not have the necessary processing for you. In this sense, the sample data load is emphatically part of your evaluation. It addresses compatibility from a different angle.

Each candidate will show a number of significant features. You will get them to concentrate on those features needed for the most important business requirements, plus a few that demonstrate impressively – the so-called 'wow factor'.

Reassure prospective users of relevance

Audience members should be able to see 'their own job' on the screen during the demonstration. This helps to convince them that the new product will be feasible to adopt and that it will help them to do their job.

Engage stakeholders

By consulting audience members, you are engaging them. You will get formal feedback on both candidates and this does feed into the final decision.

This continues your change management work. It addresses people's thinking and fears at a higher level. If they can see 'their job', they can also see how their job will be different. This helps people to think about how they might adapt to the new world.

Collect formal feedback for later choices

You will arrange for the audience to score your demonstrations. Your feedback form and analysis spreadsheet to summarise audience reactions will inform a later stage (when you select one or two candidates for negotiation).

10.3.2 Risks with software demonstrations to large audiences

This section concentrates on simply stating the risks associated with software demonstrations before a large audience. It does not present any mitigating actions at this stage – these will be covered throughout the remainder of the chapter.

Key people are not available

A significant risk is that the most important people are not available within a reasonable lead-time. This might be a demonstrator from the candidates or prospective audience members, especially those far away or with congested diaries.

Standard demonstration misses its audience

One or both suppliers might give a standard or 'canned' demonstration that does not relate to the audience.

Presenters lack experience and give poor impression of software

There is a danger that the demonstrators do not understand the software well enough. Presenting software products to an audience requires a challenging and rare combination of technical and social skills. A presenter might only be able to deliver a standard, pre-scripted demonstration. They might be unable to be spontaneous, for instance unable to explore a feature that was not planned, despite realising it is of enormous interest to this audience. They might be unable to answer follow-up questions from the audience.

Your meeting runs out of time

The meeting might run out of time or finish but not stick to the agreed agenda, so important aspects have not been covered. It is very easy to lose control of a software demonstration, becoming mired in detail or unhelpful comments about screens just because they are different from the incumbent software.

Demonstration concentrates on impressive features

There is a risk that the demonstration is largely of impressive 'wow' features. This can distract the audience, so limitations in the software are hidden. When this effect is deliberate, it is an example of the suppliers aiming to influence the basis of decision (see Chapter 2, Section 2.5.4).

Sabotage of demonstration

In your organisation, you cannot assume universal enthusiasm. Some people, some departments, some divisions or some interest groups will want one or both of the demonstrations to fail.

- You may experience a 'tactical no-show' to snub the project. Somebody might deliberately stay away, without notice, as a ploy to show that your process is unimportant and that they are above the corporate decision. They might even have another candidate in mind for a 'private' demonstration on another day or to purposely clash with your demonstration date.

- You might encounter deliberately obstructive questions that reflect negative attitudes. People who favour one candidate can ask awkward questions of the other. People who do not want new software at all can be negative at both demonstrations and casually dismiss any benefits presented.

- Some demonstration attendees might deliberately withhold information, or provide misinformation (such as how things are done now) in order to erode the relevance and therefore the credibility of the demonstration.

Poor meeting administration

You might suffer a simple administrative error, such as a meeting room that is double-booked. Simple mistakes can still damage the project reputation. You might suffer from a hardware or software failure before or (worse) during the demonstration.

10.4 WHO – THE PEOPLE WHO MAKE THE DIFFERENCE AT DEMONSTRATIONS

There is a peculiar psychology at demonstrations and they can 'turn bad' quickly. If an audience sees processing that looks primitive, peculiar or just puzzling, the mood in the room can swing from excitement to shock to derision in just a few minutes. It is awkward to witness a presenter's performance 'die' at the front and the software credibility nosedive. Once you have lost the positive atmosphere, it can be tricky to recover, and your demonstration can break down with a dispirited audience trudging out.

You need in-depth thinking and preparation – since damage recovery is difficult, you must drive for damage avoidance. A large part of this is getting the people right – the right audience members combined with the right presenters.

10.4.1 Length of demonstration

Both demonstration meetings will be on site (or nearby) and relatively short. Allow 2–4 hours for each demonstration. With this length, you can afford to have a large audience.

If you have a rough schedule of the sequence of the demonstration portions – another advantage of having a demonstration outline with flow – this gives people the option to slip in or out for the sections that interest them.

10.4.2 Audience

Plan for 15–50 attendees at each demonstration, depending on the size of your organisation and project. The decision about attendees is important. The attendance has a high impact upon the process. There should be a wide representation across your organisation with a mix of hands-on users and managers from the affected areas. The evaluation team should attend for continuity.

The demonstrations are another opportunity to engage new stakeholders. A new role on your project has become available, the demonstration attendee, with fresh faces making a short commitment.

Potential attendees have several options: they can attend the live demonstration physically; they can attend remotely over video conferencing; or they might view the recorded version.

10.4.3 Ensure presenters are fluent

Preparations by supplier presenters

You will not be able to micro-manage the presenters, but you can at least create an environment where they can be successful. They need to rehearse the demonstration, especially against the demonstration outline. So you need to allow them time to do this, the opportunity to ask you questions beforehand and possibly even some rehearsal time. Like all performances, some demonstrators prefer to view the room beforehand (earlier in the day or the night before if they travel up early) so they 'get the feel' of the room or have an accurate mental model of the space when they are rehearsing what they are going to say.

Presenters will need to prepare preliminary answers about any major gaps identified during scoring. Remember, the answer is not to modify the software (see Chapter 9, Section 9.14). However, if your discussions about remedies have revealed that a small supporting piece of software would be needed to fill in the gap, then presenters should be aware of this. Alternatively, you might be in the strong position that an enhanced facility will be available in the next version of the standard product. Although such preliminary discussions about remedies are not contractually binding, it reassures your audience that at least you have started a conversation to address the gaps.

The demonstration teams

Even for a small software solution, each demonstration team is likely to be at least two people – sales and technical. On an enterprise-level solution, good sales organisations engage with multiple levels and functions with team and strategic selling (Miller Heiman, 2013).

For a major sale, the demonstration team may be three to six people. There will be the sales executive who is leading the response to the opportunity, possibly a senior manager in an ambassadorial role and two to four technical people. Candidates will want several subject matter experts or 'module experts' driving the software at the appropriate stages of your demonstration.

With luck, some or all of this team will be familiar with your project, and known to your evaluation team because they attended the response meetings at detailed evaluation. This at least helps their own confidence during the presentations because there are some familiar faces in the audience instead of a group of strangers – reassure the presenters by making sure that your own familiar face is also a friendly face.

Presenters reflect supplier culture

During an IT evaluation project, if suppliers are not good to you when selling, they will normally be worse afterwards when they do not try as hard. This means that the demonstration presenter is a window into the company culture. While each person has their unique style, the supplier has chosen to place this person in front of you as their representative. The impression that they create is important. If they are fluent with their product, you assume that the eventual implementation consultant will also be proficient.

10.4.4 Chairing the meetings

Ensure you have a chairperson (host) who is prominent in your meeting and obviously in control. Mob rule will not achieve a worthwhile demonstration. Normally, the host is a senior internal manager. They need to have executive authority – for instance, they may need to outrank and silence someone making mischief. Preferably, the host should be your project's executive sponsor.

Your overall host, having framed the meeting, would normally hand over to the supplier lead. This person, who may be the sales executive or senior manager, would then control the timing of the demonstration and bring in the relevant presenter at the correct time.

Ideally, your host should attend the entire session, but if their diary is heavily congested they might 'top and tail' by opening the meeting to frame it and then returning at the end for the wrap-up session. If leaving the demonstration, they should make a point of handing over the chairperson role to another senior manager.

10.5 WHERE AND WHEN – SETTING UP THE MEETINGS

10.5.1 Venue

Determining a suitable venue involves trade-offs. You need to provide excellent facilities to the suppliers so that they shine. You want a lack of disturbance. You also want a venue that is sufficiently close and attractive that a large audience will turn up – you cannot make attendance compulsory, even though you would like to after all the work you have put in.

Ensure the facility provides good internet, with backup. You may need to check security settings, if the supplier demonstrator requires specific firewall settings or virtual private network (VPN) tunnels back to their mother system. You may need to arrange with security officers for access to equipment or temporary logins to your network at the venue.

Occasionally, the best option is simply to take your audience to the candidate supplier for demonstration. This might apply if their premises are nearby and have much better facilities than you can arrange. However, normally, the demonstration has to be on your site or at a nearby conference venue, simply because this is the best way to get maximum attendance.

Ensure the meeting room is booked and clearly publicised well in advance.

10.5.2 Dates

Give good notice for your demonstration and set the date to get the important people. You may have a small group of presenters from the candidate supplier. You must make certain that your audience represents the spread of stakeholders. It is virtually compulsory that your project sponsor attends, as they will probably be in a senior position steering this strategic acquisition.

Normally, you will keep the suppliers apart. One demonstration in the morning and one in the afternoon runs the risk that they bump into each other. Two successive afternoons might be better, or the afternoon of the first day and the morning of the second.

If you have remote attendees from other time zones, this may determine the time of the meeting. If your organisation routinely holds such international meetings, there will probably be a standard company time to start them and your demonstration arrangements should reflect this.

10.5.3 Timed agenda or schedule

Create another meeting schedule or timed agenda (see Chapter 8, Figure 8.1, for the example spreadsheet format). This allows time-pressed people to attend at least part of the demonstration rather than missing all of it.

10.6 FURTHER PREPARATIONS

Two main actions ensure that the software demonstration is relevant to your audience – an important aspect to address the known risks associated with demonstrations for a large audience. First, you exert some control over the data content of the demonstration and, second, you create an outline specification of the processing the candidates should show.

10.6.1 Provide sample data

You should capture some representative or sample data and send it to your two candidate suppliers. You will need to do this in consultation with the suppliers. For instance, they may request specific items to boost the credibility of their demonstration. This consultation is also part of the evaluation, because you would expect them to ask smart questions. Their questions about your data give an indication of their knowledge of the industry sector, their professionalism and their service orientation.

You usually provide a spreadsheet with representative information. The matrix, of course, maps easily on to computer tables. The format is ubiquitous and most software products can import spreadsheets.

You may have to sanitise or 'censor' the data to remove personal information. A quick way to do this is to scramble spreadsheet columns. Pick large blocks of data in one or more columns and simply move the block down a few rows, for instance to disassociate the person's address from their first name. Repeat to disconnect their first from their surname. Tidy up by deleting rows that are now missing data.

EXAMPLES OF DATA FOR COMMERCIAL AND PUBLIC SECTOR DEMONSTRATIONS

- Departments and staff;
- Customers and sales orders;
- Products and their parts;
- Designs or drawings;
- Suppliers and purchase orders;
- Citizens (in public administration projects);
- Administrative territories;
- Documents containing contracts, specifications or legislation.

Warning about demonstration data

Software suppliers sometimes complain that customers throw too much data at the demonstrator. Bear in mind that sophisticated software products require configuration, so you should not assume that the supplier can simply import your data without any preparation.

You should think through why you are giving the data for demonstration. Actually, in most cases, testing the system is the minor reason. It would apply if you had an unusual structure in your data, for instance a stock code that was heavily segmented, like an engineering part or the style-colour-size breakdown in footwear or clothing. Providing data is mostly to help the audience – to make the demonstration real.

You should allow the suppliers sufficient preparation time to load the data. Although most modern software products have sophisticated data load facilities, for very low volumes of data it may not be worth the overhead of configuring them. Suppliers will often simply re-key a few records.

In summary, you should only send enough data to make your demonstration credible.

10.6.2 Create a demonstration outline

You should write a demonstration outline and oblige both suppliers to use it (see Figure 10.1). Once again, this is consistent with the method philosophy that you cannot compare candidates with each other but you can measure them against the same yardstick.

There are several reasons for creating a demonstration outline:

- You will make your demonstrations more realistic. By stipulating the steps you want to see, it means the audience can relate to it much more immediately. The demonstration will flow much more smoothly because your audience will have far less need to ask to see facilities – you are 'putting the good stuff under their noses'.

Figure 10.1 Page of demonstration outline

DEMONSTRATE	COMMENTARY [NOTES]
3.4 Scenario A: Requirements & Design Change	
16. Show details available for one customer, including contact person who submits specifications.	
17. Show customer requirements tracking, with one set of customer requirements tracked as set of documents (multiple requirements for the customer's project). Show how the requirements can be organised into a hierarchy or tree. Explain separate records allow fine-grained version control such as tracking status and author.	**Project:** 9633 **Title:** Prototype coolant release valve **Requirements:** stainless steel; flow rate 1.5l/min @ 2Bar; to withstand maximum 200mBarG; non-annealed.
18. Pick one requirement. Show the links that encapsulate its relationship to external constraints (such as a document with relevant legislation), to another requirement and to one specific part (put in place to explicitly support the requirement).	
19. Identify which CAD models feature that part.	
20. Access the Work Breakdown Structure and add a new activity *Revise Design for Changed Requirement*.	Track work for revised requirement: 4. Modify finish to 'Annealed'.
21. Give this new activity its own budget.	
22. Access the relevant resource planning facility and show the current resource histogram.	[Highlight the figures that will change soon.]
23. Give this *new Revise Design* activity some estimated hours.	10 hours of Mechanical Design Engineering. 20 hours of Prototype Manufacturing. 10 hours of Validation.
24. Repeat the access to the relevant resource planning facility and show the resource histogram has been affected.	[Perhaps pushing into overload for that month.]

- You will control the content and ensure the best demonstration coverage in the time available. You make sure your chief requirements are addressed by the demonstration – either those requirements that are critical within your organisation, or requirements that reflect processing that is unique to your organisation. The selection of features to demonstrate should be based on the requirements that have high weights, mostly 4 and 5, with some 3 (see Chapter 5 for weighting).

- You will guarantee that your demonstrations address all your stakeholder groups. For instance, you can ensure that each affected department sees some relevant processing. Given that your demonstration outline relates to your requirements document, in practice you will ensure that you address some requirements (meaning show some software features) from each of the major categories in the document.

- You will inhibit demonstrators concentrating on impressive 'wow' features, while neglecting bread-and-butter facilities that are important labour-savers in your organisation.

Remember, your demonstration outline is a statement of minimum coverage. You might explain it as 'a series of waypoints' that must be passed by both 'demonstration journeys'. This means that the demonstration outline is not a script. You are not putting words into the demonstrator's mouth. Instead, you are creating high-level scenarios (Alexander and Maiden, 2004) that your audience should witness. You stipulate in the demonstration outline the major steps that you want your audience to see, in a flow. However, allow the demonstrators to use their superior product knowledge to be effective and to show innovative approaches that exploit the new technology.

Therefore, when designing your outline, you should always start with your requirements. However, filter your requirements spreadsheet down to the most important entries – those that have weights 4 and 5. Pull these across. The wording of the title of the requirement is not, of course, the description of the demonstration's step. However, it does give you a prompt for what you want to see at that stage.

You should then review the other requirements and see if there are any which are unusual or unique to your organisation. They may well be weighted lower than 4, but may be those requirements that require special processing. For instance, those you were relieved to see supported during the evaluation meetings, which means they will impress at demonstration.

You should then add extra requirements and steps to maintain the flow of the demonstration. For instance, your organisation might have a requirement to change the home address on consumer records hundreds of times a day, so this process must be really slick. You might therefore set up a demonstration flow that showed the creation of a new customer, and then amending their address as a later step, to show how efficient this is.

You would normally follow the flow of your product, or projects, or your organisational life cycle. As a simple example, it is sensible that participants see the demonstrator creating a customer, then raising their order, and then delivering their goods.

As a general guideline, you would stipulate steps that create new entries (like suppliers) before displaying changes to existing entries. It also makes sense to show reporting towards the end of a section or the demonstration so that the reports will include the new and amended information already seen. This proves that the management information is live rather than a 'mock up'.

Following your business flow is another way to assure that you have covered all sections of your requirements document and therefore all the main stakeholder groups.

10.6.3 Release your outline

When you release your demonstration outline, you should make it clear to the candidate suppliers that it contains **minimum** coverage rather than the totality of what is allowed. You should allow suppliers to ask questions when they receive your demonstration outline. These questions will often be, 'Which way do you want it done?'

For instance, in a sophisticated software product, there may be four or five different ways to create a purchase order. The demonstrator will not have time to show all, so they will want to demonstrate the way that is most relevant or most attractive to your audience. This might be the way that would be used most frequently, or the way that would save the most time, or the way that would be best for handling complex orders with flexibility. Therefore, the decision as to which of the ways to create an order should be a joint decision with you and the candidate supplier – once again, they provide the product expertise, but you provide the understanding of your organisation. Together, you can decide which is the best way to exploit the facilities.

Allowing suppliers to ask questions is also part of your evaluation. You are looking for smart questions, which show they understand your industry or public sector domain. To use the analogy of recruitment interviews, you often think most highly of a candidate who asked superb questions, rather than one who provided solid answers.

10.6.4 Prepare your feedback form

The feedback form allows the participants to contribute statistics to the final selection decision. Creating one shows that you are serious about the opinion of your audience.

You will see from the illustration at Figure 10.2 that you are not asking people to rate individual features. This would be too detailed and the evaluation team has already conducted specific matching of processing to requirements. You should create a smaller form that concentrates on general aspects, especially those subjective areas that are unreliable if assessed solely by a small evaluation team. These include, for example, usability, contribution to personal productivity or contribution to organisational profitability. Include a 'bottom line' question about whether the organisation should press ahead with the project in case positive assumptions miss the chance for a high-level alert.

10.6.5 Treble check everything

Given the substantial list of things that can go wrong (see Section 10.3.2) the only appropriate level of management for a demonstration is over-management.

Make sure your room booking is secured and official. Make sure refreshments are booked and adequate for the numbers. Make sure technical support people are booked to be on standby in case facilities do not work. Preferably, negotiate for them to arrive at the room at least 30 minutes early and to stick around (even if things appear to be working) for the first 10 minutes of the demonstration. Book redundant equipment – a spare computer, possibly a backup data projector and certainly a spare bulb (or at least know where the spares are kept).

Have an eventualities list – what if there is a power cut, fire alarm, lift breakdown, full car park or critical illness? White boards need special pens. The checklists for running training courses apply.

Make sure the technology is in place in your room permanently, or has been booked for the room. Examples of things that can cause you problems are inadequate or omitted conferencing facilities that are essential for remote participants or hardware of inadequate specification for the software. If you are providing the hardware, ensure you are aware of the system requirements. Hardware compatibility also affects projection: the demonstrator

Figure 10.2 Demonstration feedback form

Your Name (optional):

This questionnaire is to collect information on your experience of the demonstration of the prospective system.

Please be honest, please be specific. Leave your name blank if you prefer to stay anonymous.

Venue and date of demonstration: ....

Demonstration candidate: ....

	QUESTION	RESPONSE *(PLEASE CIRCLE A RESPONSE, OR WRITE IN A REPLY)* ADD EXTRA SHEETS, OR INCLUDE ATTACHMENTS, IF NECESSARY				
A.	**Process**: did the demonstration allow sufficient time to view the system?	Highly inadequate	Inadequate	Borderline	Sufficient	Generous
B.	**Process**: did you believe the demonstration gave an accurate view of the system?	Very poor	Inadequate	Adequate	Good	Excellent
C.	**System**: what is your initial view on the *capability and processing* of the system?	Clearly inadequate	Marginal	Acceptable	Good	Excellent
D.	**System**: what is your initial view on the *flexibility* of the system?	Clearly inadequate	Marginal	Acceptable	Good	Excellent
E.	**System**: what is your initial view on the *usability* ('friendliness') of the system?	Clearly inadequate	Marginal	Acceptable	Good	Excellent
F.	**Opinion on suitability**: do you believe as an *individual* you could use this system?		No	No strong view	Yes	
G.	**Opinion on suitability**: do you believe your *organisation* could use this system?		No	No strong view	Yes	
H.	**Other Comments**					

might require a high definition projector, but this might throw tiny images to the audience unless the image scaling is set correctly. This is a good way to lose 10 precious minutes at the start of the demonstration, force a seating layout change (moving people closer to the screen) and disturb the presenter's flow. Consider a technical rehearsal.

Follow up the sample data to make certain it is suitable for the suppliers, they have understood it and that it is loaded satisfactorily. Ensure that demonstrators at the candidate suppliers have digested the scores so they understand the strengths and weaknesses of their solution against your requirements. They may think through specific remedies for weak spots, because the audience will probably have questions on these areas.

10.7 HOW – CONDUCTING THE DEMONSTRATION

10.7.1 Managing audience expectations

It is prudent when opening the meeting to manage the audience expectations and set the tone for expected behaviour. Ideally, your executive sponsor does this when greeting the audience. Make it clear that the demonstration features a strong contender with modern technology. It will definitely not be the same as the current incumbent system. In the vocabulary of business process design, this is a view of the TO BE processes.

10.7.2 Timing

It is important to stick to time overall. In practice, this means staying fairly close to your timed agenda or meeting schedule (see Section 10.5.3).

Assuming the slots have been calculated to have the right length, significantly overrunning these slots will result in the meeting badly overrunning (meaning the audience will drift away) or the meeting being guillotined (meaning some stakeholders will not see the areas that interest them).

While the slots provide structure – important for coverage and flow – the demonstration may 'embellish' points if there is time within a session. If there is spare time at the end of the meeting, the presenter may show some off-topic but interesting features.

10.7.3 Effective handling of questions

Your presenters must be mindful that demonstrations should stick roughly to the outline sequence. This ensures the coverage that is so important, keeps the demonstration relevant to the audience (you designed it that way), makes sure it fits together and, of course, simultaneously safeguards the schedule. There are techniques to protect against detailed 'diversionary' questions that soak up time. While it is important for the demonstrator, as representative of a service-oriented supplier, to be seen to be responsive and not to 'fob off' questions, they have many options with their response.

- The question may simply anticipate a later demonstration point. The presenter should say that it will be covered by a later part of the demonstration. The person with the question should ask again if it is still outstanding then.

- A demonstrator can give a brief answer and ask to come back to it later, when more confident they will have time in the session.

- The demonstrator can ask if the question is of general interest – perhaps by show of hands. If only one person in the room is interested, that gives the demonstrator permission to suggest that the topic is explored in a one-to-one demonstration outside the main meeting. Such 'private' demonstrations can be extraordinarily effective. They lavish attention on one audience member, who may be an enthusiast. They also allow you to handle controversial topics away from the public gaze.

10.7.4 Recording the video and audio conference

Sometimes the prospective customer appoints a meeting scribe to create meeting notes or draw on white boards to capture key points. This formal approach might be required by your organisational culture. However, there are dangers. It may slow down proceedings, especially if the person taking notes does not understand the content of your demonstration and repeatedly seeks clarification. Having the meeting record created by one person may introduce unintentional or even deliberate bias. Remember, your analysis of feedback tests the main points (see Section 10.8).

There is a superb way to record proceedings without a scribe. Given standard facilities in video conferencing services, quite literally, you record proceedings. While this may not be appropriate in high-security environments (such as the defence industry), it is possible to capture the slides, screen demos and a synchronised soundtrack.

HOW TO EXPLOIT CONFERENCE RECORDING

You enter the details of your audio conferencing system into your video conferencing account. When you start the video conference, it dials into the audio conference so it can 'hear' the presenter and audience voices (via the desk microphone and telephone connections). This creates an integrated recording which has all of the slides shown, with the live screen demonstrations and a synchronised soundtrack of presenter commentary and audience questions.

After the meeting, a streaming version simply plays over the web via a link. A downloadable version may require a proprietary free player or might be in an industry standard video format. The downloadable version is ideal to copy (with the player software if necessary) onto the laptop of a busy senior manager. If they travel a lot and could not attend your demonstration, the recording is perfect to watch on their next trip.

You should create a simple index that shows the start time of the major sections (such as HR) in each demonstration. For some people, the recorded demo with the session index is actually better than being there. They can skip over the boring bits. They can re-watch the topics that they really need to absorb.

10.7.5 Closing the meeting

When your meeting host closes each demonstration, they should invite follow-up outside the meeting. Suggest people with questions hang back now for individual discussions or demonstrations, or that they contact the sponsor or members of your evaluation team (who might stand up if not universally known). Your process should have as many channels for communication – both formal and informal – as possible to elicit good ideas and 'ground' any misunderstanding or bubbling resentment.

Press the audience to complete the feedback forms before they leave the demonstration. The probability of getting them back nosedives if people take away the blanks – they never quite get round to it. Remember to collect the forms, of course – stand at the door. The analysis of forms is important. You need a volume of results for statistical significance.

10.8 ANALYSIS AFTER THE DEMONSTRATIONS

After you have held the demonstrations, sit down with a colleague to process the completed demonstration feedback forms. You should check-call the scores into an analysis spreadsheet (see Figure 10.3).

Figure 10.3 Spreadsheet to analyse feedback forms

Section:	Candidate I					Candidate J					Att Both
	Capab-ility	Flexibility	Usability	For Individual	For Organis'n	Capab-ility	Flexibility	Usability	For Individual	For Organis'n	
Attendee	C.	D.	E.	F.	G.	C.	D.	E.	F.	G.	
Alan	4	3	4	4	4	4	4	4	4	5	Y
Amanda	5	4	5	5	4	4	4	4	4	4	y
Belle	4	4	4	4	4	4	3	4	4	4	Y
Chris E	4	3	5	4	4	4	4	3	4	3	Y
Christopher K	3	3	3	4	4	2	2	2	3	3	Y
Elizabeth	3	3	3	4	4	5	5	5	4	4	Y
Ian	4	4	4	4	3	4	5	5	4	4	Y
Jay	5	4	5	4	4	5	4	4	4	4	Y
Jessica	4	4	3	3	4	5	4	4	4	3	Y
Melissa	5	3	4	4	3	5	4	3	4	3	Y
Nicole	4	4	4	4	4	3	2	2	4	3	Y
Sarah	5	4	4	4	4	5	5	5	4	4	Y
Sebastian	4	4	3	3	4	4	3	3	3	4	Y
Sergio	5	3	4	4	3	5	4	3	4	3	Y
Stephanie	5	4	5	4	4	3	2	2	3	4	Y
Stuart	4	4	4	4	4	3	2	2	4	3	Y
Tom	5	2	4	4	4	5	5	5	4	4	Y
Count:	17	17	17	17	17	17	17	17	17	17	
Minimum:	3	2	3	3	3	2	2	2	3	3	
Maximum:	5	4	5	5	4	5	5	5	4	5	
Std Deviation:	0.7	0.6	0.7	0.4	0.4	0.9	1.1	1.1	0.4	0.6	
Average:	4.29	3.53	4.00	3.94	3.82	4.12	3.65	3.53	3.82	3.65	

Difference Cand I - J [-ve J better]	0.18	-0.12	0.47	0.12	0.18						
Percent I is better (worse)	4.1%	-3.3%	11.8%	3.0%	4.6%						

You are looking for trends. Specifically, look for significant differences in reaction. In practice, this means comparing scores when the same people attended both demonstrations. Some people are 'high tickers' and tend to give generous scores on feedback forms: if one audience had a higher proportion of such people, it will skew your results. Therefore, when you are analysing scores and feedback comments, you need to identify those people who attended both demonstrations. You might extract some of the comments from people who only attended one demonstration, but you cannot draw their scores into your comparative statistics.

For each of the headings on your feedback form, your summary spreadsheet shows average values, possibly reinforced with analysis of the range with values such as minimum, maximum and standard deviation.

Absolute values do not mean much. You are looking for one candidate with a significantly higher average for one or more headings – a difference of 10 per cent would certainly attract your attention.

However, you should not be too concerned if the analysis is inconclusive – remember, the demonstration is more reassurance than evaluation. The demonstrations do involve additional fact gathering, some of it soft information, but they are not intended to collect 'one killer fact' that means one candidate becomes vastly preferred and the other becomes utterly discredited and a resounding runner-up. The comments and statistics from the feedback forms will be part of the pool of information at the final decision. If audience reaction shows they could make either work, this helps your negotiation. You have other information – notably the scores and reference sites – to help your project board pick the preferred candidate (see Section 10.9 for using the analysis).

10.9 DECISION-MAKING AFTER DEMONSTRATIONS

The demonstration phase might contribute part of the decision-making criteria. Alternatively, you may simply summarise the feedback.

When presenting feedback from the demonstrations to your project board, you should dwell on the audience reaction to the demonstration if:

- strong trends attack the current rank order of pole position and runner-up;
- one candidate should clearly be left behind now.

If the demonstrations are less dramatic, there is a straightforward gate. You simply seek permission to go into the next stage, to take up the reference sites (see Chapter 11). Normally, you press ahead with two candidates. Verify how many references for each candidate are required. Usually this is two, so you will conduct four reference site interviews.

Having confirmed the number of referees, agree how you should conduct the reference site discussions. The options are to visit the sites, or to hold a telephone interview. Generally, the telephone interview has the relative advantage (see Chapter 11).

EXECUTIVE PERSPECTIVE: A US GENERAL MANAGER'S ANALYSIS OF THE EXPERIENCE

I have been personally involved in a couple of transitions from organizations with multiple homegrown financial tools to a full-blown enterprise software implementation. This process has many potential mistakes, which can be made during the course of the implementation, some of which can significantly limit the operation of an organization. In my opinion, there are three major causes for these types of issues:

1. Business requirements not understood.
2. Software selected not able to deliver a system to meet those requirements.
3. Organization not committing the proper resources to the implementation of that system.

The cross-functional team approach software selection method with quantitative output, which was utilized, significantly reduces the risk associated with those potential causes. Following these key activities from the methodology will greatly enhance the chance for a successful enterprise software implementation:

1. Defining your needs via interview/workshop.
2. 'Possible' requirements definition document as a starting point.
3. Compiled and agreed requirements weighting meeting.
4. System selection method roadmap briefing for executive staff.
5. Compiled and agreed Request For Information document.
6. Compiled and agreed longlist/shortlist process.

During this selection process, I was in the unique position of representing a remote office in another country. The overall methodology of this process enabled myself to work as an effective team member primarily remotely, but also able to participate locally during key portions of the project.

10.10 CHAPTER SUMMARY

TAKE-AWAY POINTS

Demonstration meetings are crucial for building confidence – not just confidence in the solutions, but also confidence in the project process and your evaluation team. They root the candidate solutions more firmly in the organisation. People can begin to believe their new IT is going to work. However, the credibility of your demonstration meetings is paramount. A demonstration process that is not capable will discredit a candidate and the entire project. This is why it is important to ensure the high levels of resource and management necessary to put on a good show.

10.10.1 The next chapter

Having captured the internal audience reaction and gained permission to proceed, you are now going to get more information – very different information – from your reference sites. Not only will these points of view be heard from outside your own organisation, they will also be from existing users rather than prospective users such as yourself.

10.11 REFERENCES

Alexander, I. and Maiden, N. (2004) *Scenarios, stories, use cases: Through the systems development life-cycle.* John Wiley & Sons: Chichester.

Miller Heiman (2013) 'Strategic selling: Comprehensive strategy for complex sales'. Knowledge Center, Miller Heiman Group. www.millerheiman.com/Our_Products/ Manage-Opportunities/Strategic-Selling (10 November 2014).

10.12 FURTHER READING

10.12.1 Books and articles

Highmore Sims, N. (2006) *How to run a great workshop: The complete guide to designing and running brilliant workshops and meetings.* Pearson Business: Harlow.

Karia, A. (2014) 'Own the room: Presentation techniques to keep your audience on the edge of their seats'. AkashKaria.com.

Thomas, P., Paul, D and James, C. (2012) *The human touch: Personal skills for professional success.* BCS, The Chartered Institute for IT: Swindon.

10.12.2 Related formats by download

Demonstration attendee feedback form; feedback analysis spreadsheet from http://shop.bcs.org/offtheshelfextras.asp.

11 REFERENCE SITES: REAL CUSTOMER FEEDBACK

'Only a fool learns from his own mistakes. The wise man learns from the mistakes of others.'

Otto von Bismarck (1815–1898)

11.1 WHAT YOU CAN LEARN FROM THIS CHAPTER

- Understand the realistic objectives for the reference site phase, which might be different from your first thoughts.
- Recognise the tools and techniques for taking up reference sites.

11.2 OVERVIEW

11.2.1 The value of reference sites

Reference sites collect important information, but sometimes also 'soft information' (Wiebe, 2010).

- This helps protect your organisation from an ill-informed final selection decision.
- It usually cannot be collected accurately via paper and desk exercises.
- The information is often best not sought directly from the candidate suppliers.
- It acts as free advice from experienced users of the product – a type of implementation consultancy. Their tips help you to avoid their mistakes.
- Reference site discussions and their consequent new relationships are your first steps towards joining the user community.

However, reference site information is general advice, so the usual guideline applies – you must extract from it that which is relevant to your organisation and project.

11.2.2 Note of caution about references

It is unusual for a reference site to match your organisation and its exact processes. Therefore, each reference site will have experiences of the software that you will never come across. This means a chunk of their experience is not relevant to you.

Be clear that you are not asking, 'Should I use this product?' You are asking, 'What has your use of the product been like?'

11.3 WHY – OBJECTIVES OF REFERENCES

Reference sites are not really to verify whether the candidate is 'a good one' in the conventional judgemental language. No competent supplier will provide you with a 'bad' reference site, and your evaluation process so far will have eliminated unsuitable suppliers.

You must not allow another organisation to determine the fitness for purpose of the product for **your** organisation. That is your job as an evaluation team. The reference site does not know your full requirements. They may have requirements that you do not have that make the software ideal for them – but not for you.

Instead, your first objective should be to get feedback on those aspects of the software and supplier that are not suitable for evaluation via documentation, demonstration or direct supplier answer. These are often intangibles.

- One example is usability. A good question could be: 'At demonstration, a couple of people thought the Goods Receipt screen was confusing – do your own Goods Inwards people have problems with that screen?'

- Another good example is the service mentality of the supplier. You could ask any supplier at any stage in your evaluation – in writing or verbally – whether they are strongly customer oriented. However, they will all answer positively. This is a question better asked of the customer.

- Reference sites already running your volume of data are more important than supplier assertions about performance.

Second, another important objective is to get free advice – a form of implementation consultancy. This is probably the most important aspect of your contact with the referees (see Section 11.6 for example questions).

The third objective is reassurance of your senior managers, whom you will soon require to make the final selection decision. The reference sites are an opportunity for them to gain intelligence – albeit indirectly – from their peers, the management of the reference organisation. You can seek information about how practical their project proved to be, what the resource implications were and what dangers they had to steer around.

11.3.1 Selection of sites

You are, of course, reliant on the suppliers to put forward the reference sites. However, this stage provides yet another opportunity for a better outcome by you articulating your needs to the candidates. Good reference sites are compatible and mature.

Compatible means that they are in a similar industry or public sector area, using similar product modules (if there are optional sets) and using a software version that is close to the one that you would buy.

Mature means that their implementation is advanced enough to have hard experience of what went right and what can go wrong. Experience is sometimes described as staying around long enough for your mistakes to catch up with you.

EXECUTIVE PERSPECTIVE: AN ENTREPRENEUR'S EXPERIENCE OF IMPROVING RESEARCH DURING SELECTION

I found the method to be logical and straightforward. It gave me guidance in my decision-making and allowed me to choose a solution using my head and not from gut feel.

I had had a previous bad experience with the choice I had made for my website software and content management system. The technology was appropriate but it was other factors such as supplier stability and data security that needed to be considered to ensure my solution was right for my business. The method encouraged me to think about the relative importance of a broad range of requirements – not just the technical features of the solutions on offer.

11.4 WHO – REFERENCE SITES ATTENDEES

11.4.1 Your interviewing team

It is best to have at least two interviewers from you as prospective customer – but probably no more than two, as increased audience size often means that your interviewee will be less willing to talk freely. Your options for the internal team are as follows:

- Select two people from your evaluation team, or put together a mix with one existing team member and one new face, to deepen the roots of the project. If Procurement has not previously been involved, you might now involve a colleague from that department.

- One standing member and a rotating guest second interviewer, who attends selected portions of the reference site conversations for their specialist topic. For instance, an in-house project manager – who will pick up the project after contract – might join your meeting for the specific discussion about implementation (see Section 11.6 for example questions).

- A two-person team to drive the conversation, but an extra person who is an observer rather than an active participant – not questioning, but possibly acting as scribe.

11.4.2 The reference site interviewee

It is probably better to have only one interviewee (at a time) from the reference site. Again, your interviewee is more likely to talk freely without a colleague present – especially if people were the major source of issues on their project.

When requesting your reference site contact details, it is best to send in advance, via the supplier, some detail of the questions you would like to ask. At the very least, indicate the major areas, such as usability, interfaces, training or support. Better still is to give prior sight of your specific questions.

Either will help the candidate suppliers to understand your objectives and it will therefore help them to find the right referees. Nobody wants, say, technical IT staff floundering with questions about business processes and strategy or (equally) an executive sponsor referee floundering with questions about database compatibility.

Providing an indication of your topics of interest is especially important if your requirement and associated questioning has a wide scope. You may have to take more than two people as interviewees and combine their answers to cover the full range of your topics.

11.4.3 Supplier involvement

You need to choose between accompanied and unaccompanied visits or calls. With the supplier present, you will probably get better technical information and some social ice breaking. Without them, customers talk more freely. Usually it is best without, although you can still be collaborative by sending your notes to the interviewee, with the option to pass them on to the supplier.

11.5 WHERE AND WHEN – MEETING LOCATION AND FORMAT

11.5.1 Trade-off between site visits and telephone interviews

Actually visiting the premises of the reference site has one major advantage. You may gather informal information at the coffee machine, when people are talking off the record. However, this advantage is offset by several significant disadvantages.

- The site visit is more intrusive – more of a burden on your referee, who is doing you a favour.
- It is harder to schedule meetings, given congested diaries and 'grace and favour' service levels.
- It will usually garner only a little extra information compared to the telephone.
- You may gain a bad impression by encountering somebody who does not understand, or simply does not like, the software or the supplier – irrespective of the software facilities or the supplier talents.
- You must treat the suppliers evenly, so if you have a site visit for one supplier, you have an obligation to find another one for the other supplier.

Therefore, it is usually best to conduct reference site conversations by telephone or video conference. People will usually talk freely – definitely more freely than you emailing questions and requesting written replies. You should take advantage of the normal opportunities in a conversation to build a rapport, before asking the valuable (but awkward and embarrassing) questions such as, 'Where did you mess up?'

In practice, you would normally aim for four telephone interviews – two reference site calls for each of the two strongest candidates. You can have more if possible, but avoid fewer. Four calls normally strikes a balance between project risk and workload – yours, the candidate suppliers and the referees.

MORE ADVANCED AUDIO CONFERENCING FOR REFERENCE CALLS

Assuming telephone interviews rather than site visits, an audio conference is the preferred technology – it is one of the easiest forms of meetings to organise. Taking your call, to a landline or mobile, places very few limitations on the time slot because it relies on facilities that are nearly ubiquitous. In addition, it may be that your organisation's two interviewers are not even in the same room.

One hybrid approach is a call from three different locations with two participants from your organisation and one telephone interviewee. You supplement speech with data conferencing facilities (desktop or document sharing) between yourself and your colleague interviewer. This allows one interviewer to witness the note taking of the appointed scribe. You can also type private messages to adjust the direction of questioning.

11.5.2 Meeting length and scheduling

The meeting length and the number of questions interact, of course. As a guideline, allow 40–60 minutes per reference site call.

Allow lead-time for the suppliers to find suitable reference site contacts and conduct the normal negotiation over diaries. You should provide as much flexibility and as many potential slots as possible – including perhaps some slots out of standard business hours if you can.

11.6 HOW – EXAMPLE QUESTIONS

Your reference site discussions should be semi-structured interviews (Easterby-Smith et al., 2012). The best questions are usually more to do with process and people. The evaluation team looked at the capabilities of the technology during the detailed evaluation meetings and demonstration. The best questions relate more to, 'What do **we** have to do?'

See Figure 11.1 for an example format to collate questions. Responses would go into the **Notes** column, made much wider just before the interview.

Preparing questions in advance is partly to save time and reduce mistakes. Mostly, it is to ensure that you have been fair and asked the same questions of the reference sites of both suppliers. This does not mean you must ask all your questions of all four interviewees. However, there must be mirroring, such that if you ask a question of one of the referees, you must ask the same question of (at least) one referee from the other candidate. Once again, the principle applies of measuring candidates against the same yardstick.

Figure 11.1 Questions for reference site

REF	QUESTION	NOTES
	Customer's Experience of the Supplier	
26	How was the quality of training?	
27	What was the performance of the implementation consultants?	
29	How have you found the attitude of supplier staff (friendly, adversarial, condescending, helpful)?	
31	If you did it all over again, would you choose the same company?	
	Estimates	
32	Have cost estimates proved accurate?	
34	Have time and duration estimates proved accurate? What has been the ability of the supplier to meet schedules and deadlines?	
	Project Learning	
36	What do you know now that you wish you had known at the beginning of the project?	
41	What should we take back to the senior management in our organisation to improve our chance of success?	
	Customer Contribution	
42	Have you experienced customisation issues?	

11.6.1 Investigating the product

- 'What would you summarise as the main strengths of the solution?'
- 'What would you summarise as the major limitations of the product?'
- 'And what is the single biggest weakness?'
- 'What is your view on the usability of the product?'
- 'Was there anything unusual about the product that was revealed by your installation, which you weren't expecting?'
- 'Has performance degraded as you loaded production volumes of data?'

11.6.2 Researching the supplier

- 'Was the sales and demonstration process representative of your subsequent experience as a customer?'
- 'How did your training go?'
- 'Have the supplier estimates for project effort and duration proved accurate? What has been the ability of the supplier to meet schedules and deadlines?'
- 'How would you rate the helpfulness of the support desk?'

11.6.3 Assessing impact during implementation

- 'Was the resource load on your internal people more or less than expected?'
- 'How difficult was it to gather or generate the necessary data to set up the product?'
- 'How much did you need to change your processes?'
- 'Do you think you are using the product to its full potential?'
- 'What should we take back to the senior management in our organisation to improve our chance of success?'

11.6.4 Wrapping up an interview

- 'What do you know now that you wish you had known at the start of your project?'
- 'If you had it to do all over again, would you still choose the same product and supplier?'
- 'Is there anything else that you think I should know about?'

This is an effective final question. It relies on any rapport that you have built up during your conversation. It creates a slight moral obligation on your interviewee to disclose anything they were previously not sure they would say.

SPREADSHEET TO SUMMARISE LEARNING

As well as your 'discussion record' notes (see Figure 11.1), you may create a matrix that is a kind of project log or learning register. This spreadsheet would summarise your learning and feedback, to help you report to your decision-making body. The matrix approach can be particularly useful – when you place the answer fragments alongside each other – where there were strong contrasts in your interviewee reactions.

11.7 THE 'ANTI-REFERENCE SITE'

11.7.1 Handling a request to take up an anti-reference site

A critic of one of your top two candidates may know about a failed implementation. Alternatively, somebody who does not want a new solution at all may have got wind of a spectacular project failure. They may ask you to speak to a contact they have at the 'failed project'. The contact is unlikely to be volunteered by the candidate supplier.

As an evaluation team, you are obliged to take up the request to talk to such an 'anti-reference site'. It is an extra information-gathering step, on top of the 'positive' reference site interviews. You must be seen to be fair and receptive to information, even negative information – perhaps especially negative information.

11.7.2 Learning from failed projects

Actually, as well as being seen to be fair, talking to people involved in an unsuccessful project can be an enormous educational resource. The failed implementation may have had problems with project management or change management – not with the off-the-shelf solution. Statistically, this is the most likely explanation.

If their project failed for non-technical reasons, the 'bad example' customer might, notwithstanding, endorse their supplier. They may have been tolerant of the customer mistakes, supportive and not overtly driven by profit.

There are strong learning experiences from failed implementations. Project management issues, such as losing the project sponsor partway through the project, will allow you to go back to your project board and emphasise the critical nature of senior sponsorship during your implementation phase. Collecting practical information on what can go wrong can be used to reassure your own senior management that, while problems do occur, they can be managed if the risk is understood and mitigated.

11.7.3 Consciously seeking reference sites with problems

This is a very advanced technique, and the suppliers may be unable or unwilling to oblige. You may specifically request that the candidate suppliers avoid glowing references. You may prefer to avoid ringing endorsements that are almost sycophantic because they come from raving fans. You may prefer the learning experience of hearing about at least one project that was heading towards disaster, but averted it ultimately. To use again the analogy of recruitment, this is similar to the job interview question, 'Tell me a situation where you turned something around'.

11.8 BUILDING RELATIONSHIPS

11.8.1 Send your interview notes

One way to help both your interviewee and yourself simultaneously is to send them your notes from the conversation. Assuming you use the recommended table format for questions, you can type notes during your chat, tidy them up after the meeting and email them promptly. Of course, you will need to capture your notes diplomatically and this may involve a few euphemisms – 'problems' are 'issues' while 'company politics' is 'the organisational dynamic'.

This will allow your referee to verify that you have understood their comments. From the perspective of your referee, sending your notes means that you are prepared to be open and collaborative. It is also providing them with a practical document to use during future reference site calls – happy customers that give references usually become targets for multiple requests.

11.8.2 Contribute to the user community

If a referee expresses an interest, keep them posted about your project progress – especially whether you bought the same product that they are using. It is possible that you will learn something about the software that is relevant to their use of it. So you might drop a quick email with a pointer, such as an obscure announcement for a complementary product that they might not have seen, or a link to an article that you sense will help them.

It motivates your referee if your demeanour makes it obvious that you would enthusiastically join the community of users if this product becomes the one for you. If you show you are a collaborative customer, you will be a valuable asset and their investment in your organisation will eventually help the user community.

11.8.3 Recognise networking opportunities

Your reference site interviews are an opportunity to build relationships with people who may help your project later. If networking is 'building relationships before you need them', your reference site conversations are a form of networking. Potentially, your reference sites are almost an informal 'buddy system'. Once again, it is prudent to build relationships with all your referees, because you do not know which product you will eventually implement.

Leave the door open for later contact. Invite interviewees to get back to you later if something occurs to them after the conversation, or if they find something in your notes. Similarly, if the atmosphere during the conversation seems right, ask if you can get back to them. If you select 'their' product (and enthusiastic users regularly identify closely with the software), you might ask if you can visit them later. This means that, without committing time now, you have left the door open to an excellent networking opportunity. You will invest more in such relationships when you have a clear winner.

11.9 CHAPTER SUMMARY

TAKE-AWAY POINTS

Do not expect another organisation to gauge a solution's fitness for purpose against your own requirements. The reference site is about their experiences in the past and not the fit in your future. Focus on what the reference sites sensibly can give you:

- free advice from an experienced customer on practical issues;

- the opportunity to learn lessons, such as avoiding unintended consequences of project decision-making;

- a chance to investigate soft issues (like the candidate's customer focus) that cannot be directly asked of suppliers.

11.9.1 The next chapter

As a prospective customer, you are now as sophisticated as you can be. You are informed by the accumulated knowledge of requirements with their weights for importance, the scores with their gaps, the demonstrations with their audience feedback and the soft information from the reference sites. You now have all the information you need to negotiate.

11.10 REFERENCES

Easterby-Smith, M., Thorpe R. and Jackson, P. (2012) *Management research*, 4th edition. SAGE Publications: London.

Wiebe, J. (2010) 'Hard and soft information'. OneMind, WordPress. http://onemindblog. wordpress.com/2010/03/07/hard-and-soft-information (10 November 2014).

11.11 FURTHER READING

11.11.1 Books and articles

Cadle, J., Paul, D. and Turner, P. (2014) *Business analysis techniques: 99 essential tools for success*, 2nd edition. BCS, The Chartered Institute for IT: Swindon. Especially sections 'Investigate Situation' and 'Manage Change'.

Thomas, P., Paul, D and James, C. (2012) *The human touch: Personal skills for professional success*. BCS, The Chartered Institute for IT: Swindon.

Willis, G. (2004) *Cognitive interviewing: A tool for improving questionnaire design*. SAGE Publications: London.

11.11.2 Related formats by download

Semi-structured reference site interview form, with some standard questions, from http://shop.bcs.org/offtheshelfextras.asp.

12 CONTRACTS: NEGOTIATION AND AGREEMENTS

'We're overpaying him, but he's worth it.'

Samuel Goldwyn (1879–1974)

12.1 WHAT YOU CAN LEARN FROM THIS CHAPTER

- Understand how to guide your negotiation to the critical outcome of coming to agreement, while protecting both customer and supplier organisations from common pitfalls.

- Appreciate that negotiation for software and services requires crucial technical input from candidates.

- Be aware of the dangers of adopting 'traditional' and 'adversarial' negotiating tactics rather than a collaborative approach.

12.2 OVERVIEW

Negotiation is another example of collaborative work to ensure successful IT adoption, but at this stage tension is higher. You are reliant on the supplier's understanding of the technology and prior projects, for instance to estimate the number of implementation days. However, you may fear that they are padding such an estimate for commercial gain. You face the classic dilemma of engaging highly skilled knowledge professionals and the question of whether they are using their superior knowledge for your benefit, or for their own.

This chapter aims to make you a more capable software negotiator, including setting worthy objectives and recognising the supplier viewpoint.

By this stage of your project, you want to come to agreement with the preferred supplier. You want to buy, usually from your top scorer. This is **not** a commodity purchase. You have established the suitability of one or possibly two candidates. Do not buy on price now unless the candidates are truly interchangeable.

By this stage of your project you also want to exploit your negotiation position. You have a good position now, but your window of opportunity is closing. The relative power positions change once you sign the contract – the large pool of customers for an off-the-shelf solution can flip from an advantage (spread of development costs) to a disadvantage (competition for attention).

EXECUTIVE PERSPECTIVE: A DIRECTOR'S EXPERIENCE OF NEGOTIATIONS BASED ON SCORED FIT

As project sponsor, I led our negotiation team. The negotiation for our ERP solution was one of the most structured, objective and ultimately successful I have ever conducted.

The methodology highlighted the functionality that was critical to meeting the real needs of the business. This enabled us to easily focus on key areas that were important to us and was a great tool to enable the negotiation to stay focussed.

We engaged in negotiations with two candidates, both of whom provided a very good fit to our requirements. Although not aware of the detail, they were both aware that they were in a close competition, which I felt helped to drive the discussions to a good solution.

12.3 WHY – OBJECTIVES OF A SUCCESSFUL NEGOTIATION

You are negotiating for a software product with supporting services – such as implementation, data migration, training and helpdesk. There may be an even wider context where the software product is one component within a larger services package such as an IT outsourcing deal. You might summarise this packaging of components by using the term 'the solution'.

DEFINITION OF SOLUTION FOR NEGOTIATION

The **solution** is the result of taking a **software** product and applying the supplier **services** to configure and implement it.

The service element means you are not buying a tangible artefact. Later you might measure, say, success against a service level agreement, but the customer experience of the service itself depends on their own contribution. Supplier response times are not the determining factor if you never report the fault (see Chapter 1, Section 1.6).

12.3.1 Your true objectives for the negotiation

The real prize during software procurement is not a few extra percent discount from list price. Your major objective – indeed your overwhelming objective – is to achieve the workforce productivity and organisational effectiveness of successfully adopting the strongest candidate. This benefits every user and your whole organisation.

There are two supporting aims. One is to agree some 'free modifications' as part of your contract (see Section 12.9). The other is to agree to attach three critical project documents to contract (see Section 12.7.3).

Winning the prize can be problematic if your organisational culture is obsessed with cost reduction, whatever the impact on value. At a more personal level, if your lead negotiator is from finance or procurement and believes negotiation is all about discounts, this can cause problems. If they are prepared to walk away if discounts are not conceded, their behaviour can actually be counter-productive. The discount is trivial in the scheme of things compared to the overall benefits of adopting the best off-the-shelf solution.

12.4 WHAT – DECISIONS AND PREPARATION BEFORE THE NEGOTIATION MEETINGS

Some of the aspects covered in this section may already be agreed, either by earlier discussion or by reference to organisational standards (such as to always negotiate with two providers). If not, you will need to present one or more of these issues to your project board for their decision.

12.4.1 Review project information

You are now informed by the accumulated knowledge of the:

- requirements, including their weights for importance;
- evaluation visits, with their detailed responses and exposure to supplier culture;
- scores, with their gap analysis;
- demonstrations, with their audience feedback and your analysis of it;
- soft information from the reference sites;
- accumulated issues, concerns and requests from multiple project board meetings.

Assemble this knowledge now, to ensure you have all the information you need to negotiate (see Section 12.7).

12.4.2 Decide the number of candidates

If not determined by your procurement framework, you will need a decision as to whether you negotiate with one or two candidates at this stage. Some organisations are surprised that there is such a choice because they assume that it is always in their interest to play off one supplier against at least one other. However, given the complexities of procuring one of the most sophisticated items humankind has ever created, you should balance the advantages and disadvantages of dual or sole negotiation. The largest task in negotiating for the solution is to agree your 'scope of supply'. There can be 20–40 item lines in your negotiation plan, each an aspect you need to agree (see Section 12.5).

Negotiating with two candidates

If you go ahead with two candidates, this has the advantage of being the more traditional way to progress to contract. The competitive pressure is much more overt when both candidates know they are in a two-horse race.

However, it is a great deal more work – possibly three times the work of single sourcing – because the two candidates are not identical when it comes to commercial terms and contracts. So there are no economies of scale, and you have the additional work of comparing multiple line items that you have negotiated across the two candidates.

Negotiating with a single candidate

If you go ahead with a single candidate, it is far less work. You can concentrate on your preferred candidate. If yours is a small order compared to their turnover, they may take you more seriously if you give them preferred status.

Reassure yourself that you are not exposing yourself to a supplier with a monopoly position. You always have your runner-up – this is the background threat and competitive pressure. You know how much you will lose if you fall back to your runner-up, but the preferred supplier does not. You have your scores, and your analysis of the differences between the scores.

12.4.3 Decide whether to disclose the rival and rank

If you have two candidates for negotiation, your position on disclosure might now change. At previous stages, you should have let candidates know how many candidates were on the longlist or shortlist, but not given the names of competing suppliers. This was to prevent supplier collusion, for instance price fixing if you listed two resellers of the same product.

By this stage of your project, they have probably guessed anyway, so you are not revealing much and you can avoid suppliers wasting energy speculating. If you are confident you have genuine rivals, they will not be colluding to suppress the value of your contract. They will be trying to win it.

Telling the candidates the other candidate's name may increase competitive pressure and give you some extra negotiating options.

You also need to decide whether to let candidates know the two fit percentages and therefore their rank order. This is a balance of judgment. Normally, it is in your interests to disclose at this stage. The vendor at pole position will probably not become complacent, whereas the runner-up may well raise their game. This is especially true if your scores are close.

It is ethical, and mandated by some procurement frameworks, that you disclose the same information to all the bidders at the same time.

12.4.4 Decide your response to a parked runner-up

If you have decided to negotiate solely with your preferred supplier, you need to decide what to tell the runner-up. It is normally better to tell them they are parked – they will soon guess this anyway because you will go quiet for some weeks while contracting.

If you fail to agree with your preferred candidate and need to execute Plan B, you will need to re-activate your runner-up. You need to be diplomatic in announcing the fact that this candidate is your Plan B, but, actually, you have little to lose and something to gain. If you do not manage their exit, they may lapse into anti-competitive behaviour (see Chapter 2, Section 2.6.3).

12.5 THE SCOPE OF SUPPLY

The scope of supply refers to the total 'package' of software, services, training and annual support agreements, and you will negotiate all its dimensions. There are several and each has its own subtleties and pitfalls.

12.5.1 Modules needed to meet requirements

Where a software product is broad, with multiple modules, there are often core or foundation modules with optional, supporting or specialist modules. You need to agree which of the optional modules you need to meet your requirement. This might have been decided at the detailed evaluation phase during the responses to your requirements (see Chapter 8). However, it might not be a clean decision. With large software products, you have the phenomenon that there are multiple ways to meet requirements. A rudimentary facility may be part of the core software, but more attractive processing may require an add-on at extra cost. You will need to make your best guess at this stage whether it is worthwhile paying the premium for the benefits of the extra module.

12.5.2 Number and type of user licenses

If the modules represent the 'breadth' that you will adopt, the 'depth' is the number of licences or seats. This determines how many people can access the software – inside your organisation and at partner organisations. If you intend suppliers or customers to access your solution directly, they will need their own logins.

You also have to decide the best licensing model since there will often be more than one approach available. Large software solutions usually have different prices for concurrent and named users.

- **Concurrent** users are usually more expensive, because there is a re-usable pool with a ceiling and anybody can log in as long as the total number of active connections is below your ceiling.

- **Named** users are usually cheaper, because the login is tied to a person (sometimes an email address) so it is not transferable.

Software licenses often come with a graded capability – almost 'strengths' – like platinum, gold and bronze memberships. The license that gives unlimited access to all facilities will of course be the most expensive, but a sub-set of users will need it. The less capable level may satisfy most users. There may be a much cheaper, third level for light use – variously described as visitor, guest, read-only or reporting users. You will need to decide the mix you need of different user capabilities.

These two dimensions – call them concurrency and strength – might combine to create a 2x3 pricing matrix. For instance, the product has one price for a concurrent full-strength or platinum user while there is a different per-seat price for a named bronze or read-only user.

Issues with establishing a user license mix

As you can see from this example, one of the reasons that establishing your scope of supply can be problematic is that it involves estimates and projections. If you have an enormous user population who will only use the solution for a few minutes per day, concurrent licensing is probably in your interests. However, if everybody will login to the solution in the morning and stay connected all day, you may as well have the (cheaper) named user licenses.

Unfortunately, it does not even come down to simple statistics, such as a headcount for your organisation. First, you cannot rely on licence counts from your incumbent software if it is more primitive and less widely used than the new solution you are buying. You are attempting to assess the impact of the new solution, and think through how your organisation will look with TO BE processes and therefore projected usage or uptake.

Second, you need to account for anticipated changes in the size of your user community. In most conventional licensing models, you cannot give back licences for a refund. If your projected number of employees is declining, it is easy to over-license. However, if your projected number of employees is growing rapidly, it is usually in your interests to 'buy ahead' since you will get volume discounts at the main negotiation that will probably not be available if you add a small number of licences after, say, one year. On the other hand, your user population may fluctuate or be unpredictable (such as variable, seasonal demand for workers). Therefore, you might take up a subscription model priced per user per month (if available and worth the expected premium). This is a mix of license type and charging model (see Section 12.5.3).

12.5.3 Best charging model

Another dimension of your negotiation is the high-level charging model. Different software suppliers have different charging models. One supplier might have multiple charging models for you to choose the best one. With such flexibility comes responsibility for decision-making.

Charging might be a straightforward **cost base** – in return for the capital cost, you buy access. Sometimes, it is best simply to pay the gate money rather than deal with the uncertainty of more contingent charging models. The 'clever' charging models might actually not work out to plan, and cost you more.

The negotiation candidate may offer a **subscription model**, with a monthly fee that covers the combined cost of software, user licenses and services. This gives you the option to rent more or less seats per month and is usually the only way to flex your number of users both up and down. This is often the model with cloud-based solutions.

Sometimes the charge you pay will be **based on savings**. This can be attractive to save capital. However, it introduces the complexities of accurately identifying the savings that can be attributed to using your new solution.

Some software charges are based on a sort of **ratio or commission scheme**. For instance, some supply chain solutions charge so many thousands of dollars per year for so many millions of dollars worth of materials handled.

This all means that you have to reach a decision based on understanding the charging model options and mapping them onto current and projected metrics for your organisation.

12.5.4 Agreeing services and charges

Your organisation might prefer to negotiate a fixed price for major phases such as implementation. However, this immediately introduces a large number of issues associated with calculating the resource required to implement. Suppliers will be nervous about quoting a fixed fee until they have a well-defined implementation project, with sponsor, project board, implementation team members and a project plan that is both detailed and resourced (people are allocated to tasks). You are unlikely to be able to feed such firm and detailed information into your negotiation. It will cause substantial delay to concluding negotiations if you 'divert' to create the resourced plan.

Usually, services are costed assuming day rates for different levels of expertise – such as implementation consultant or project manager. These rates will be associated with an estimated number of days for each role.

One common resolution is to agree the firm day rate for your contract, but recognise the quoted number of days is an estimate and may need to change after contract, during full implementation planning. It will be prudent – if you adopt this approach during negotiation – to outline in your contract the mechanism for re-estimating and adjusting the days. It is also prudent to agree a mechanism for changing the day rate, or agreeing the rate for future phases.

12.5.5 Implementation phasing affects costs

Providing services usually involves considerations of project phasing. Implementations with lumpy or uncertain resource requirements carry supplier risk, which must attract a price premium. If you can guarantee to the supplier that you will draw down your service days within a specified range of dates, it is much easier for them to plan and resource, so you will get a better price. Therefore, it is ideal if you can think through some of the basics of your implementation schedule – for instance, agreeing that the start of your implementation phase will definitely skip over your imminent financial year end.

12.5.6 Support and maintenance

The support and maintenance agreement is a significant portion of your 10-year costing. The charge is recurring, typically annual, with the first year paid with your initial software order. It is usually a percentage of the software cost, with a mechanism for increasing it. At a typical figure of 20 per cent, it means that every five years you spend the equivalent of the software cost. In a 10-year costing, you effectively buy the software three times – originally and twice more. Software suppliers are often firm during negotiations, since maintenance is crucial to their future revenue stream and important to fund future development. Notwithstanding, you do have some options to explore.

- A maintenance agreement is normally obligatory, so it is rarely worth trying to exclude one from your scope of supply. Nor would you want to, since you want updates and access to the helpdesk. (Dropping maintenance from scope just might apply if you have an enormous IT department who commit to skill up and bring support entirely in-house.)

- Software suppliers are also extremely reluctant to drop the percentage figure. You might attempt this, but do not risk goodwill by pushing too hard in the negotiation. More subtly, you may be able to base your percentage on the final **negotiated** cost, rather than the list price of the software.

- There are usually mechanisms for annual increases, perhaps based on X per cent per year, or Retail Price Index. You may find some movement if you ask for the lower of these two.

- If you are buying ahead with more seats than you can currently use (see Section 12.5.2), you might reduce your maintenance charge in the first year or two by a type of de-scoping. You might ask to make your annual charge pro-rata to the number of users **in use**, rather than the entire pool of licenses (your total user count). This concession presumes a smaller initial load on the supplier helpdesk.

12.5.7 Relative level of risk

Effectively, the exposure to risk at both customer and supplier is one more dimension to your scope of supply. For instance, a fixed-price contract transfers the risk of overrun to the supplier. So far, so attractive, you may think. Nevertheless, the risk needs to be funded, so it will invite a price premium. This means that it affects your negotiation. You should agree internally the level of risk that is acceptable to your organisation – it may be culturally risk-averse or risk-taking, and your project may conform to culture or make a conscious effort to buck the trend.

12.5.8 Impact of decisions on negotiation stance

Your decisions about user licensing (see Section 12.5.2) are clear examples of the complexities of negotiating for new software. As you can now see, it involves a combined understanding of the supplier's technology and the customer's organisation. This means that a healthy decision relies on knowledge that is held by both candidate and customer negotiators. It is a form of collaborative estimating and illustrates why a combative approach to your negotiation is likely to be counter-productive.

12.6 WHO – NEGOTIATION TEAM MEMBERS

12.6.1 Participants from the customer

You have a new role on your project – that of negotiation team member. You can now draw on the large group of people who have experienced your project. To assemble your negotiation team, you can choose from your sponsor, interviewees, RFI assessors, evaluation team members, demonstration attendees, reference site interviewers and decision-makers from your project board.

You should be careful not to include negotiation team members entirely on their rank or role in your organisation. For instance, it might be tempting to include your chief financial officer, especially if they will authorise the eventual purchase order (rather than your project board or a capital approval committee). However, if they are not familiar with your project background (or are not experienced software negotiators) this might actually be a drawback. They might unwittingly become that person 'who knows the price of everything and the value of nothing' (Wilde, 1892).

Having considered who is to fill the new roles of negotiation team member, you will put your team together and brief them. As with other occasions on your project, diplomacy is necessary because you are dealing with people who are either senior to you or in another department with several organisational rungs to the common boss. If your project board has no strong views, use the following as a guideline to your negotiation team membership.

Project sponsor

Recruit your project sponsor for their seniority and to lead your negotiation team. If your project sponsor cannot make the negotiation meetings, you will need another senior manager to represent your organisation.

Evaluation team members

You should select one or two members from your evaluation team. They provide continuity with the evaluation process. For instance, they hold your 'corporate memory' of commitments made during the evaluation meetings and demonstrations.

Representative from procurement

You should usually include a representative from your purchasing or procurement department. Partly, they are formal support for the process of negotiating. They should have professional negotiation skills, and good instincts or some training in reading the other party. Partly, including a procurement representative is engaging a stakeholder group, since your project board will often want the reassurance of eventually 'running the deal past procurement'.

On some projects, you may be lucky enough to have a project scope such that one of your evaluation team members represents your procurement department anyway. This evaluation team member is a perfect choice for your negotiation team because they have negotiation experience, your evaluation project history and an incentive to procure successfully the solution they have helped select.

Extra people to balance

It is poor negotiation technique to face a superior force. Irrespective of filling the roles above, you may need to add extra negotiation team members to provide balance on grounds of team size or seniority.

You may need to add members simply to avoid the supplier having numerical superiority during your negotiation meeting. This is not because you plan a physical brawl, but is a pragmatic piece of meetings management to have an equal number of brains. For example, if the supplier has two main negotiators and one observer – tasked with watching for reactions and taking notes – you are at a disadvantage if you only have two negotiators and they are busy all the time.

You may also need to add members to match seniority. If the supplier is a small developer with the owner heading the negotiating team, consider putting forward a very senior manager such as your CEO. Again, this is not merely an exercise in display plumage.

- Negotiators need to be empowered to make decisions **during** the meeting. An experienced and very senior negotiator from a candidate will be unimpressed if they feel they are talking to mere messengers who cannot make business commitments. Your counterparts need to be confident that if they cut you a deal some higher authority that is shadowy, absent and remote will not overturn it.

- If you cannot secure the full-time presence of, say, your CEO, arrange for them to open your meeting and publicly hand over to the empowered negotiation team when leaving your meeting.

- If you cannot organise your CEO part-time, consider a letter of authority, for instance an email from your CEO to each candidate, to show robust support for your project, your process and your negotiation team. Make sure it is sent separately to each supplier if you have two negotiation candidates and they still do not know who their rival is (see Section 12.4.3). Arrange for other senior stakeholders (like Sponsor and CFO) to be copied and mentioned to give the email more gravity.

12.6.2 Approval to negotiate

Refer to your procurement approval processes, or seek explicit project board approval, to ensure the negotiation team are empowered.

- There may be a top budget figure that you are allowed.

- There may be other limits to authority, such as the number of staff you can commit to the implementation.

- There may be tolerances (with upper and lower limits) and therefore a 'target box'. This means that you can continue if you are within tolerance, but need to escalate the issue if you are outside your parameters.

- There may be specific rules of engagement, such as where you are **not** allowed to drive a hard bargain. One classic example relates to the cost of service – often the biggest component of the implementation cost. The service cost component is nearly always calculated by number of days times day rate. The number of days will be estimated by the supplier, using their experience, their understanding of your project, information they glean during the negotiation and possibly sophisticated estimating metrics. Fundamentally, the customer negotiators simply do not know enough for you to argue with their number. If a supplier estimates 100 days, it is usually counter-productive to say, 'Make it 75'. You may only increase the risk of project failure, which will cost many times the theoretical saving. So you should 'attack' the day rate, if anything. You will rely on reading your counterpart during the negotiation and assessing the integrity of their estimating process. Of course, you have downward competitive pressure to inhibit this portion of their revenue running away, and possibly a useful comparison to the equivalent estimate from the other candidate.

In short, your evaluation team need to be clear when they are 'the one' and when they are 'the conduit'. As part of agreeing this, in addition to any reference to organisational standards and your project board, it is prudent to hold a meeting with the person who will ultimately 'foot the bill'.

Assuming they are not on your negotiation team, determine whether they have additional stipulations that will later reassure them that the team have negotiated thoroughly. Part of this discussion might be incentives – your evaluation team might be rewarded with a share of the savings.

12.7 PREPARING TO NEGOTIATE

Candidates have always been important stakeholders during your selection project. Even though you are about to enter into a more adversarial environment, remember that the candidate remains important to you. The successful supplier will probably become one of your most significant partners – perhaps your most important partner. You should avoid a negotiation that demotivates the supplier (Weiss, 2014). As usual, since you do not know which of two negotiation candidates will win your business, you need to treat them both well.

12.7.1 Gap analysis

Your gap analysis may have revealed weaknesses in the software product or service offering of the candidate (see Chapter 9, Section 9.13.2). You may already have held discussions about closing gaps. Your negotiations will need to firm up any commitments. For instance, you may be augmenting the main solution with a small supplemental software product and prefer to source this from the supplier of the main solution. Such objectives need to be added to your negotiation agenda so they are not forgotten in the heat of your meeting (see Section 12.8 about your plan and agenda).

12.7.2 Consider service aspects

There is usually more flexibility in the delivery of the candidate's service than in the software, which is inherently more inflexible. Therefore, you should consider the service aspects that you want to agree. For example, standard support hours may not be long enough for your organisation and, while you have discussed 24×7, it may be important to agree this exceptional level of support formally. Another example, for a multinational customer organisation, is the preference to have local offices in the nations where you operate. If the supplier has no office in Mexico, say, but expects to open one within the next 12 months, you will want to get the commitment recorded and a firm date written into your contract.

12.7.3 Think through the must wins

You will be drawing up a list of dimensions for your negotiation discussion. Partly this will be brainstorming. Partly it will be by extracting points from project documents, such as your gap analysis by filtering your scoring spreadsheet.

When you have a list of negotiation topics that is reasonably complete, go through the list again. Identify the topics where you must win – meaning you have low tolerance (or no tolerance) to disagreement on the point. Alternative terms for these 'must win' points are 'deal breakers' or 'show stoppers'.

Three must win attachments to contract

One clear example is to attach to contract your three project working papers developed from using this evaluation method – your requirements document, your candidate scores and your linking document of definitions with language ladders (see Chapters 5 and 9).

In my experience, it should be a 'deal-breaker' if the candidate supplier refuses to recognise these documents as contractually significant. You will have made it plain (and in writing) during your initial supplier briefing that you intend these attachments to contract, so it will be no surprise. However, you are approaching crunch time and the supplier may not have invested time thinking through the implications when they were one of 20 candidates on your longlist.

> You should refuse to contract with a supplier who will not attach these critical documents to contract. The reason is that their refusal invalidates many of the protections in the method. Remember you have taken multiple unsubstantiated statements during your evaluation and used them to shape your scores. The essential defence is that these statements had contractual significance because in due course the supplier was going to 'sign up' to their own scores.

Be clear that no software supplier will warrant their software as compliant to your requirements specification. Their software product complies only with its own specification. However, you have not evaluated, and you will not buy, bare software. You will buy the software wrapped in services to create the solution.

With some suppliers, you should stipulate at negotiation that your contract should recognise your scores and percentage fit of their **solution** (see Section 12.3) to your requirements document.

Other suppliers will not countenance any mention of the software at all, even 'hidden inside' the definition of the solution. In this case, you should stipulate that the **services** they provide would create a 'customer experience' with the percentage fit in your scores.

Unfortunately, you may need to enter the realm of 'weasel words' to find a mutually acceptable phrase for exactly what is an 85 per cent fit. However, any 'word-smithing' is worth the effort because it is crucial that your contract records the customer expectation, by recognising your calculated percentage fit and your supporting definitions.

12.7.4 Estimate your total spend and potential savings

You should estimate what you think you are going to spend on your project, for the software plus the services, plus the support for the first year. You will typically have list prices that were provided during your evaluation. Your estimate of total spend will take these figures and apply the percentage discount that you believe is achievable.

While it may be only an internal estimate, it does give you some benchmark for the success of your negotiation. Closing the deal with the highest-scoring candidate, while simultaneously achieving slightly more than your target saving, should be useful to reassure any old-school onlookers that you have not 'rolled over' during the negotiation.

12.7.5 Request standard contracts

There will often be multiple contracts – to license the software, to agree terms for the services and to formalise the service level for support. You should secure copies of the standard contracts for your legal department before the negotiation. This avoids an ill-fated battle of contractual terms. Changing contractual clauses takes time, so start early because legal people are not allowed to hurry – their job is to make sure their company does the right thing. Prior study of standard contracts is therefore another example of stakeholder management and lessens disagreement amongst your project managers, the supplier's commercial managers and two sets of legal advisers.

12.7.6 Consider financial and budget year ends

Research the financial year end (FYE) of the negotiation candidates, and work out the dates for the end of year and quarter. Sales executives at publicly quoted software suppliers are often under pressure to book the revenue this period. If you can be flexible about timing, closing the deal before the deadline can yield advantageous terms. On contracts lasting many years the initial effect can be diluted, but concessions do impress observers and you might win recurring savings on annual charges.

In public sector deals, year end can work the other way – budgets must sometimes be spent before the fiscal deadline or they are lost. Suppliers will want to know this.

12.8 NEGOTIATION AGENDA WITH RELEVANT TERMS

12.8.1 Format for negotiation preparation

For a general explanation of negotiation with its terms and techniques, see *The Economist*'s *Pocket Negotiator* (Kennedy, 2001). See Figure 12.1 for an example of the spreadsheet you use to prepare for a significant negotiation. The examples in rows are a sub-set of typical entries, column headers are explained in this section.

Figure 12.1 Format to prepare for negotiation

CC Solution Selection - Commercial Terms Negotiation - Two Shortlisted Candidates

Ref Request	Open	Best	Worst	BATNA	Nego Priority	Calc Method	Est Value
A. Costs & Terms							
010 Attachments to contract (Part A)	Attachments to contract must include: a) RDD (b) scores (c) linking definitions.	Must agree	Must agree	Delist supplier - Must agree	0 Must	Risk	CoPQ
020 Price: software - user licensing type or agree ratio(s) of named to concurrent	Clarify position re concurrent user licensing as option or equivalent named users. Agree ratios.	Concurrent	Named but with agreed ratio of named to concurrent	Named users	0 Must	Lower license count	PMSI
040 Price: agree cost for extra users (possibly 200-300) within two years of initial implementation	Discuss future pricing.	Further discount of 5%	As quoted already discounted) for 1 year	No agreement - calculated risk we face monopoly pricing	0 Must	Discount	PMSI
050 Price: fixed cost for software - given agreed set of (a) modules (b) user numbers (c) licensing model (d) outline implementation sequence/timetableof CRM (3mn), PLM(6-7 mn) & ERP(9mn)	Confirm - may need to come back to this if other dependencies remain.	Quoted less £200k	Quoted less £100k	No agreement - calculated risk we face monopoly pricing	0 Must	Discount	PMSI
055 Price: phased uptake - pay for users in blocks as system rolled out - avoid over - licensing	Year One - possibly HQ users only.	Pay just before needed	In full upfront	In full upfront	0 Must	Interest earned	£25,000
060 Price: services - system installation (days x rate)	Agree day rate, number of days, discuss if can fix.	£800/day	£950/day	List (RFI)	0 Must	Discount	PMSI
120 Price: maintenance & support charge - percentage rate & final software cost	Discuss basing support on percentage of negotiated cost rather than list price - discuss percentage value.	Standard percentage of negotiated cost	Standard percentage of list cost of software	Normal IT industry terms are to base it on package list price & cost of bespoke work.	0 Must	Discount	PMSI
170 Price: invitation to independent audit of number of licenses in use, or software locks	Discuss terms, need for audit and/or technology for license management.	No audit/checks	Standard terms	Resist audit - change terms	4 Could	Lower license count	£2,500
B. Implementation							
300 Support: agree support hours & service level, especially during implementation	Discuss level of service - especially early phases of 2012 - UK only.	Bronze, even year one	Gold	Follow the sun (wasted until international)	0 Must	Discount	PMSI
C.I Specifics To One Candidate Including Requested 'Free Mods' -							

Open or opening offer is the position at which you believe you should start the discussion.

Best is the best outcome you dare hope for. It is the upper limit of achievement and you should stop negotiating if you get to this level. Save your energy and goodwill credits for another agenda item.

Worst is the worst or least you will accept. You keep negotiating if the position is below worst. Of course, your target range is indicated by the spread between Best and Worst.

BATNA is the Best Alternative To a Negotiated Agreement. This is the fallback position if you cannot resolve the negotiation on this point. Sometimes, your 'best' alternative is to walk away, but you should have as few of these as possible. To avoid a negotiation that breaks down for the wrong reasons, you should always put some prior and cool-headed thinking into what your alternative might really be.

Estimated value is an attempt to value the win or concession. It is your estimate of what that particular item on your negotiation agenda is worth to your organisation. This is simple to calculate if the line item is percentage discount to list price, whereby you can value a 10 per cent discount. It is much harder to estimate for a line item that is less tangible, such as the improved productivity from an enhanced software feature (see Section 12.9). Nevertheless, it is still useful to think through. It improves your perspective on what is worthwhile.

EXPLOITING SPREADSHEETS BEFORE AND DURING NEGOTIATIONS

Spreadsheet processing allows you to create your negotiation plan and with little effort turn it into your published negotiation agenda. You extract negotiation items from your scoring spreadsheet. You note items directly into the agenda matrix during your preparation meetings. You use formulae to calculate the value of wins and concessions, for instance estimated percentage discounts. You hide (or delete) whole columns and exploit views to derive your published agenda quickly from your internal plan. You record each agreement during your meeting and can use filtering to find outstanding items. The updated spreadsheet meets the need for electronic notes to play back your agreements, since handwritten notes would not be considered credible by the legal teams at either customer or supplier.

You can also use spreadsheets if you are offered complex pricing options with software licences or service days. For instance, you may be offered quantity discounts if you take the number of seats that you will need in two years time rather than those needed today. In this case, the discounted cash flow figure, produced rapidly during a recess, will allow you to make a rational decision that balances the cost of capital against the savings.

12.8.2 Compiling your negotiation plan

Having clarified your negotiating authority and the criteria or parameters to negotiate, you can now put together your negotiation plan. With a few minutes of reformatting effort, this will also serve as the published negotiation agenda during your meetings.

Populate your spreadsheet with all of the entries you have noted so far. Ensure you have processed the relevant project documentation, such as your scoring matrix for the gap analysis or your notes from the reference site interviews.

Some of the entries will be **straightforward numbers** – such as the number of seats, the day rate for implementation consultancy or the number of service days for training.

Some agreements will be triggered by **context or time**; for instance, to agree the day rate for implementation consultancy if the original estimate of days is exceeded, or if your implementation will span supplier financial years and you want to avoid the nasty surprise of next year's rates. Agreeing such items in advance is a defence against the software product being used as a Trojan horse, where you experience a price hike or 'fee gouge' once you have committed to a particular solution.

Some of the entries will be less easy to express, but you still need a **reminder to discuss** them. For instance, you cannot know the names of the optional modules, but you still need a place marker on your agenda to discuss them.

Some negotiation objectives will relate to **project process**. For instance, if the supplier proposes a change in the implementation consultancy team, you as customer wish to examine CVs, interview candidates and reject a replacement if they are provably unqualified.

12.9 FREE MODIFICATIONS

Free modifications are in one way simply another set of entries on your negotiation plan. However, the separate section here reflects their importance to your negotiation. Be clear that there is a world of difference – at the negotiation and for the future years of using the new solution – between 'free mods' and 'paid mods'.

12.9.1 Distinguishing between free mods and paid mods

Some of the most valuable entries on your list of negotiation items are 'free modifications' because they affect the productivity of all users. These are entries where you have identified a gap between your ideal processing and the actual processing against one of your requirements. In practice, they are mostly driven by entries on your scoring spreadsheet with high weight but low score (see Chapter 9, Section 9.14).

Free modifications (which are good) are entirely different from paid modifications or customisations (which are bad). Free modifications are enhancements to the standard product that appear in the next major version – or possibly the next-but-one version. The enhanced processing should reflect your needs and close the gap to your requirement.

- You will need a brief description of the enhancement you seek. If such improved processing is embedded in the standard version, it will be created at the supplier's R&D cost. It will not come from your implementation budget.

- More importantly, the new feature will be supported through the standard maintenance agreement. It will be released when built into the next major release.

- It will be supported by standard arrangements, understood by the supplier helpdesk staff as normal and included in standard training courses.

- An important, but less obvious, advantage is the large pool of experienced user staff who understand how to operate the software. When you recruit in a few years, the new person will understand 'your' new feature because they used it in the standard software at their previous employer.

In practice, requesting free modifications means that you want to shape the development wish list. Some of the enhanced processing that you request will possibly already be identified. It will already be within the pool of enhancement requests. Your negotiation objective is to make sure that (some of) the enhanced features that are valuable to your organisation make the cut and are included in the next round of development. If an item is not already identified but is important to you, your objective is to have it added to the development pool and immediately float to near the top.

12.9.2 How not to do it

One of the common pitfalls with adopting off-the-shelf solutions is for the customer to pay for enhancements – customisation or tailoring. This is expensive and risky, hence the flat statement above that paid modifications or customisations are bad. Contemplating customisation at negotiation stage is tremendously ill advised for the following reasons:

- You can probably do without them. Actually, you can almost certainly do without them.

- You do not yet understand your exploitation of the software well enough to specify changes with any reliability.

- Customisation can cut you off from future releases of the software.

- It can make your version of the product so exotic that only a handful of people understand how to maintain the code as developers and operate the solution as users.

- If you commission modifications inexpertly, you can end up repeatedly paying every two or three years for your adaptations to be 'put back in' to the standard product every time a new version is released. This explains many software acquisitions that experience unexpected costs.

12.9.3 When you are likely to win free mods

You are more likely to win a contractual commitment to free modifications if one or more of these circumstances apply:

- The software producer, while creating standard off-the-shelf products, is quite a small software house and finds it practical to respond to the requests of a single customer (or a committed prospect).

- You are negotiating with one of the senior technical team (or perhaps even the technically-orientated founder) who simultaneously understands your need and can accurately assess that developing your new feature will be moderately easy.

- Your contract, once signed, will represent a substantial proportion of the annual turnover of the supplier – because either your contract is enormous or the supplier is small.

- The software product, while robust enough to be credible during your evaluation, is relatively young and you can contribute to its maturity by injecting your considerable operational knowledge.

- The supplier is trying to break into a new market niche and you are a serious operator in that specific niche. This makes you an important 'index customer' and they are prepared to make extraordinary effort to win your business because it is a gateway to lucrative future contracts in your niche.

- Your new feature becomes regarded as a 'strategic enhancement'. This means it will be useful to a wide user base and attractive to prospective new customers. Your requirement is not merely parochial to your organisation, but actually represents a market demand that is not currently being met by the product. This is most likely if your organisation has processes that are specific, but mature and capable, making you a role model for other organisations in this niche. You are arguing pragmatically that, by including the strategic enhancement, the supplier will find it easier to defend or grow their market share.

If several of these apply, negotiating may expose win-win items.

12.9.4 When you are less likely to win free mods

You are far less likely to win free modifications if one or more of these circumstances apply:

- If you are dealing with a very large, global supplier of enterprise software, they will have a very formal process for adding entries to the wish list and especially for deciding which new features are incorporated in the next round of development. They may have a development plan stretching forward multiple years. Given the scale of their operation, the gap that you have identified may amount to little more than a pothole on their roadmap.

- If the negotiators are remote from a highly centralised development operation, such that they are only one of many distant voices when requesting new features.

- If promises of new software versions have a severe and negative impact upon revenue recognition (see Section 12.11.4).

- If the feature you request is only relevant to a business process that is eccentric or entirely specific to your organisation.

- If the processing you request implements rules or procedures that are contrary to recognised best practice.

You should still bid for your free mods, because any win is valuable. However, you should not risk breaking the deal with unreachable objectives – lower your expectations about the proportion of your requests that will be successful and how soon the new processing will be available.

12.10 THE SUPPLIER VERSION OF THE AGENDA

It is not in your interests to surprise a negotiation candidate with a lengthy agenda packed with specifics. The supplier needs preparation time and a chance to consult colleagues. You should supply a copy of the negotiation agenda several days before your negotiation meeting.

Actually, it is not a copy, but a version. Consistent with the method philosophy of using one document for all parties (to avoid transcription errors) you exploit spreadsheet facilities to create the supplier version of the negotiation agenda. The agenda is actually your plan, with most of your columns hidden or deleted. For instance, you never show your column for the least you will accept. See Figure 12.2 for an example of the negotiation preparation spreadsheet turned into the supplier agenda.

If your negotiation team work from prints rather than a shared laptop, there is another safeguard when using the same document for customer and supplier. Format your 'private' entries (such as BATNA) in a small font to avoid your notes being read upside down from across the table.

If you build your agenda in a spreadsheet and email the original to the negotiation candidates, make sure you password protect the format (to lock columns). Alternatively, create a cut-down version or convert your original to a read-only format such as PDF. Never send your raw spreadsheet that allows the recipient to unhide your confidential columns.

Do not make the mistake of one supplier before a negotiation who responded to our agenda with their own template spreadsheet for calculating the deal value. The sales executive had hidden the two columns for their internal price and mark-up, but by sending the raw spreadsheet, they allowed us to unhide it. The IT manager was delighted, although we never did work out if it was an innocent blunder or a crafty double-bluff with dummy figures to manage our expectations.

12.11 WHERE AND HOW – THE NEGOTIATION PROCESS AND MINDSET

12.11.1 Venue for negotiation meetings

Negotiations are best held face-to-face for all the reasons to do with social animals, empathy, bonding, positioning and body language, that must be outside the scope of this book. Attending virtually by video or audio conference is rarely effective. Consistent with the shortlisting philosophy of investing more time in fewer candidates, you have to accept some people travelling to the critical negotiation meetings.

Figure 12.2 Shared negotiation agenda revealing only some columns

CC Solution Selection - Commercial Terms Negotiation - Two Shortlisted Candidates

Ref Request	Open	Agreed Inc Customer Resp'y - Candidate I	Actions - I
			See actions below at General Meeting Notes
A. Costs & Terms			
010 Attachments to contract (Part A)	Attachments to contract must include: a) RDD (b) scores (c) linking definitions.		
020 Price: software - user licensing type or agree ratio(s) of named to concurrent	Clarify position re concurrent user licensing as option or equivalent named users. Agree ratios.		
040 Price: agree cost for extra users (possibly 200–300) within two years of initial implementation	Discuss future pricing.		
050 Price: fixed cost for software - given agreed set of (a) modules (b) user numbers (c) licensing model (d) outline implementation sequence/timetable of CRM (3mn), PLM (6-7 mn) & ERP (9mn)	Confirm - may need to come back to this if other dependencies remain.		
055 Price: phased uptake - pay for users in blocks as system rolled out - avoid over-licensing	Year One - possibly HQ users only.		
070 Price: services - user training (days x rate)	Agree day rate, number of days, discuss if can fix.		
090 Price: services - vendor project management (days x rate)	Agree day rate, number of days, discuss if can fix.		
100 Price: payment terms - effective retainer held till satisfactory completion	10% & exchange small advance payment if necessary.		

You should hold negotiation meetings at your own premises or in a neutral venue such as a hotel or meeting facility. You should not negotiate at supplier premises – you are playing away from home and therefore relatively disadvantaged. You might also expose yourself to the risk (however unlikely) of covert surveillance of your out-of-meeting discussions.

12.11.2 Mindset dangers during negotiation

Your approach to negotiation is an exercise in balance – you should be positive and collaborative, sharing as much as possible, without compromising your interests.

Some of the dangers you face include falling into using counter-productive vocabulary. Remember not to allow your negotiating position to get in the way of your organisational interests (Sebenius, 2001).

- Your interests lie with coming to agreement – by this stage of your project you are keen to acquire the software from the team across the table. Conceivably, the negotiators from either candidate could deliver you an excellent solution.

- You should safeguard the tone of the negotiation from 'legalistic objectors' who one-sidedly criticise any deal, concentrating on the flaws, negatives and risks (however unlikely).

12.11.3 Completing your agenda

You work through your agenda, probably in the order that you have sequenced it. It is sensible to agree your scope of supply (such as which modules you need) before you negotiate the cost elements. You simply cannot price it until you are clear what you are buying and how much of it. As you reach a conclusion for a point, update your Agreed column.

One negotiation approach is that 'it's not agreed until it's all agreed'. This principle means that no point is closed off until you have reached agreement on your entire agenda. Since you have published your full negotiation agenda, this is a reasonable principle to apply to your meetings. It prevents a concession being agreed (and then frozen, as you thought) but eroded by later 'salami slicing' techniques.

During your meeting, there will be a few items where you may only be able to reach provisional agreement because one or other negotiation team needs to escalate the issue for approval. Update your Agreed column accordingly, to record the provisional status and the need to revisit your resolution.

It will be important to stick to plan. Suppliers might offer special prices on modules you have not asked for, provided you include them in the initial order. As a rule, do not take them. Your requirements have not shown any need for them. Even if it is something you would consider later, you do not know if these modules are fit for purpose.

12.11.4 Recognising non-negotiable items

There will be some entries on your agenda that will prove to be not on the table for negotiation. This is one of the many advantages of agreeing before the meeting your positions at Best, Worst and BATNA. You hope that none of these non-negotiable items correspond to a BATNA of 'refuse to buy the solution' – but at least you have primed yourself for the situation before the heat of your negotiation meeting. If you do encounter a deal-breaker during your meeting, it is normally best to call a recess and discuss with your negotiation team whether you should continue negotiating.

You should recognise during your meeting that there are some genuine 'no-go' areas for the supplier negotiators. For instance, large software producers will normally have strict rules on revenue recognition – when they can book the value of the deal. These are internal rules of engagement to avoid commercial teams selling 'vapour-ware' or 'vision-ware' but then not delivering the promised software.

The software giants are usually international organisations, with part of their corporate structure in jurisdictions subject to Sarbanes–Oxley regulations. They will have a role of 'revenue police' who inspect a prospective deal and have the power to block it for false profit accounting.

Sometimes it is not simply a negotiating tactic when a supplier says, 'I'm not allowed to do that.' They really do have a constraint. For instance, throwing in some vaguely defined 'jam tomorrow' future order has no traction if it would be from, say, a sister organisation where you lack authority to negotiate. The supplier commercial team are not allowed to recognise the revenue, so they cannot justify the extra discounts you seek in return for a supposedly bigger order.

Likewise, your requests for product enhancements might comprehensively founder on the rocks of revenue recognition. You should establish during your negotiation – ideally before it – whether promises of enhanced software mean that the entire value of your deal cannot be recognised until the new processing is actually live. This would be the supplier equivalent of a deal-breaker – negotiators will not make contractual commitments to enhance software in the circumstances. This is one reason why your free modifications are rarely a 'must have' negotiation item, but a bonus item. You may have to settle for an agreement that your requested enhancements will be added to the wish list, but no more. Given the benefits, it is still worth trying. If you adopt this software product, you can always join the user community and lobby for your enhancements at the user group.

12.12 AFTER YOUR NEGOTIATION

12.12.1 Seek project board approval

Go back to your project board for their approval of the deal (if you negotiated with a single candidate) or for their final selection (if you negotiated with two). If you have two candidates with very similar scores, equally satisfactory demonstrations and strong reference sites, the deciding factor may become the commercial terms.

However, if several indicators show that there is a clearly preferred candidate and an emphatic runner-up, the final decision-making probably comes down to whether there is such a massive difference in commercial terms (in the favour of the runner-up) that it overthrows the rank order based on all other criteria. If you have this 'Mini versus Rolls

Royce' situation (such that the inferior candidate is cheaper), remember to refer to the evidence from your evaluation so far, such as your gap analysis between candidates (see Chapter 9, Section 9.13.2).

12.12.2 Compile the contract pack

With a major software acquisition, you rarely have a single contract document. There will usually be a front document with a large number of attachments. There may be as many as 10 appendices. The supplier will provide many, for instance their service level agreement for support arrangements. However, you will provide some of the attachments. From your point of view, having used this method for its safeguards, the most significant contribution to the contract is the three project working papers. You supply in a read-only format the authorised and baselined version of your requirements document (see Chapter 5), your scores for that candidate supplier and your definitions document with its language ladders (see Chapter 9).

12.12.3 Offer debrief to candidates

It is both a professional courtesy and in your pragmatic interests to offer candidates some feedback on their performance during your evaluation. You need to decide how far back you go – probably candidates that were left behind at your longlist stage have not invested much in your process. However, the shortlisted candidates – the three or four for detailed evaluation – have put a lot into your process. The runner-up suffers the worst position, because they have done all the work of the winner (including investing time in negotiating) and have passed across some of their best ideas, but have won none of the revenue. Therefore, you should offer at least the runner-up your debrief, so they get something back for all the work. You may want them to enter a new race in the future.

A scrupulous debrief does not divulge commercially sensitive information such as pricing. However, you are in a strong position to help a supplier to understand their market position and the strengths and weaknesses of their product in relation to your requirement. Some candidates might invite comment on their sales performance and may even ask you to identify the stronger members of their sales team, or the most effective behaviours.

12.12.4 Notify other stakeholders affected

After your deal is agreed, you have several updates to make in order to keep the relevant stakeholders informed.

- If you have not done so yet, your evaluation team will want to know all about the negotiations. Especially if they will become implementation team members (see Chapter 13).

- You may need to reassure other people you enlisted before your negotiation, such as your procurement department.

- Remember to advise your CFO or financial controller to update the cash plan for some significant payments in the next two months as invoices fall due. While services are often charged in arrears based on days consumed in the month, software and support is often paid in advance.

EXECUTIVE PERSPECTIVE: AN IMPLEMENTATION MANAGER'S EXPERIENCE OF CONTRACTUAL SAFEGUARDS

The methodology imposes an innovative step at contract agreement stage, as the evaluation scores are formally agreed and accepted by purchaser and vendor. The vendor can challenge the evaluation scores and bid for an improved score subject to provision of reasonable justification. The major benefit is that the agreed final evaluation records become an integral part of the contract. Anyone who has experience of software vendors' contract terms will realise the significant benefit of this commercial innovation.

As evidence of the contractual strength of this approach, I recall a point during project implementation when we were disputing a required time registration process for customer invoicing. The point was quickly won, as we as purchaser were able to point directly to the evaluation record in the contract, where the vendor had clearly stated full compliance. The vendor had to accept the £30,000 costs of the required modification, but more importantly the project avoided the more damaging costs of dispute and associated delay.

It is not unusual for sales specialists dealing with complex technology to be creative in their performance assertions, but this approach means they remain responsible for their statements right through implementation to project sign off.

12.13 CHAPTER SUMMARY

TAKE-AWAY POINTS

The main objective of a software procurement negotiation is to come to agreement. Do not allow an unhealthy obsession with cost or discounts to mean you lose the deal. The real prize is the significant workforce productivity improvement of your whole organisation that is within reach if you adopt the solution with best fit. This is especially the case if you can agree that the standard software will be a closer fit to your needs in one or two years.

Thorough preparation beforehand, a cool head during the negotiations and a collaborative approach will yield substantial dividends.

12.13.1 The next chapter

The next chapter introduces implementation – the installation, configuration, training and data loading for the new software. Specifically, the chapter covers how the learning and material from your evaluation process will continue to be useful and will contribute to a successful adoption of the successful candidate solution.

12.14 REFERENCES

Kennedy, G. (2001) *Pocket negotiator: How to negotiate successfully from A to Z*, 4th edition. Economist Books: London.

Sebenius, J. (2001) 'The negotiator's secret: More than merely effective'. Working Knowledge, Harvard Business School. http://hbswk.hbs.edu/item/2480.html (10 November 2014).

Weiss, J. (2014) 'HBR guide to negotiating'. Harvard Business Press Books, Harvard Business School. http://hbr.org/product/hbr-guide-to-negotiating-ebook-tools-video/an/14201H-KND-ENG (10 November 2014).

Wilde, O. (1892) *Lady Windermere's fan: A play about a good woman*. Methuen Drama (Bloomsbury): London.

12.15 FURTHER READING

12.15.1 Books and articles

Blackstaff, M. (2012) *Finance for IT decision makers: A practical handbook*, 3rd edition. BCS, The Chartered Institute for IT: Swindon.

Holt, J. and Newton, J. (2011) *A manager's guide to IT law*, 2nd edition. BCS, The Chartered Institute for IT: Swindon.

Kennedy, G. (2008) *Everything is negotiable*, 4th edition. Random House Business: London.

Nickson, D. (2008) *IT procurement handbook for SMEs*. BCS, The Chartered Institute for IT: Swindon.

12.15.2 Related formats by download

Negotiation agenda spreadsheet from http://shop.bcs.org/offtheshelfextras.asp.

13 IMPLEMENTATION: PREPARING THE GROUND

'It's not the progress I mind, it's the change I don't like.'

Mark Twain (1835–1910)

13.1 WHAT YOU CAN LEARN FROM THIS CHAPTER

- Understand the transition from evaluation to implementation, so you ask smarter questions during the evaluation and the implementation planning.
- Appreciate the aspects of your implementation that must be the customer responsibility.
- Be aware of the lasting benefits of the method even after your selection is complete.

13.2 OVERVIEW

This chapter is written assuming that you stay with the project as it switches from the evaluation phase to the implementation phase, possibly as the project manager or an implementation team member. If not involved in the implementation, be sure to hand over lessons learnt, issues to watch and working papers such as the contract.

Your involvement in implementation will mean very different vocabularies, challenges and relationships. Specifically, power positions shift once you have signed the contract.

You have put a great deal of effort into a successful evaluation and procurement process. You got the best solution. However, success is by no means automatic. Actually, the real effort starts now, so you cannot rest on your laurels. You need to make your implementation project work. You have a lot to lose and so does your crucial new partner, the successful supplier.

There is a critical window of opportunity at this stage. Plenty of users understand your organisation and its processes. Multiple people at your supplier understand the standard software. However, during the first few months, few people understand both the organisation and the solution alongside each other. Implementation staff from customer and supplier who have been exposed to the evaluation process are better educated in this combination.

Some deliverables from your project process may still be in use one or two years after signing contracts, such as the scope documentation to help you concentrate on the objectives. They help avoid scope drift or scope creep – especially if there has been a long period between starting the evaluation and beginning your implementation. Losing sight of the objectives and scope may happen if there has been little continuity of staff. (It is extremely risky if no evaluation team members went forward to your implementation team **and** none of the supplier response team joined your project as implementation consultants.)

Your scoring documentation continues in its important role of clarifying assumptions, performance and expectations for both the customer and the supplier.

If you read this chapter at the beginning of your selection project, it is worth reflecting that, even before your project has picked the winner, there are opportunities for implementation planning and change management. In fact, the whole evaluation process has the effect of bringing forward the implementation planning. To meet your requirements, candidate suppliers must think through how their solution would be configured to meet your need.

This evaluation process probably places a similar amount of work overall upon the candidate suppliers as a conventional evaluation. However, their cost of sales budget is directed less into defining the prospective customer needs and more into preparing for implementation. Therefore, one benefit of the method may be less obvious but is important – earlier, and probably better-digested, implementation planning.

13.2.1 Specific nature of chapter

This chapter cannot be a general introduction to multiple substantial disciplines: IT implementation; IT operations; IT service management; organisational change. It concentrates on specific aspects of the implementation that relate to this method. It can only make a small contribution and you should:

- draw on the experience of your new supplier and your internal implementation team;

- refer to relevant organisational standards, perhaps because yours is an ITIL environment (Office of Government Commerce, 2009);

- see Further Reading for some useful suggestions;

- see the BCS extras page http://shop.bcs.org/offtheshelfextras.asp for the companion article on the interaction with other IT approaches.

EXECUTIVE PERSPECTIVE: AN EVALUATION TEAM MEMBER'S EXPERIENCE OF TRANSFERRING TO IMPLEMENTATION

As the formal system selection process had been very rigorous, it was easier to plan and execute the system implementation. Each member of the selection team understood the available functionality of the chosen system, its complexity and hence the time scale and resources required to implement the system in their respective areas.

We are now in the final stages of the system implementation and we feel that the system selection methodology gave us a lot of confidence in the system and its capability to meet our business needs, both in the immediate and in the long term.

13.3 CHANGE OF POWER POSITIONS

The balance of power has shifted now that you have signed up with a single supplier. You now rely heavily on a single successful supplier – specifically on the knowledge of their staff in support and implementation consultancy roles. There would be a huge switching cost to move away from your new solution – both an intellectual switching cost to do with unlearning and, of course, the more obvious (but probably lower) financial switching cost.

You are now one customer voice amongst many. The advantage of a solution with a large customer base has become the mirror image disadvantage. You are competing for resources at your chosen supplier.

For example, you may be seeking software development resources to create features that are important to you in the next version of the standard product. However, these will go on to the development plan (or sometimes a less formal 'wish list'). Depending on the supplier circumstances and your negotiation outcomes, you may not have a contractual commitment to these enhancements (see Chapter 12). Therefore, you will need to lobby and hope your features float to the top of the list. (This lack of final control reminds you why you scored candidates earlier based on what is actually there today, not on future features.)

More immediately, you seek skilled and knowledgeable staff from your supplier. The supply is limited and it is tough to increase the supply of qualified staff at short notice. Competition for implementation experts will be particularly keen if there is another large implementation at another new customer at the same time. Honestly, the supplier cannot do much to stop this bottleneck emerging given that they had multiple uncertainties about landing both contracts at the same time.

Maybe you can do little about the new power positions and competition for resource. However, you should at least be aware of them and recognise them. Be conscious of your behaviour and adopt a style to help get your fair share (or more) of resources.

13.4 SUPPLIER RESPONSIBILITIES DURING IMPLEMENTATION

There are certain aspects of the implementation phase that you should rightly expect to be the responsibility of your successful supplier:

- They will help you set expectations, for instance recommending the number of training days for the various combinations of module and user type. This will help you to schedule delivery dates, especially when they supply information about the availability of their trainers and consultants (see Section 13.5.2).

- The supplier will understand their own technology. They will execute the solution design, although you will own it (see Section 13.5.2).

- Your supplier will train the customer users (direct training) or train the implementation team members for cascade training (train the trainers).

- The supplier will contribute to data migration – typically, your staff extract your old data while the supplier maps, reformats and loads it.

- The supplier should stress the importance of change management. However, they cannot impose or effect change – it is not their responsibility to manage or motivate your staff.

13.5 CUSTOMER RESPONSIBILITIES

A common mistake when buying software is making suppliers responsible for aspects of the implementation that cannot possibly be part of their remit. Such transfer is extremely ill advised, rarely successful and cannot end well because it puts your supplier in a position of responsibility without authority. Your responsibilities as customer include the following.

13.5.1 Monitor delivery

Fundamentally, your implementation team must ensure that facilities delivered are as good as agreed during negotiation (unless there is a conscious decision for a variation). You can always refer back to your scoring matrix and scoring definitions with the language ladders for a record of your expectations (see Chapter 9).

13.5.2 Plan the project

You must own your own project plan, and it is best if you, as the customer, manage the project planning process (even though it relies heavily upon supplier input).

- You must prioritise both clearly and ruthlessly. Stick to scope, checking your project initiation or scoping documentation to avoid scope creep or scope blur.

- You must conform to internal project approval mechanisms, because you understand them better than your supplier does.

- You must own your solution design even though technical experts at the supplier have created it for you.

For more on the actual implementation plan, see Section 13.6.

13.5.3 Allocate resources

Perhaps the most crucial customer responsibility is to allocate resources and then to protect them.

Build your implementation team

You need to find the right internal people and convince them to commit to your implementation project. Of course, you want the most talented and dedicated people, so their current managers will be reluctant to release them. Part of your change management activities is to explain to your organisation that it is profoundly in their personal interests that your implementation is successful. People who transfer into your implementation team face hard work and an uncertain outcome. You need to convince them it is not a poisoned chalice or a career cul-de-sac.

You need terms of reference for people who are seconded into your implementation team, or transfer full-time as their new post. These personal terms of reference should avoid uncertainty and create commitment. For instance, they should cover the circumstances for extending (or reducing) their secondment. There should be an explicit description of when and how they will return to their 'normal' job at the end of your implementation.

It is becoming increasingly common for implementation teams to have a substantial element of interim or contract staff, sometimes including the project manager. Large enterprise-wide projects are especially subject to this.

Allocate project resource

To prevent delays, start early with the process of allocating resources to your new implementation team. They need office space, desks and whiteboards. They need substantial IT equipment, including desktops, laptops, possibly servers and logins for the new solution.

Get everybody up to speed

If you have been immersed in a project for multiple months, it is easy to forget that most people do not have your level of understanding. Get everybody on your implementation team (full-time members and part-time contributors) up to a comparable and effective level of understanding. One technique is to book training courses as soon as possible because there will be a lead-time to delivery.

Create an induction to the implementation phase – both a verbal briefing and a document. Include relevant project background, such as your evaluation process. These resources are especially important if no evaluation team members transferred into your implementation team.

Provide data for migration

You understand your own data structures and content so it is normally your responsibility to extract the old data to migrate into the new software. Planning this (mapping old data to new) and extracting old data into an agreed format requires experienced resource. Only a limited number of people can do this work, and they already support the legacy solution. Resource competition is likely. See the techniques that follow to avoid resource starvation.

Defend the implementation team from distractions

The contemporary working environment is plagued by distractions (Friedman, 2006). In the specific context of implementation planning, you need to defend your implementation team members from being pulled off their new role. For instance, you should lobby for them to be 'back-filled'. This means their old position is filled with another member of staff, new recruit or temporary worker. This will safeguard you from an important evaluation team member being diverted if a crisis emerges in their old department.

Your working practices also need to defend against 'Continuous Partial Attention' (Stone, 1998). Thinking through the implementation requires groups concentrating on issues for long periods. Working out how your organisation will exploit the substantial facilities of your new software is a demanding process involving creative thinking at increasing levels of detail. It is difficult to perform this invention to a schedule so you need to lobby for an environment in which people can alternate between solitary research, reflection and creativity, and periods of group work to interact, communicate and share (Cain, 2012).

13.5.4 Ensure your consultants are proficient

A common model is for the supplier's consultants to work within your implementation team. A second model is for the supplier team to work alongside yours under their own project manager or team leader and be responsible for specific deliverables. A third model, when the supplier delivers a service (data migration is a good example), means that you may never meet the people involved and will have very limited influence on who does the work. On some implementations, you might have all three different models for different parts of the work. This section mainly addresses the first model, and to some extent the second, where you have more direct involvement with the implementation consultants.

You should check that your supplier – especially if using a separate implementation team from the sales team – has conducted an effective handover. This involves more than throwing your specification 'over the wall'. It will take both formal meetings and informal updates.

Be aware of the risk that 'the supplier A Team' made your sale, but your implementation becomes the responsibility of 'the B Team'. When you are agreeing the allocation of implementation consultants, you should review their CVs. You are not simply looking for their technical capability, so you should also interview candidates. As with other types of recruitment, you are looking for a fit of personal chemistry and culture. You should be honest and if somebody is technically proficient, but somehow cannot get on with other implementation team members, you should address this issue quickly.

You might need to change them as a last resort, but you first need to manage them. Highly technical people can often be focused, difficult people and lack social skills. However, unless they are threatening or conspicuously lazy, try to accommodate and manage them first. If you replace them, your choices will be constrained by skills and schedules.

Chemistry is particularly important once the team has formed (Straker, 2009). Partly, once you have started your project, a group dynamic will develop that you must protect. Partly, if you have had several successful introductions, the temptation is to 'lower your guard' and not go through your due diligence processes as part of engaging a new consultant.

13.5.5 Manage expectations and change

Organisational change is another huge topic that this book can only mention. In the context of a selection project, IT sets a platform that creates the possibility that you can realise your benefits. The change management determines whether you actually do. Implementation projects that assume the technology itself will deliver benefits hit problems. Accordingly, one often-quoted model for change is the triangle of people, process and technology (Lane, 2011). Communication is vital to a successful implementation, especially with enterprise–class software that cuts across organisational silos.

Managing expectations and the organisational dynamic now has particular effect on the implementation, because you have already acquired software that fits. There is an argument that you cannot actually 'manage' organisational change, but you can at least try to shape the conversations by participation (Rodgers, 2006). Whatever your change philosophy, you definitely need multiple channels of communications, as follows.

Some of these are **formal** – pages dedicated to the project on your intranet, emails, perhaps a newsletter and, of course, meetings. As well as special project meetings for implementation planning and project management, if you are exploiting enterprise software, you probably need a standing agenda item at commercial board meetings or senior management team meetings in the public sector.

Some communications channels are **informal**. The conversations at the coffee machine, in your staff restaurant and over a drink after work are also important. There is also a style called 'management by wandering around'. This can be effective because people can express concerns in an informal environment. With this technique, your mug of coffee and a bag of pastries to share are important working tools.

Prepare your '**elevator speech**'. This is another informal communications channel where you have to sell the project in however long it takes to travel between floors in the lift.

You may be able to blend the formal with the informal at a **salon** (Gray, 2014). This is a meeting with some structure, a light agenda and ground rules. However, it is held in an informal, social environment, usually with food and drink. It deliberately seeks diverse views from people with different perspectives who contribute, without reference to role or seniority, in an environment where it is safe to disagree. A salon can be useful in exposing knowledge that is hidden in your organisation. It reduces bias towards vocal or powerful people, while gathering the full breadth of information about messy, controversial or emerging subjects.

Your **web searches** should seek out implementation case studies and 'war stories' to make your planning more realistic and your explanations more compelling. You should research examples that are relevant to your niche, your organisation and possibly your new software product. Another under-appreciated advantage of a high profile, off-the-shelf solution is the ready-made anecdotes.

Successful change relies on engaging people early, which you have done by using the method's numerous consultations and bursts of decision-making. If people are engaged and feel listened to, your implementation is much more likely to be successful. In short, committed users will make software with problems work, whereas 'perfect' software with antagonistic users will not be successful.

13.6 YOUR IMPLEMENTATION PLAN

13.6.1 Who – contributors to your plan

For a large project, the implementation plan is created by a joint effort across many parties over multiple weeks.

- Your project or programme manager (see Section 13.5.2) who needs to engage with the project board for your implementation. If your project does not yet have a board, the project manager needs to engage with the senior management team to create one.

- Your standing implementation team. Most projects of any size need some full-time members. Even the tiniest project needs one full-time member, but any project large enough to consider using a formal method, such as this, will probably need at least two full-time members on your implementation team. Large projects covering multiple offices and countries can have tens of people on the implementation team.

- Representatives from affected departments.

- Implementation consultants from the software supplier.

- Other consultants, interims and contractors.

You should also get back to the contacts you made at your reference sites (see Chapter 11). They may now be prepared to volunteer further information because you are part of 'the club'. They may even be prepared to volunteer resources, such as sight of their own implementation plan. Many users of sophisticated software become attached to it and are (rightly) proud of their successes exploiting it. Unless you are a direct competitor, they are often amazingly willing to help you.

Find out the date of the next user group meeting as soon as possible. You might even arrange to meet your former referees for a private chat there.

13.6.2 What – the aspects to plan

Remember that this chapter cannot be a full treatment of implementation planning, but there are points worth making about exploiting previous learning from your evaluation.

Data structures in your new solution

Some of the data that you need for your new off-the-shelf solution will be available in your old software. Other data will require generation, and this means not only the eventual data entry, but also the more challenging prior decisions as to what that data should be (see Section 13.6.3).

Modules in your new solution

There is a substantial suite of decisions around the modules that you are going to use, especially the order in which you implement them. You need to understand the dependencies between modules.

That understanding will come partly from your evaluation work, including detailed evaluation and the negotiations, and partly from your supplier.

Your supplier may have standard documentation on module dependencies, but might not if there are multiple customer choices, such that maps need to be project-specific. The diagram at Figure 13.1 is adapted from a large implementation of ERP and PLM (see Glossary). The original became known as the Jigsaw Diagram because the tongues on the pieces indicate if a module depends on others. The illustration is simplified to show the idea and the notation – on the real project, the original had 33 jigsaw pieces.

Figure 13.1 Module interlock during a hypothetical implementation

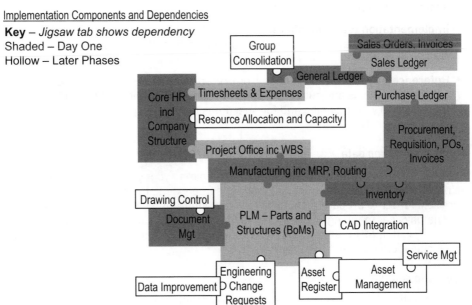

If the new solution is replacing a legacy system, another factor is how the transfer will take place ('big bang' or process-by-process) and when (it may need to be on a boundary such as year end).

Another approach to planning is to list all the modules you contracted to buy and categorise them into implementation phases. It may be appropriate to think in terms of tranches of end-user capability and have that drive the module selection.

13.6.3 How – the planning process

The project process so far will contribute considerably to your implementation planning.

- **Evaluation team members**: they should understand some of the interplay between solution and organisation, having been involved in matchmaking of software to requirements. Draw on former evaluation team members (see Chapter 8) for some of your decision-making meetings, even if they are not on your implementation team full-time.

- **Implementation consultants**: with luck, some of the consultants will have supported the sales cycle for your project, perhaps as presenters during your detailed evaluation meetings. If not, suggest that the supplier's project manager makes the connection between sales team members and implementation team members – a basic point, but one that can be overlooked in the race to implement.

- **Definitions and language ladders**: this documentation from scoring in effect contains specific statements about the features to exploit against each requirement. This is because they contain specific statements of what processing was expected when awarding the points (see Chapter 9). You can remind yourself at the start of a planning meeting what the evaluation team expected when picking this solution.

- **Implementation team members**: they probably attended the demonstrations. They will have had time to reflect on exploiting the features they saw (see Chapter 10).

- **Reference sites**: the experiences from referees inform your understanding with real situations and outcomes. Consult your interview notes, both for issues that relate to your planning and for anecdotes to help you explain things better (see Chapter 11).

Mapping to solution data

Your evaluation has already involved some work to map your current data structures to the new data structure within the solution. To some extent, the mapping was a mental exercise in order to prepare responses to your requirements document, but there was also the physical mapping needed to load your demonstration data. Any preliminary decisions will inform and probably accelerate your implementation, especially knowledge about data that has 'nowhere to go'.

Mapping to solution processing

Your evaluation has clearly revealed how the facilities of the new solution support your requirements. Your gap analysis has also revealed missing or under-weight facilities compared to these requirements. You may have held early discussions about how to close these gaps. Access any preliminary decisions made, either by talking to people who attended these discussions or by checking meeting notes (see Chapter 9, Section 9.14).

Process and change team

Note that in a large organisation with a substantial implementation of enterprise software, a different team on a separate project with its own phases and external consultants may deliver the change method and process redesign. This means that your implementation project is part of a much larger programme and part of your responsibilities as a team will be to interact with the change programme manager or team members.

Project scheduling tool

Assuming that you are providing the project manager (see Section 13.5.2), they will need a project scheduling tool. The project plan will inevitably involve tasks, dates, dependencies and resources (mostly people assigned to tasks). It will be too complex and fast changing to manage on paper or spreadsheet. It is important to use a tool that your organisation (and your project manager) is familiar with, but it is also important to agree formats for exchanging your plan electronically with your supplier team.

13.6.4 Hardware or provisioning platform

Again, this chapter cannot possibly address the full breadth of the subject of hardware capacity planning or the different sorts of provisioning such as cloud or local servers. However, knowledge from your evaluation project to date will inform the choice of platform.

- During your original requirements definition exercise you will have captured requirements about security, confidentiality and the constraints of the legislative environment in which your organisation operates. These requirements – which may be constraints, because they **must** be met – will shape the platform you use, such as the choice between installing your solution locally on your servers through to a full-blown online subscription model.

- Your evaluation may have made preliminary working assumptions that you will standardise on hardware the supplier recommends.

- Your negotiation may already have covered provisioning as part of your integrated bundle of hardware and software.

13.6.5 Decisions about replacing your old solution

There are multiple options as to what to do with your incumbent software, soon to become your legacy or old solution. You may move it to the sidelines and possibly only use it to look up old information. Alternatively, you may formally decommission it, removing your old software and data. There are complex, interlocking decisions to be made here by the implementation team in consultation with your business representatives.

Once again, you can refer back to your requirements document. There will probably be requirements about interfacing to your old software. There may be requirements about migrating old data or statistics on data volumes. You might have scored your incumbent software at longlist or shortlist stage. Its scores will help to decide its fate (see Chapters 7 and 9).

13.6.6 Populating your new solution's databases

Large software products almost inevitably involve multiple databases: live or 'production'; a test environment; an experimental 'sandpit'; the training database, to match workshop exercises; sometimes a baselined reference copy of migrated data; maybe even the database used for your sales demonstration. Your implementation plan will need to determine which databases will be installed, in what order, to match the overall project schedule and how they will be populated, if there is a choice.

EXECUTIVE PERSPECTIVE: A DIRECTOR'S EXPERIENCE OF TWO IMPLEMENTATIONS USING THE SAME APPROACH

The standard method adopted for the software and hardware selection allowed our newly appointed IT manager and a consultant to work through the requirements definition, longlisting, scoring, shortlisting and contract.

A core team represented the transformed business functions and at each checkpoint the selection process was discussed, modified if necessary and then approved by the senior management team and our US parent. Our parent had more functional heads, a more mature IT department and a different sales model. They could therefore intelligently question the UK team's assumptions, so it helped to have a rigorous process behind us.

Many suppliers were keen to be involved with a relatively small company because of the strength of our brand, augmented by a credible evaluation process. The systems were installed in time for the start of the new trading regime with minimal disruption to customers.

As a bonus, the features within the chosen solution also meant that it could potentially be exploited later to support a Pan-European acquisition that increased our presence in France and Benelux. A few years later, we ran a mini-project that built on original project deliverables and followed the now-familiar method against a candidate list of one – the newly installed UK system. Starting with the old requirements, the capture of differences in requirements and the consequent fit-gap analysis gave us clarity. We gained the confidence to extend the exploitation of our UK system to the rest of Europe.

13.7 CHAPTER SUMMARY

TAKE-AWAY POINTS

Signing the contract with your successful candidate is simply a milestone on the overall project. Not only is your project work incomplete, but also the larger risks are almost certainly still in front of you. Effective software that fits well is a foundation for success, but most implementation issues are non-technical. It is entirely possible to install software with a superb fit, but have an unsuccessful project overall because of poor data quality, inadequate training, ineffective process redesign or a hostile user base because you have not managed expectations, fears and the change process.

There is a major shift of roles when you move into your implementation phase and an associated shift in power positions. Your supplier's superior technical knowledge in the early stages of implementation makes them a crucial force.

Your evaluation process feeds valuable knowledge and documentation into your implementation. Project working papers continue to be valuable as a record of expectations, promises and earlier decisions. This documentation is especially valuable if very few people who have been involved in your evaluation carry forward into your implementation.

13.7.1 The next chapter

This is the last chapter to illustrate the core method. The next chapter concentrates on some important themes within the method.

13.8 REFERENCES

Cain, S. (2012) 'The rise of the new groupthink'. NYTimes.com, The New York Times. www.nytimes.com/2012/01/15/opinion/sunday/the-rise-of-the-new-groupthink.html (10 November 2014).

Friedman, T. (2006) 'The age of interruption'. NYTimes.com, The New York Times. www.nytimes.com/2006/07/05/opinion/05friedman.html (10 November 2014).

Gray, P. (2014) 'IT leaders, bring back the salon to benefit from different perspectives'. TechRepublic, CBS Interactive. www.techrepublic.com/article/it-leaders-bring-back-the-salon-to-benefit-from-different-perspectives (10 November 2014).

Lane, D. (2011) *The chief information officer's body of knowledge: People, process, and technology*. John Wiley & Sons: Chichester.

Office of Government Commerce (2009) *ITIL V3 foundation handbook*. The Stationery Office: Norwich.

Rodgers, C. (2006) *Informal coalitions: Mastering the hidden dynamics of organizational change*. Palgrave Macmillan: London.

Stone, L. (1998) 'Continuous partial attention'. Linda Stone, WordPress. http://lindastone.net/qa/continuous-partial-attention (10 November 2014).

Straker, D. (2009) 'Form, storm, norm, perform'. Changing Minds. http://changingminds.org/explanations/groups/form_storm_norm_perform.htm (10 November 2014).

13.9 FURTHER READING

13.9.1 Books and articles

BCS, The Chartered Institute for IT (2014) 'Boo hoo: Avoiding the lure of the big bang'. www.bcs.org/content/conWebDoc/52727 (10 November 2014).

Bingi, P., Sharma M. and Godla, J. (1999) 'Critical issues affecting an ERP implementation'. Information Systems Management, Auerbach Publications Inc. http://carl.sandiego.edu/gba573/critical_issues_affecting_an_erp.htm (10 November 2014).

Castellina, N. (2012) 'ERP implementation and training: A guide to getting your business in gear'. Aberdeen Group. http://aberdeen.com/research/7402/ra-enterprise-resource-planning/content.aspx (10 November 2014).

Gray, P. (2014) 'The $1.78 victory of automation process over human discretion'. TechRepublic, CBS Interactive. www.techrepublic.com/article/the-1-78-victory-of-automation-process-over-human-discretion/ (10 November 2014). (Avoidance of the Happy Path.)

Hughes, B. (2008) *Exploiting IT for business benefit.* BCS, The Chartered Institute for IT: Swindon.

Morgan, J. and Dale, C. (2013) *Managing IT projects for business change: From risk to success.* BCS, The Chartered Institute for IT: Swindon.

Morris, J. (2012) *Practical data migration*, 2nd edition. BCS, The Chartered Institute for IT: Swindon.

Paul, D., Cadle J. and Yeates, D. (2014) *Business analysis*, 3rd edition. BCS, The Chartered Institute for IT: Swindon. (Especially chapters 'Stakeholder Analysis and Management' and 'Delivering the Business Solution'.)

13.9.2 Useful websites

BCS Practitioner Certificate in Solution Development and Architecture: http://certifications.bcs.org/category/15625

BCS Practitioner Certificate in Integrating Off-the-shelf Software Solutions: http://certifications.bcs.org/category/15638

14 VIEWPOINTS BY THEME

'Having not said anything the first time, it was somehow even more difficult to broach the subject the second time around.'

Douglas Adams (1952– 2001)

14.1 WHAT YOU CAN LEARN FROM THIS CHAPTER

- Identify more routes to explore the method, by pointing to the aspects that support certain themes.
- Appreciate the provisions in the method that help project communications.

14.2 OVERVIEW

This chapter reviews the selection approach by looking at themes. It takes as read the earlier method Chapters 3 to 13. If you have jumped into the book at this section, you will see pointers to other chapters and sections.

The sections in this chapter are mainly intended either for advanced practitioners or for specialist interests such as quality, process, organisational development or change managers. They may want quick referrals to the tools the method provides to improve integration, communications, consultation and engagement.

14.3 COMMUNICATIONS

'Project teams that treat communication as reporting, joint working as an opportunity to inform and training as telling are setting up to fail. That one-sided view builds nothing except a black box from which outsiders are excluded. They should instead make communication and engagement a two-way affair in the course of which the team will learn useful things'.

(Morgan and Dale, 2013)

Table 14.1 examines six crucial aspects of project communications in order to show how they are supported by the selection approach.

Table 14.1 How the approach helps communications

Communications theme	How supported by method	Chapter
Business engagement	Consultation during requirements definition interviews or as reviewer when requirements document is circulated.	4, 5
	All project meetings aim for consensus – or at least majority – by stressing the corporate significance of the decisions.	Intro
Project sponsorship	Formal appointment of project sponsor, by project board, to match scope of project.	3
	Defined contributions by sponsor, especially at stage gates.	3, 5, 7, 9, 11, 12
Project management	Formal limits of authority, such as the evaluation team making recommendations (not the decision) or parameters set for the negotiation team.	9, 12
	Clearly defined role and contributions, especially at stage gates.	3–13
Stakeholder management	Multiple roles that contribute to decision-making, engaging stakeholders as sponsor, RFI assessor or project board member.	3–13
	Multiple roles that contribute to fact-gathering, engaging people as requirements interviewee, evaluation team member, demonstration attendee or reference site interviewer.	4, 8, 10, 11
Organisational change	Contributing to the process by one of the many available roles means the project is deeply rooted in the organisation.	3–13
	Early internal discussion about changes to organisational process during evaluation meetings.	8
	Tailored and targeted demonstrations of prospective new solutions to large number of attendees allows them to visualise 'their new world' before final decision.	10

(Continued)

Table 14.1 (Continued)

Communications theme	How supported by method	Chapter
	Reference site calls explore process changes, the organisational impact and lessons learnt by external referees.	11
Benefits realisation	Expectations are clear and documented using scores and definitions and reinforced during negotiation.	5, 7, 9, 12
	Gap analysis clarifies shortfall to aspirations, with exploration of remedies before and during negotiation.	9
	Standard project process allows effective engagement of independent consultants with vertical and process expertise.	1

14.4 DEFINED RESPONSIBILITY WITH CONSULTATION

Another theme of timely consultation occurs repeatedly in the method, so the relevant people are engaged at the appropriate time. Some selected examples follow.

- You consult the senior management team to establish the project board members (see Chapter 3).

- You consult the project board in order to appoint your executive sponsor (also see Chapter 3).

- You consult the executive sponsor to determine your interview list (see Chapter 4).

- One of your questions for requirements definition interviewees is to ask who would be a good evaluation team member or implementation team member (see Chapters 8 and 13).

- You ask project board and evaluation team members who should attend the demonstrations (see Chapter 10).

- You repeatedly consult suppliers to respond to your requirements (see Chapters 7 and 8) and then, crucially, to verify their own scores (see Chapter 9).

At Figure 14.1, the format used is the Responsibility Chart (nicknamed role-responsibility matrix) from GDPM (Andersen et al., 2009). The activities listed at left reflect the steps in the method diagram at Figure I.1. (For further information on the steps, follow this method diagram's chapter numbers.)

Figure 14.1 Responsibilities and consultation as GDPM Responsibility Chart

Proj Responsibility — Key:
- X - Executes the work
- d - Takes decision jointly
- D - Takes decision solely/ultimately
- P - Manages progress
- T - Transfer of information/knowledge
- C - Must be consulted
- I - Must be informed eg copy documents
- A - Available to advise
- S - Provides support eg technique/documentation

#	Activity	Senior Mngmnt Team (SMT)	Project Board (PB)	Project Sponsor	Project Manager	Evaluation Team	Interviewees	Negotiation Team	Implementation Team	Software Suppliers	Hardware Suppliers	IT Procurement Advisors	Change Mngmnt Advisors
1	Authorise project	D	C	C	P							T	T
2	Determine scope	I	D	C	P	I		I		I	I	S	S
3	Study feasibility inc cost	I	C	d	d	C		I		C	A	S	S
4	Establish phasing	I	D	C	P	I	I	I		I	A	S	S
5	Research best practice (desk search)		I	I	P	I			I	A		X	T
6	Capture requirements (interviews)		I	C	P		C				A	X	C
7	Document requirements (RDD/SoUR)		I	C	P	I	C		I		I	X	I
8	Weight requirements		X	C	P		I		I		I	S	I
9	Trawl marketplace			I	P					C		X	
10	Evaluate longlist (RFI)			I	D	X				C		S	
11	Review longlisting and shortlist		X	C	A					I	I	S	
12	Detailed eval of shortlist (RDD/SoUR)			I	P	X				C		S	
13	Score for fit			I	P	X				C		S	I
14	Analyse gaps			I	P	X		I	I	A		S	A
15	Review eval and select demos		X	C	A					I	I	S	C
16	Demonstrate preferred candidates	C	C	C	P	C,T	C	I	I	X	I	S	C
17	Check reference sites		I	I	X	C		I	I	C	I	S	A
18	Negotiate terms		I	I	P			X		C		S	
19	Agree contract	d	d	C	P			C		C		S	I
20	Install system	D			P	C	I		X	C	S	A	A

At top left on the chart, note the key for the types of involvement used in any cells with an activity–role combination. For instance, D marks the decision-maker. The Responsibility Chart is excellent for tracking involvement, especially where you have multiple participants, often part-time, making different contributions. As well as clarifying the position for the contributors, the matrix is an excellent briefing document as new people join the project. You can also run simple integrity and completeness checks, for instance to verify each step (row) has someone managing it (D, d, P or X).

EXECUTIVE PERSPECTIVE: AN IMPLEMENTATION CONSULTANT'S EXPERIENCE OF OWNERSHIP AND CULTURE

Working with an external consultant, the client's project team had applied the tools and techniques described here to:

- Define the business needs and requirements for a company-wide system.
- Qualify vendors and evaluate their product offerings.
- Build the business case to justify the proposed investment.

Joining the team at the start of the implementation phase, I was impressed by:

- The quality of the solution chosen, and the supplier's commitment to the implementation process.
- The commitment and enthusiasm of the team members – who had been involved in the selection process – and their ownership of the solution.

However, successful implementation is a challenge that should not be underestimated, especially when a key objective is to replace the dysfunctional systems used to control and manage projects, including the business change initiatives.

The role of the project sponsor as a change champion is critical in any successful implementation as new processes are developed and validated and the organisation recognises the need for behavioural changes – among the managers and 'other ranks'. The temptation to re-introduce familiar but flawed methods of working must also be resisted if the expected business benefits are to be realised. Critical issues during implementation included:

- Continuity of management responsibility through selection and implementation.
- A clear vision of the expected business benefits and timescales.
- Good communication of the planned changes throughout the organisation.
- Recognising and explaining the impact that the new system will have on working practices, and the rules that are embedded in the software. This may be of particular importance when existing informal and flexible systems allow people to avoid basic management disciplines, such as change and version control.

The benefits of a structured approach to system selection were clearly demonstrated by the quality of the selected solution. When system selection is the start of a process of business transformation, the implementation process demands an equally rigorous approach with the full support of senior management.

14.5 OTHER SECTIONS OF THE BOOK

Specialist quality, process improvement or method managers in an organisation will want to know how the method integrates into other organisation standards. See the

Introduction, Section I.1.2, for positioning of the selection method and Section I.3.1 for the importance of adapting the approach.

Managers of quality schemes and standards will want to know how the major pieces of documentation fit together. See Section I.3.2 for the interlock of main method deliverables.

14.6 CHAPTER SUMMARY

TAKE-AWAY POINTS

Defined roles, consultation and communications are essential to project success. The techniques assembled in this method inherently support them.

14.6.1 The next chapter

The next chapter has concluding remarks, summarises the most important points and signs off with more Executive Perspectives.

14.7 REFERENCES

Andersen, E., Grude, K. and Haug, T. (2009) *Goal directed project management: Effective techniques and strategies: 4*. Kogan Page: London.

Morgan, J. and Dale, C. (2013) *Managing IT projects for business change: From risk to success*. BCS, The Chartered Institute for IT: Swindon.

14.8 FURTHER READING

14.8.1 Books and articles

Nickson, D. and Siddons, S. (2006) *Project management disasters: And how to survive them*. Kogan Page: London.

Paul, D., Cadle J. and Yeates, D. (2014) *Business analysis*, 3rd edition. BCS, The Chartered Institute for IT: Swindon. (Especially the chapter on stakeholder analysis and management.)

Thomas, P., Paul, D. and James, C. (2012) *The Human touch: Personal skills for professional success*. BCS, The Chartered Institute for IT: Swindon.

14.8.2 Related formats by download

Role-Responsibility Matrix (GDPM Responsibility Chart) for selection project from http://shop.bcs.org/offtheshelfextras.asp.

15 CONCLUDING: RECOMMENDATIONS AND RESOURCES

'Life can only be understood backwards; but it must be lived forwards.'

Søren Kierkegaard (1813–1855)

15.1 SUMMARY

Projects to select off-the-shelf IT solutions are common, but under-appreciated and often high risk. They are damaging if they fail, entirely or even partially, which is also common.

This book has presented a systematic method to yield a successful procurement. The approach is proven (see Appendix 2). It optimises project, process and organisational risk. It defends against skewing your selection by a small management elite, by the IT department or by the candidate suppliers.

You should tailor your use of the approach to suit your organisational culture, your exposure to risk and the specifics of your project including the requirements, the type of software, the number of departments covered, your budget and the visibility of the result to your external partners.

The most important themes of this book are as follows:

- Engage your stakeholders throughout the project, including treating the candidate and successful suppliers as valuable collaborators. Change management is not something that can be tacked on to the end of a project (Hindle, 2010).

- Drive all aspects of your evaluation by your requirements such that the basis of decision is always informed by requirements or by criteria that are derived from them.

- At each stage, assemble enough – but only enough – evidence to make the decisions necessary to pass through the stage-end gate.

- Determine the basis of decision before you make that related decision, and then measure those criteria that form the basis of the decision both fairly and consistently.

By following the method stages relevant to your project, you become a much more sophisticated, informed purchaser of software products. You should now appreciate the wider project context and use appropriate techniques and processes to realise the benefits you need. You have been given insight into the viewpoints of multiple stakeholders – your decision-makers, prospective software users, colleagues in the IT department and candidate suppliers.

It is worth a reminder of the size of the prize. The prize is not just selecting the correct supplier and software product. The prize is actually landing on the right side of the chasm between success and failure.

Using a systematic method during IT software procurement is a form of due diligence. This involves a balance between over-investing in the due diligence process (making it unnecessarily expensive and wasteful of resource) and the cost of failure if something goes badly wrong (because your due diligence investigations were too lightweight). During your IT selection, always bear in mind the damage that can be caused by an ill-fitting solution.

- Many IT projects are simply abandoned (see *Introduction*). More common, but less visible, are the projects that stagger on, while delivering substantially below expectation, for several years. An unsuccessful software product implementation wastes time, money, talent and 'organisational will' (because the organisation becomes more cynical next time similar benefits are predicted).

- It can be catastrophic to the organisation if a single project intended to provide an enterprise solution does not deliver. As well as the many local difficulties caused by missing the opportunity for enhanced work automation, such non-delivery can knock you off course in meeting your strategic vision. It does not need to be as brutal as an outright project failure – an underperforming project with poorly implemented enterprise software is enough to delay your vision by years.

- Your software needs to recognise increasingly stringent audit requirements that apply to public sector bodies, to publicly quoted companies and to suppliers where customers direct standards (such as in the defence or aerospace industries). The security or confidentiality of your data and the success of your IT projects are dimensions for audit. Your external financial and quality auditors will have increasingly lengthy checklists to test the integrity of your IT solutions and the governance of your IT projects.

Given asymmetric risk, your due diligence should err on the side of caution. It is better to do 'too much' evaluation than face the ordeal of a failed implementation. It is better to 'fail to limit' your due diligence effort to precisely the right amount than fail to find a software product or procure the wrong one. Given the countless things that can go wrong, the only appropriate level of management is over-management.

I will leave you with two more user experience stories to reinforce the importance of a thorough selection process when procuring new software off-the-shelf.

EXECUTIVE PERSPECTIVE: A SUPPLIER'S EXPERIENCE OF CONTRASTING APPROACHES ON THE SAME PROJECT

I was recently involved in an opportunity with a customer who had an urgent business need and compelling reason to select an end-to-end solution and it was all systems go to select a system urgently. However, they did not use any selection method initially, and due to the urgency rushed the process by pre-selecting two vendors, provided little information regarding what they were actually looking for and asked for a couple of demonstrations. This resulted in a difficult decision to distinguish between the solutions. To us, the process felt biased towards the other vendor, since communication was poor and meetings were always at short notice with no alternatives. We therefore assumed the other vendor must have been getting more chance to respond favourably as this poor level of engagement did not feel like the company wanted to do business with us. Our approach focused on a strategy to beat the competition, not to address the requirements (especially as these were not clear).

The initial selection process culminated in the board being unable to make a decision. There were far too many risks. The business users were not bought-in, and the board just saw risk rather than benefit. As vendors, we felt as though we had not been given the chance to demonstrate the true capability of our solution for their business.

The company decided to re-start the selection process, and an external consultant was hired to facilitate the selection process, but also to develop the business processes. A systematic method was then followed to identify the solution capabilities to enable the 'TO BE' process. Requirements were documented and weighted, and the vendors requested to demonstrate against key requirements.

The process was monumentally different from the first time around with information open, two-way communication and a clear basis of decision. We were clear on what we needed to do to demonstrate our capability, and the project team was clear on how to differentiate between vendors.

The selection process did not take any longer than the first time around, but the project benefited from having clear aims and objectives. The opportunity for success with the project is much greater, with all of the project team including the key business users on-board to make it a success.

EXECUTIVE PERSPECTIVE: A DIRECTOR'S EXPERIENCE OF RIGOROUS EVALUATION THAT DODGED SUBSTANTIAL WASTE

My role was that of director within a start-up company offering online digital products. Investors had started to become more nervous about lending money to fledgling 'dotcom' start-ups. I had been charged with developing a business plan – outlining in particular the costings for building an IT platform – enabling the business to sell and deliver the majority of its products entirely online.

Whilst starting from scratch with a business can be exciting, there are many unknowns. We had a basic idea of the format our digital products would take and an even more basic idea of how we were going to deliver these. I knew we needed some help in identifying the hardware and software platforms necessary. I'd also read extensively about how most start-ups rushed to build bespoke systems and how disastrous this had proved. It was at this point that I sought specialist advice about procuring off-the-shelf software.

After preliminary discussions, we set to work on putting together a document that would contain a comprehensive list of highly specific requirements. This 'wish list' would be used as the basis for identifying and selecting a short list and ultimately a single software vendor whose product(s) best fit our requirements.

To kick-start the Requirements Definition stage, we began by building on a 'Pizza Base' Requirements Definition Document (RDD). This document contained a wide range of requirements assembled from previous projects and best practice research in our area.

Over the coming sessions we slowly built up the number of requirements through:

- closely examining and refining the business model;
- clarifying our customers' wants and needs;
- identifying areas where the business could differentiate itself from its competitors.

During a number of intensive question and answer sessions, we were able to capture all the requirements deemed important to the success of the project.

The surprising outcome of the requirements definition and vendor selection approach was that the leading edge, 'best fit' software solution, although phenomenally expensive, was fatally flawed. This was only discovered as a result of following the process rigorously and identifying the critical software functionality necessary to support the business model.

This also highlighted a serious problem with the business model, which would mean we would not be able to generate sufficient revenue to justify spending a huge amount on bespoke software. The project was shelved before further time and money were wasted.

15.2 REFERENCES

Hindle, K. (2010) 'Implementing business change'. In Paul, D., Cadle J. and Yeates, D. (eds), *Business analysis*, 2nd edition. BCS, The Chartered Institute for IT: Swindon.

15.3 FURTHER READING

15.3.1 Books and articles

AMED (2014) 'Good reads'. The AMED Network, The Association for Management Education and Development. www.amed.org.uk/page/good-reads (10 November 2014).

Jenner, S. (2012) *A senior manager's guide to managing benefits: Optimizing the return from investments.* TSO: Norwich.

15.3.2 Useful websites

BCS support for Business and IT Skills: http://shop.bcs.org/business.

APPENDIX 1
SIZING QUESTIONNAIRE: TO SCOPE A SELECTION PROJECT

Figure A.1.1 gives sizing metrics to collect as part of scoping and risk assessing your project. Adjust the questions for your organisation – for instance, the number and names of sites. Ask relevant knowledgeable staff to research the figures now, and to guess where possible the equivalent figures in five years' time.

For some numbers, the most important distinction is one versus more-than-one (rather than the exact value). For instance, single currency versus multi-currency or single-language screens versus multi-lingual.

The larger the numbers and the greater the difference between today and five years, the more likely that the project will be risky and that the eventual solution will be more sophisticated and expensive. Some of these figures will also feed the volumes section of your requirements documentation (see Chapter 5, Section 5.5.5).

You can download the spreadsheet format from: http://shop.bcs.org/offtheshelfextras.asp.

Figure A.1.1 Metrics to assess size and risk of selection project

Project: [Add rows if needed for specifics or to track some metrics by site] Completed By: Date:

Ref	Factor	Today	5 Years	Notes
(A) Business Size				
10	Turnover			
20	Funding amount (if start-up)			
30	Value of asset base			
40	Number of assets tracked			
50	Number of employees			
60	Number of separate sites			
70	Number of products/services			
80	Number of overseas locations			
90	Number of customers tracked			
100	Typical length of sales cycle (days)			
110	Number of sales orders per year			
120	Number of purchase orders per year			
130	Percentage of stock specifically procured for projects			
140	Typical stock valuation			
150	Number of people booking time			
160	Number of hours booked per year (if time-based business)			
170	Percentage of exports (portion of turnover overseas)			
180	Number of different bank accounts			
190	Number of different payrolls			
200	Number of legal entities requiring own P&L			
210	Number of entities requiring own balance sheet			
220	Probable number of acquisitions in the next 5 years			
230	Annual IT budget			
(B) Size/Sophistication of New Software				
2000	Number of named users envisaged on the new system			
2010	Number of concurrent users envisaged on the new system			
2020	Number of mobile users connected to the new system			
2030	Number of different organisations accessing software			(a)
2040	Number of different databases supported by new system			
2050	Number of time zones supported on same server			(b)
2060	Number of currencies			
2070	Local of solution vs Head Office [see Notes]			(c)
2080	Number of languages (multi-lingual)			
2090	Number of interfaces to other systems			
2100	Number of database transactions per month, if calculable			
2110	Number of EDI transfers per month			
2120	Number of new documents per month			
2130	Number of new web pages per month			

(Continued)

Figure A.1.1 Continued

Ref	Factor	Today	5 Years	Notes
(C) Current Systems				
4000	Number of named users on the network			
4010	Number of concurrent users on the network			
4020	What is/was cost of current system			
4030	How much already paid to supplier (%age of total)			
4040	Percentage overrun to original budget			
4050	Number of people supporting the current system			
4060	Annual maintenance/support cost for the existing systems			
4070	Annual license cost for the existing systems			
4080	Data volumes			(d)
4090	Number of Virtual Machines under management			
(D) Project				
6000	Target ROI/ROCE, if set			
6010	Expected project duration (months) if known			
6020	Expected date to start implementation, if determined			
6030	Expected live date, if determined			
6040	Size of project team			
6050	Number of interviewees to capture requirements/criteria			
6060	Number of early project documents to read to capture requirements			
6070	Can interviewees be grouped			(e)
6080	All interviewees internal, or customers [see Notes]			(f)
6090	All interviewees internal, or suppliers [see Notes]			(g)
6100	Budget for system/implementation, if determined			
6110	Budget for project work (such as external consultancy)			
6120	Internal cost of the project/implementation, if tracked			
6130	Number of IT suppliers expected on shortlist			
6140	Number of IT suppliers that will be engaged			

Notes

(a)   Allow for suppliers & customers
(b)   If same server, states or countries with different zone or daylight saving dates need sophisticated timestamps
(c)   1 = Solution at Head Office; 2 = will report to parent in same country; 3 = will report to parent overseas
(d)   Break out by business category or software type if necessary, eg ERP, CAD
(e)   1 = can group into small workshops; 3 =interviewed individually; 2 = mix
(f)   1 = all internal; 2 = need to interview sample customers
(g)   1 = all internal; 2 = need to interview sample suppliers

APPENDIX 2
COMPARATIVE METRICS: EXAMPLE PROJECT PROFILES

Figure A.2.1 gives summary sizing metrics on the projects that have used this method. They have different profiles by number of interviewees, number of requirements, number of candidates and spend. This shows both the flexibility of the approach and the need to adapt its use to the scale and risk profile of your project (see Introduction, Section I.3.1).

Headings on table:

> **Interviews:** number of interviews to capture requirements.
>
> **Nbr Rqts:** number of requirements in requirements documentation.
>
> **Longlist:** number of candidates on initial longlist.
>
> **Det eval:** number of candidates for detailed evaluation.
>
> **Project £000s:** project budget.

Note there are gaps in reference numbers because the original table tracks other types of projects. This list is filtered to projects selecting IT hardware and software.

Figure A.2.1 Summary metrics for projects using this method

Ref	Project Metrics During Option/Solution Selections	Year	Interviews	Nbr Rqts	Longlist	Det eval	Project £000s
01	Fluids Manufacturing Package (MRP)	1992	45	243	8	4	£664.7
02	Counsellor Management	1993	20	131	6	2	£7.0
03	Newspaper Distribution	1993	2	80	20	2	£1.6
04	In-House Braille	1994	2	0	5	0	£5.0
05	Document Transmission	1994	2	14	8	0	£0.7
06	Customer Relationship Management (CRM)	1995	3	84	43	3	£7.1
07	Youth Training Administration (West Lancs)	1995	10	108	11	6	£60.0
08	Youth Training Administration (East Lancs)	1995	2	167	1	1	£41.8
09	New Standard Desktops	1995	2	20	2	1	£2.0
10	Pen Computing Laptop	1995	2	20	2	1	£3.6
11	PC card HDD & modem	1995	1	3	1	1	£1.1
12	Client management system	1996	2	163	1	1	£50.0
13	Business advisory service support	1996	2	162	2	2	£180.0
14	Financials & order processing	1997	1	127	250	6	£200.0
15	Financials & MRP	1997	51	320	200	7	£600.0
16	Laptop specification/selection	1997	2	42	2	1	£2.8
17	Telephony & WAN	1998	2	80	3	3	£60.6
18	Mechanical/electrical CAD, visualisation & stress analysis	1998	80	182	10	2	£5,000.0
19	Remote desktop	1998	1	10	1	1	£1.3
20	NT desktops & server	1998	2	33	1	1	£12.4
21	Pan-European ERP & materials management	1999	30	198	1	1	£179.8
22	ID card, access control, time, attendance & work-booking	1999	43	260	61	5	£1,162.0
23	National ebusiness feasibility	2000	98	317	0	0	£57.8
24	Web storefront - spares from 17 legacy ERP systems	2000	4	228	8	0	£68.6
25	Mobile telephones/network	2000	2	50	1	1	£0.5
26	ERP & digital rights management	2001	3	235	19	3	£22.0
27	Learning management system (LMS)	2001	53	217	1	1	£30.9
28	Networked colour laser mopier	2001	2	9	3	1	£7.4
29	Global engineering resource/skills management	2002	10	61	4	4	£29.4
30	Web-based CSCW	2002	2	360	3	2	£13.2
31	Accounting	2002	1	200	1	1	£0.8
32	Desktop & virtual office communications	2002	1	200	2	2	£6.0
33	XP desktop	2002	2	20	1	1	£1.4
35	XP Tablet PC feasibility/specification	2003	2	50	11	1	£2.0
37	ERP for design/import	2004	6	333	36	1	£183.3
38	Telephony, email & ISP evaluation	2004	2	166	2	1	£8.7
43	Audio/video/data conferencing	2005	1	100	7	1	£10.9
44	Global ERP for engineering/construction consultancy	2005	28	416	103	3	£1,069.0
45	Web retailing & SaaS	2005	2	202	8	3	£13.2
46	Service charge management - full replacement hardware	2006	4	115	5	1	£56.3
47	Support contract - supplier assessment/selection	2006	4	29	10	3	£30.0
48	Consultancy services - replace bespoke business system	2007	6	280	2	2	£121.4
54	Central HR	2009	38	236	0	TBD	£160.0
56	Rota	2010	24	151	0	TBD	£35.0
57	PLM/ERP/CRM/SCM	2011	11	387	102	3	£1,370.6
58	Asset & Service Management	2011	5	25	24	1	£700.0
59	'Extendend' HR	2012	1	0	1	0	£1.2
60	Asset Intelligence	2012	11	107	7	1	£288.0
61	Integrated HR & Payroll	2012	12	302	OOS	OOS	£539.3
62	Community Fire Protection	2013	80	325	8	TBD	£54.0
Count/Total:			50	722	7,568	1,008	88	£13,125

APPENDIX 3
CHECKLIST: DETAILED METHOD STEPS

Table A.3.1 shows the main steps in the method. For more information, see the related chapter number shown on the high-level headings.

Note, **WBS** is Work Breakdown Structure – see Glossary.

You can download this checklist in Microsoft Project or Excel format from: http://shop.bcs.org/offtheshelfextras.asp.

Table A.3.1 Method checklist

WBS	Task
1	Project scoping (Chapter 3)
1.1	Prepare resources
1.1.1	Distribute sizing spreadsheet for completion
1.1.2	Capture metrics for business case calculations – such as value of saved hours
1.1.3	Get organisational background documentation from website, operations manuals, published plans or internal strategy documents
1.1.4	Research sources of likely requirements such as meeting minutes
1.2	Compile scoping input list
1.2.1	Research scoping list sources
1.2.2	Extract entries from research and existing material
1.2.3	External proof and review
1.3	Scoping workshop
1.3.1	Agree presentation with project sponsor (and workshop chair if different)
1.3.2	Write glossary if needed

(Continued)

Table A.3.1 Continued

WBS	Task
1.3.3	Create scoping input lists – numbered and titled
1.3.4	Triage entries in meeting
1.3.5	Distribute output lists for confirmation
2	Requirements definition interviews (Chapter 4)
2.1	Confirm interviewees list, with groupings to workshop
2.2	Email introduction from project sponsor
2.3	Make requirements definition interview appointments, or organise assistant to do so
2.4	Create prompts as topic notes or matrix of questions
2.5	Organise 'props' for meeting room, such as sample products
2.6	Create and send pre-interview briefing sheet
2.7	Generate note-taking formats
2.8	Conduct semi-structured interview programme
2.9	Adjust interviewee list as necessary – confirm with PM or sponsor
2.10	Collect background for appendices such as current system
3	Requirement documentation (Chapter 5)
3.1	Ensure collected samples are marked to tie to interview session
3.2	Organise notes into requirements catalogue
3.3	Get business volumes (collection maybe delegated)
3.4	Create requirement categories – agree with sponsor
3.5	Mark category onto all requirements
3.6	Write or dictate new requirements
3.7	Incorporate standard requirements
3.8	Process any written submissions of requirements
3.9	Transfer selected requirements from scoping workshop output
3.10	Transfer from business volumes document
3.11	Back-check to collected samples and sweep notes, especially volumes
3.12	Attach current system samples as appendix

(Continued)

Table A.3.1 Continued

WBS	Task
3.13	Create or update glossary if necessary
3.14	Standard appendices
3.14.1	Interviewee list
3.14.2	Paste interviewee-supplied samples from current systems, or scan paper samples
3.14.3	Glossary of terms (as appendix or separate document if shared across projects)
3.14.4	Pre-interview background document
3.15	Release for comment by sponsor, PM, all interviewees (depending on version)
3.16	Requirements revisions after comments
3.16.1	New requirements
3.16.2	Changes to existing requirements
3.16.3	Retitle requirements to match reworded content
3.16.4	Moves to 'project notes' appendix if not requirement
3.16.5	Proof
3.16.6	Update revisions history section
3.16.7	Release notes – last appendix of project notes will be suppressed from supplier copies
4	Weights for importance (Chapter 5)
4.1	Voting spreadsheet
4.1.1	Compile voting spreadsheet including voter name, coloured columns, transfer requirement titles, fill category
4.1.2	Mark rotating lead voters with dashes – every 10 or divide number of scored requirements by number of voters
4.1.3	Create agreed weight distribution chart
4.2	Other preparation for weighting meeting
4.2.1	Confirm weighting team
4.2.2	Create name cards for weighting team members
4.2.3	Standard meeting tasks including date, venue and notify attendees

(Continued)

Table A.3.1 Continued

WBS	Task
4.2.4	Print standard document to define weights
4.2.5	Print sample page of voting spreadsheet
4.2.6	Compile meeting progress spreadsheet
4.2.7	Example of weighted attribute scoring mechanism – article on BCS extras page
4.2.8	Print spares of prime section of requirements and own copy for revision annotations
4.2.9	Create presentation or check standard is suitable
4.3	Meeting brief
4.3.1	Introductions (if new members)
4.3.2	Introduce next project stages, especially scoring mechanism
4.3.3	Definitions for weights
4.3.4	Explain outcomes needed from weighting meeting
4.4	Requirements revisions after weighting meeting
4.4.1	Splits, deletes and modifications – from mark-ups
4.4.2	Moves to 'project notes' appendix
4.4.3	Reword and retitle
4.4.4	New requirements
4.4.5	Update revisions history section
4.4.6	Align voting spreadsheet with new requirement numbers and titles
4.4.7	Proof then modifications
4.4.8	Release notes – last appendix suppressed
5	Longlist (Chapter 6)
5.1	Longlist sources to trawl marketplace
5.1.1	Trawl online technology articles
5.1.2	Trawl online product databases – niche
5.1.3	Check vertical magazines, e.g. *Manufacturing Management*
5.1.4	Ask suppliers, customers, possibly competitors
5.1.5	Contact Computer Users Information Service, CUIS

(Continued)

Table A.3.1 Continued

WBS	Task
5.2	Creating longlist
5.2.1	Load from previous projects
5.2.2	Load any suppliers already contacted on project so far
5.2.3	Prepare telephone call notes – project information, ask if interested, dates RFI out/in, who best contact
5.2.4	Ring new potential candidates
5.2.5	Load new suppliers from latest trawl of marketplace
6	Request for information – RFI (Chapter 7)
6.1	RFI creation
6.1.1	Check if tendering regulations apply for this project (e.g. OJEU, GSA)
6.1.2	Ensure have up-to-date, weighted requirements
6.1.3	Rules for inclusion: high weight or 'litmus test'; discriminates; can test by documented closed question; not concomitant; not seatbelt; spread of sections
6.1.4	Extract RFI criteria from requirements
6.1.5	Create RFI – all items numbered, in separate rows
6.1.6	Write project background for candidates (extract from requirements document)
6.1.7	Consider attaching or extracting glossary
6.2	Finalising RFI
6.2.1	Include terms or include project glossary
6.2.2	Complete background – company, project, method, response, timing
6.2.3	Complete 'answers' – assessment criteria
6.2.4	Circulate to sponsor or PB for approval
6.2.5	Ensure supplier version has answers removed
6.3	Distribute RFI to longlist
6.3.1	Prepare covering email
6.3.2	Distribute RFI email with attachment – BCC to list or individual emails – candidates should not see each other

(Continued)

Table A.3.1 Continued

WBS	Task
6.3.3	Clarify if enquiries – broadcast general answers to all candidates as appropriate
7	Mark RFI responses (Chapter 7)
7.1	Receiving responses to RFI
7.1.1	Collate replies
7.1.2	Check copied to project inbox – forward if not
7.1.3	Acknowledge safe receipt
7.1.4	Mark status on longlist matrix
7.1.5	Save attachments including response and appendices to folder per candidate
7.1.6	Save covering email as document in same folder
7.1.7	Check supplier/product name is in each document name – rename if necessary
7.1.8	Print each candidate's main RFI with attachments
7.1.9	Print all notifications of withdrawals ('turndowns') as evidence for meeting
7.2	Prepare marking spreadsheet
7.2.1	Ensure have columns with criteria (transfer from RFI) plus candidates across page
7.2.2	Setup headings to mark categories
7.2.3	Filter to suppress headings for assessment meeting
7.2.4	Setup format of price-performance Bubble Chart – X = Cost, Y = Points, Bubble = PPI
7.3	RFI assessment meeting (marking)
7.3.1	Setup working room for RFI marking (need space to spread out, and screen visible)
7.3.2	Assess to marking scheme – one RFI question for all candidates, then next question
7.3.3	Agree shortlist with project board
7.3.4	Contact suppliers with through/park outcome
7.3.5	Send non-disclosure agreement to shortlisted suppliers

(Continued)

Table A.3.1 Continued

WBS	Task
7.3.6	Send requirements document (less internal appendices) and project background document
8	Evaluation 'tour' arrangements (Chapter 8)
8.1	Agree dates with shortlisted suppliers – get directions
8.2	Organise itinerary, hotels, transport, tickets
8.3	Notify evaluation team of arrangements
8.4	Brief evaluation team
8.5	Create control spreadsheet for meeting sequence and schedule to reflect availability of evaluation and response team
8.6	Print requirements documentation as notes format (reduce to 70 per cent, each meeting with watermark for candidate name)
9	Evaluation meetings – open/close for suppliers (Chapter 8)
9.1	Opening meeting (before first main evaluation session/category)
9.1.1	Introductions
9.1.2	Verify time constraints on attendees
9.1.3	Highlight objective of sessions
9.1.4	Introduce next stages (briefly, to give meeting context)
9.1.5	Stress need for pace
9.1.6	Stress benefit of brief introductions – save time for main sessions
9.1.7	Explain general demonstration OK – if gives shorthand for later responses
9.1.8	Verify Appendix 1 conditions OK
9.2	Evaluation meetings with suppliers
9.2.1	Collect samples – tag to requirement number
9.2.2	Conduct end-of-day reviews with evaluation team
9.3	Closing meeting (after last evaluation session)
9.3.1	Advise scoring meeting dates – confirm supplier contact for period if evaluation team have queries
9.3.2	Advise date outcome will be available
10	Scores for fit on weighted attribute matrix (Chapter 9)

(Continued)

Table A.3.1 Continued

WBS	Task
10.1	Scoring formats (inputs to meeting)
10.1.1	Create empty WAM spreadsheet including column headings
10.1.2	Load requirements titles (from voting spreadsheet or requirements document direct)
10.1.3	Add columns if needed for more candidates and enter candidate names across scores columns
10.1.4	Set all candidate scores to 0.1
10.1.5	Fill down category keywords
10.1.6	Insert sub-totals at change of Category to Requirement Number, Weight, Maximum and all Fit Xtd columns
10.1.7	Adjust formulae at total and sub-total lines for Count and Average
10.1.8	Transfer weights from weighting meeting as necessary
10.1.9	Add percentage fit to one sub-total entry and copy to others
10.1.10	Protect sheet, test can only input to Title and Match columns
10.1.11	Print sample page of (unfinished) scoring spreadsheet for meeting
10.1.12	Generate definitions document format by merging standard framework with requirement number/titles
10.1.13	Create definitions front and version control sheet
10.1.14	Add 'purpose of definitions' sheet if necessary
10.1.15	Print sample definitions page for scoring meeting
10.1.16	Create schedule and progress control spreadsheet from requirement ranges
10.2	Run scoring meeting
10.2.1	Brief scoring team in scoring spreadsheet and definitions
10.2.2	Hand out scoring process reference sheet
10.2.3	Show sample page of scoring spreadsheet – explain weights transferred from voting
10.2.4	Show sample definitions
10.2.5	Explain scoring will be blind – weight should not influence process of agreeing score for fit

(Continued)

Table A.3.1 Continued

WBS	Task
10.2.6	Advise team to lay out their notes in a way that aids reliable product recognition amongst the group
10.2.7	Give summary statistics especially number of scored requirements
10.2.8	Score for fit in range 0–3 – remember need specific definitions of scores for each requirement (will be attached to contract)
10.2.9	For each requirement, identify variations in the packages – the spread of capability
10.2.10	Discard golden features – over-capacity or over-provision where solution does more than required and surplus is not beneficial
10.2.11	Record basis for allocating points, only define the scores you allocate, rather than all four (not a ranking, some candidates will score the same)
10.2.12	Record the capability needed for each score in scoring definitions (one definition per requirement per score used)
10.2.13	Record the scores for each candidate on the scoring spreadsheet
10.3	Verifying scores with candidates
10.3.1	Copy scoring spreadsheet to generic supplier version
10.3.2	Unhide all columns and rows
10.3.3	Add in general/common version new columns for supplier applications (difference in current score versus application, supplier comment)
10.3.4	Delete columns such as source (if used), weight and extended scores
10.3.5	Delete surplus sheets
10.3.6	Create 'cut down' versions – one per supplier showing only their scores, not competitor
10.3.7	Email to confirm scores with IT suppliers – send definitions and cut-down matrix for their scores – remind requirements document not changed
10.3.8	When returned, review supplier bids for more or less points – adjust scores – adjust definitions if necessary
10.4	Analysis of scoring spreadsheet
10.4.1	Review fit established (so far)
10.4.2	Form initial opinion on whether should go ahead
10.4.3	Find mandatory not yet scored, due to lack of information (5 and 0.1)

(Continued)

Table A.3.1 Continued

WBS	Task
10.4.4	Find others not yet scored, due to lack of information (All and 0.1)
10.4.5	Find any mandatory requirements with score of 0 ('fatal flaws' or apply to drop weight 5 to 4)
10.4.6	Find mandatory requirements with score of 1
10.4.7	Revise opinion on whether should go ahead (stop/go recommendation)
10.4.8	Analyse scores for trends or highlights for meeting
10.4.9	Create chart of fit
11	**Selecting demonstration candidates (Chapter 9)**
11.1	Preparation
11.1.1	Standard meeting tasks including date, venue and notify attendees
11.1.2	Confirm recommendations with evaluation team
11.1.3	Assemble briefing notes and handouts – recommendations and decisions needed
11.1.4	Distribute handouts before meeting if beneficial
12	**Demonstrations (Chapter 10)**
12.1	Specification
12.1.1	Filter requirements document scores to high weight and high score (usually 3+, 2+)
12.1.2	Select requirement section and title/number combination
12.1.3	Transfer list and build table around it – add demonstration step numbering
12.1.4	Distribute for comment
12.2	Demonstration data
12.2.1	Research and collate demonstration data
12.2.2	Check data to outline for gaps
12.2.3	Send outline and data to demonstration suppliers
13	**Reference sites (Chapter 11)**
13.1	Request reference sites with contact details and appointments
13.2	Create questions list
13.3	Send ahead to referees

(Continued)

Table A.3.1 Continued

WBS	Task
13.4	Send courtesy copy to suppliers
13.5	Conduct interviews – update questions table with notes
13.6	Play back notes to referee
14	Selecting preferred for negotiation (Chapter 12)
14.1	Preparation
14.1.1	Standard meeting tasks including date, venue and notify attendees
14.1.2	Create presentation with summary of progress
14.1.3	Create or update and review chart of fit
14.1.4	Distribute handouts before meeting if beneficial
14.2	Final selection discussion – review scores, demonstrations, reference sites
14.2.1	Discuss overall match between the candidates and business requirements
14.2.2	Discuss technical fit of each product
14.2.3	Discuss fit of the supplier services
14.2.4	Discuss investment likely to be required
14.2.5	Discuss ability of suppliers to meet the implementation schedule
14.2.6	Discuss calibre of supplier resources and strategic alliances
14.2.7	Discuss chemistry between your organisation and the supplier
14.2.8	Agree number of negotiation candidates
15	Negotiation and agreement (Chapter 12)
15.1	Analyse scores for important shortfalls to negotiate (high weight, low score)
15.2	Compile/agree negotiation sheet including Best, Worst and Open
15.3	Distribute negotiation agenda to internal negotiation team for information and agreement
15.4	Conduct negotiations
15.5	Document agreements in Agreed column
15.6	Follow up outstanding points
15.7	Compile contract from supplier and customer content, especially attaching requirements, scores, definitions

INDEX

ABC ratings 159–60

Adams, Douglas 231

adaptation of selection method 4–8

adoption policies 19

advisers 80–1

Agile (management framework/ methodology) 2

Agree (requirement outcome) 81

agreeing recommendations (scoring meetings) 151

allocating resources (implementation phase) 220–2

alternative full marking 113

'anti-competitive' behaviour 35

anti-reference sites 188–9

approval to negotiate 201–2

areas serviced by off-the-shelf solutions 17

'artefacts' 22–3

audio conferencing 186

avoiding pitfalls 22–4, 238

back-checking 100

back-filling 222

background/briefing section (RFI process) 104–5

'basis of decision' 6, 10

BATNA (Best Alternative To a Negotiated Agreement) 205–6, 210, 213

benefits of selection method 3–4

benefits realisation (communications theme) 233

'best outcome' (negotiation preparation term) 205–6, 213

'bidding up' 152, 153

Bismarck, Otto von 182

'black hat thinking' 36

'bleeding edge' adoptions 90

'blind responses' approach (RFI process) 98

booking scoring meetings 146

boundaries 40, 41, 44–5

breaks (during meetings) 125–6, 149

bubble charts 115–16

business engagement (communications theme) 232

business need 72–3

business volumes 76–7

'buy-in' 14, 44, 53, 136

'buying signals' 128

Carroll, Lewis 1

'cast iron' contracts 28

cataloguing 69–70

categories (scoring meetings) 150

censoring data 170

chair role (evaluation team) 123

charging models 197–8

checks and balances (evaluation process) 130

Cloud First policy (USA) 16

'cloud of points' 44, 45

COBIT (management framework/ methodology) 2

collaboration 23–4

'Collaborative Business Relationships' (BSI standard) 24

Collected (requirement characteristic) 77

commission scheme charging models 198

communications themes 231–3

compatible reference sites 183

competitive advantage 24

complex software 22–3

compliance requirements 19

concurrent users 196–7

'configuration' 11, 107, 158

consistency 58, 97

consistent attendance (evaluation team) 122

'consistent comparison' approach (RFI process) 97

consultants (implementation phase) 222–3, 226, 235

consultation 233–4

'Continuous Partial Attention' 222

contract pack compilation 214

'copycatting' 90

core member (assessment team member) 109

cost base charging models 197

Cost of Change Curve 12

costing parameters (RFI process) 105

COTS (commercial off-the-shelf) 16, 17

'critical factor' requirements 82

critical partnerships 34–5

culture clash 31

'current version' approach (RFI process) 98

current volumes 76

'customisation' 11, 107, 158, 207–8

data retention 77

data structures (implementation plan) 225

'deal-breakers' 203

debriefing candidates (negotiation process) 214

decision-makers (demonstration audience members) 164

decision-making cycles 43–4, 82–3

defence mechanisms 130–1, 155–6

definitions document 135, 140–6, 240

Delete (requirement outcome) 81

demonstrations
  analysis of 178–9
  audience of 164, 167–8, 176
  chairing meetings 169
  closing the meeting 178
  conducting 176–8
  creating demonstration outlines 171–3
  and decision-making 179
  and determining applicable stages 7, 8
  executive perspective on 180
  feedback forms 165, 174, 175
  handling questions 176–7
  'impresario' role 165
  length of 163, 167
  number of candidates 163
  objectives of 165
  psychology of demonstrations 167
  releasing demonstration outlines 173–4
  and requirements 164, 165, 172–4, 177, 179–80
  risks of 166–7
  sample data 170–1
  setting the date 170
  strength of candidates 164
  strengths/weaknesses of demonstrators 166, 168–9
  and supplier relationships 164
  timing 176
  treble checking 174, 176
  venue for 169
  and video conferencing 177

desk enquiries 100

'desk-based' approach (RFI process) 97

detailed requirements document 70–1

determining applicable stages 5–8

development costs 20, 159, 193

diffused knowledge 23–4

'discriminatory' questions 100

'doing your homework' 13

Drucker, Peter 16

DSDM (management framework/ methodology) 2

due diligence 12, 32, 58, 65, 121, 160, 223, 238

economic complexity 21

economic feasibility 48–50

effective behaviours (supplier relationships) 35–6

electronic note-taking 133

Ellison, Larry 91

email addresses 91, 108

emergency ejection and substitution (evaluation process) 131

encapsulated knowledge 21

'escalating family' of requirements 74

estimated costs (RFI process) 113

'estimated value' (negotiation preparation term) 205–6

European Public Procurement Rules 36

'Evaluation and Selection' phase 6, 7

evaluation process
  advantages of teams over individuals 122
  chair role 123
  and 'configuration' 11
  consistent attendance 122
  defence mechanisms 130–1
  demonstrations see demonstrations
  determining applicable stages 6–7
  and due diligence 121
  emergency ejection and substitution 131
  and evidence-based decision-making 11
  executive perspectives on 124, 130, 239–40
  and feasibility studies 40, 47–51
  following the subject leader 133
  guest evaluators 122
  and implementation phase 217–19, 221–2, 224–5, 226–8
  material used 125

meeting administration 124–6

new internal stakeholders 121

note-taking 131–3

object of evaluation meetings 121

overt/covert techniques 129

philosophy of evaluation 128

preparing the evaluation team 126

reference sites see reference sites

requirements as driver of 6, 237

and requirements document 73

response team 123, 124

review sessions 129

and RFI process 96–8

schedule of evaluation meetings 126, 127

scoring see scoring

and shipping version 11, 128

skill sets of attendees 123–4

and specialisation 10

and staged decision-making 11–12

standing evaluation team 122

and supplier relationships 32, 121

team member selection 23

team mindset and vocabulary 128–9

team roles 122–3

time management 125–6

tracking roles 123

and transferring risk 28

venue of evaluation meetings 124

evidence-based decision-making 11, 116–17

exclusions 40

executive perspectives
  contractual safeguards 215
  contrasting approaches 239
  demonstrations 180
  early, formal consultation 47
  evaluation process 124, 130
  formally measuring fit 118
  implementation phase 218–19, 228, 235
  make–buy decisions 20
  negotiation 193, 215
  premature shortlisting 87

reference sites 184
requirements capture 57–8
scope 40–1
selection process 3–4, 136–7
supplier relationships 29
weighting workshops 79
executive sponsors 5, 51–2, 80
explicit concessions 145–6
extra team members (negotiation process) 201

facilitator (assessment team member) 109
fact checking (scoring meetings) 150
fairness/unfairness (supplier relationships) 35
feasibility costing 48–50
feasibility studies
    economic feasibility 48–50
    and evaluation process 40, 47–51
    feasibility costing 48–50
    organisational feasibility 50
    and scope 39–40
    stop/go decisions 50–1
    strategic feasibility 47–8
    technical feasibility 48
feedback forms 165, 174, 175
finalising provisional scores (scoring meetings) 151
Finance (requirements category) 73
fit 137–8, 139–40, 144, 148
'flashy office syndrome' 124
'flat weights' 157
flexible content (scoping workshops) 45
FMR (failed mandatory requirements) 157, 158
follow up (evaluation meetings) 126
formal risk management 28
free modifications (negotiation process) 194, 207–10
functional scope 40
functions (scope decision level) 42–3
FYE (financial year end) 204

gap analysis 10, 157–8, 159–60, 202
Gates, Bill 91

General Services Administration (GSA) 2
'gifted amateurs' 21
Goldwyn, Samuel 192
Good To Great (book) 18
GOTS (government off-the-shelf) 16
Greenleaf, Robert K. 120
guest evaluators (evaluation team) 122
guiding principles of method 10–11
gut feel (scoring meetings) 147

Handy, Charles 27
hardware costs 113
Hawthorne Effect 60
'high tickers' 178

implementation
    allocating resources 220–2
    aspects of the implementation plan 224–6
    and consultants 222–3, 226, 235
    contributors to the implementation plan 224
    customer responsibilities 220–4
    defending implementation team 222
    and evaluation process 217–19, 221–2, 224–5, 226–8
    executive perspectives on 218–19, 228, 235
    hardware/provisioning platform 227
    managing expectations 223–4
    mapping 226
    old software decision-making 227
    planning process 226–7
    populating the new databases 228
    and power positions 219
    project scheduling tool 227
    and reference sites 224, 226
    and supplier relationships 222–3
    supplier responsibilities 219–20
implementation phase (negotiation process) 198
'implied threat' of demonstrations 164

importance of finishing (evaluation meetings) 125
'impresario' role 165
incumbent solution 18, 93–4
industry bodies 90
influencers/advisors (demonstration audience members) 164
information system 60, 64
initial licence costs 113
Interfaces (requirements category) 73
interlock of main deliverables 8, 9
internal costing 49
ISO 11000 (management framework/methodology) 2
issues section (definitions document) 142
IT consultancy 24
IT reports 90
IT systems (scope decision level) 42–3
ITIL (management framework/methodology) 2

James, William 135
joint costing 49

Kierkegaard, Søren 237
knowledge workers 27, 30
KPIs (key performance indicators) 75

lack of commitment 24
'language ladders' 141, 142–5, 152, 154, 203, 220, 226
launch events 53
lead qualification 32
'limited ambition' approach (RFI process) 97
Lincoln, Abraham 27
listings services 90
longlists
    creating 87–91
    including/excluding candidates 92–3
    and incumbent solution 93–4
    knowledge of contacts/colleagues 89
    length of 91–2
    previous research/lists 89
    and progressive shortlisting 87

researching published information 87, 89

and RFI process *see* RFI process

sales exhibitions 89–90

spreadsheet for collating 88

and suppliers 86–7

'Major factor' requirements 82

make–buy decisions 20, 24

manageable processes 13

management commitment 63–4

managing expectations 56, 58, 91, 136, 176, 210, 223–4

managing information (scoring process) 154

'Mandatory' requirements 74–5, 82, 83, 157, 158

mapping (implementation plan) 226

'marching down' the scoring matrix 149, 150

market analysts 90

marketplace risks 91

marking schemes 107, 110–11, 141

Marx, Chico 163

material (evaluation meetings) 125

material (for scoring verification) 152

mature reference sites 184

measurable/testable requirements 75, 77

measurement, consistency of 6

measurement, yardstick 6, 10, 12, 14, 69, 97, 155, 161, 171, 186

'mechanical' processing of notes 70

medium-technology approach 106

meeting administration (evaluation process) 124–6

Merge (requirement outcome) 81

'mind-share' 89

'minimum success units' 51

'Minor factor' requirements 82

mitigating risk 12

model answers (RFI process) 108

Modification (RFI coded response) 107, 110, 111

module costs 113

modules (implementation plan) 225–6

modules (negotiation process) 196

monitoring delivery 220

MoSCoW (Must, Should, Could, Won't) rules 79

Move (requirement outcome) 81

'must win' negotiation topics 203–4

named users 196–7

negotiation

agreeing services and charges 198

approval to negotiate 201–2

charging models 197–8

completing the agenda 212

contract pack compilation 214

debriefing candidates 214

decision-making prior to negotiations 194–6

disclosing rival candidates 195

estimating spend and savings 204

executive perspectives on 193, 215

format for negotiation preparation 204–6

free modifications 194, 207–10

and gap analysis 202

impact of decisions 199

implementation phase 198

mindset dangers 212

and modules 196

'must win' topics 203–4

negotiation plan compilation 206–7

non-negotiable items 212–13

notifying affected stakeholders 214

number of negotiation candidates 194–5

objectives of 193–4

and parked candidates 196

and project board 213–14

relative risk levels 199

requesting standard contracts 204

scope of supply 196–9

service aspects 202–3

spreadsheets 204–6

and supplier relationships 192, 199, 203–4, 213, 214

supplier version of agenda 210, 211

support and maintenance agreement 199

team members 200–2

and user licenses 196–7

venue of meetings 210, 212

'Negotiation and Contract' phase 6, 7

networking opportunities 190

new internal stakeholders 121

non-negotiable items 212–13

Non-prescriptive (requirement characteristic) 77

non-technical complexity 56, 189

'Not significant' requirements 82

note-taking (evaluation process) 131–3

notifying candidates (RFI process) 117

objectives (scope decision level) 42–3

Observer Effect 60

officers 80–1

Official Journal of the European Union (OJEU) 2

one-to-one interviews 60, 62–3

'open' (negotiation preparation term) 205–6

operational system 64

optimistic working assumptions 100

organisational change (communications theme) 232

organisational feasibility 50

organisational strategy 18

organising requirements 69–70

'out of the box' processing 11

Outside scope (RFI coded response) 107, 110, 111

overt/covert techniques (evaluation meetings) 129

Ovid 56

paid modifications (negotiation process) 207–8

'parking' candidates 87, 117, 196

Partial (RFI coded response) 107, 110, 111

peace of mind 13

'pet products' 92, 115, 160, 161

Peter, Laurence J. 39

physically processing of notes 70

PID (project initiation document) 51, 52–3

'playing down' 152, 153

Positive (requirement characteristic) 77

power positions 34, 219

pre-conditions of selection 1–2, 18–19

premature evidence 100–101

PRINCE2 (management framework/methodology) 2, 52

Production Control (requirements category) 73

project boards 5, 114–17, 160–1, 213–14

project coverage (scope decision level) 42–3

project initiation 6, 7, 51–3

project management (communications theme) 232

project notes 69–70, 92

project phases, establishing 51

project planning (implementation phase) 220

project reputation 100

project scale adjustment 5

project scheduling tool (implementation phase) 227

project scope see scope

project sponsorship (communications theme) 232

projected volumes 76

proven methodology 13

providing data (implementation phase) 221

providing information to candidate suppliers 30, 32–3

provisioning, choice in 22

provisioning platform (implementation plan) 227

'qualifying out' 34

'quick no' approach (RFI process) 98

RACI (Responsible, Accountable, Consulted and Informed) matrix 62, 63, 123, 126

RAM (responsibility assignment matrix) 123

reasons for selecting off-the-shelf solutions 20–2

recorder (assessment team member) 109

reference sites

   attendees 184–5

   building relationships 189–90

   example questions 186–8

executive perspective on 184

and failed projects 188–9

and implementation phase 224, 226

meeting format 186

meeting location 185–6

objectives of 183–4

selection of 183–4

value of 182

Referenced (requirement characteristic) 77

relative risk levels (negotiation process) 199

replacing inadequate processing 19

representative samples 100

required features (scope decision level) 42–3

requirements

   articulating 72–7

   and 'basis of decision' 6, 10

   benefits of capture exercise 65–6

   and best practice 58–9

   capturing 59–62

   categorising 73

   and consistency 58

   defining 56–8

   as decision drivers 10

   and demonstrations 164, 165, 172–4, 178, 180

   and determining applicable stages 6, 7, 8

   document see requirements document

   as evaluation driver 6, 237

   executive perspective on 57–8

   and evaluation process see evaluation process

   and existing documentation 59–60

   importance of 56–8

   interview programme 62–3, 64–5

   management commitment 63–4

   managing expectations 56, 58

   measurable/testable 75

   mutually exclusive 75

   one-to-one interviews 60, 62–3

   organising 69–70

   revising 78

   and RFI process 96, 98, 99–107, 110–14, 116

and scoring see scoring

selecting interviewees 62, 64

separating 73–5

small workshops 60–1, 62–3

validating/agreeing/refining 77–8

'Requirements Definition' phase 6, 7

requirements document

   articulating requirements 72–7

   and business need 72–3

   business volumes 76–7

   categorising requirements 73

   circulating weights document 84

   final revision of 83–4

   formats 70–2

   measurable/testable requirements 75

   mutually exclusive requirements 75

   optimum length of statement 74–5

   organising requirements 69–70

   and scoring 135

   separating requirement 73–5

   validating/agreeing/refining requirements 77–8

   values used 81–2

   weighting workshops 78–84

   wording of 68–9

Requirements Engineering 57

response team 123, 124

responsibility charts 62, 233–4

revealing extended scores (scoring meetings) 151

'revenue police' role 213

review sessions (evaluation process) 129

reviewing project information 194

revising requirements 78

Reword (requirement outcome) 81

RFI (request for information) process

   agreeing detailed method 109–10

   assessing responses 109–13

   assessment team roles 109

   background/briefing section 104–5

   briefing the assessment meeting 110

and consistency 97

costing parameters 105

and determining applicable stages 7, 8

distributing the RFI 108

and email addresses 91, 108

estimated costs 113

and evaluation process 96–8

evidence-based decisions 116–17

and external candidate suppliers 99

and feasibility studies 51

and including/excluding candidates 92

and internal customer assessors 99

marking scheme 107, 110–11

model answers 108

notifying candidates 117

objectives 96–7

premature evidence 100–101

presentation to project board 114–17

prior planning 98–9

and requirements 96, 98, 99–107, 110–14, 116

and scoring 147, 149, 157

selecting good questions 99–100, 101–4

sequence of marking 112–13

strong RFI questions 102–4

summarising the assessment outcome 113–14

technology used 106

'turnaround' spreadsheets 106

wording of questions 101–2

risk management 12, 28

robustness of processes 13

role models 90

rotating assessor (assessment team member) 109

routine defences (evaluation process) 131

sabotage of demonstrations 166–7

safe gap guidelines (scoring process) 155

safety in numbers 21

Sales (requirements category) 73

sales executive (response team) 123

sales exhibitions 89–90

sales process 31–4

sample data (for demonstrations) 170–1

savings-based models 198

scenario format (requirements document) 71–2

schedule of evaluation meetings 126, 127

scope

and boundaries 40, 41, 44–5

determining 40–1

executive perspective on 40–1

and executive sponsors 52

and feasibility studies 39–40

scoping workshops 41–6

scope creep 218

scope drift 218

scope of supply (negotiation process) 196–9

scoring process/matrix

addressing gaps in capability 158–60

adjusting scores 153

benefits of verification 153–4

categories 150

closing gaps 159–60

defence mechanisms 155–6

and definitions document 135, 140–6

documentation 135, 140–6

elevating the requirement 145

explicit concessions 145–6

fact checking 150

and fit 137–8, 139–40, 144, 148

format of scoring matrix 138, 139–40

gap analysis 157–8, 159–60

gut feel 147

importance of 135–6

managing information 154

'marching down' the scoring matrix 149, 150

meeting administration 146

meeting process 147–9

philosophy of scoring 147

project board presentation 160–1

project example 159–60

reviewing scoring 160

and RFI process 147, 149, 157

role of 135–6

safe gap guidelines 155

scoring team 146

selecting demonstration candidates 157–8

sensitivity analysis 157

sequence of scoring 149

and shipping version 148

stage outputs 137–40

steps for completion 151–2

summary score analysis 140

threshold guidelines 154–5

time management of meeting 149–50

treatment of costs 149

verification with suppliers 152–4

and weight of requirements 148

seat costs 113

selection process

adaptation of method 4–8

benefits of selection method 3–4

and critical partnerships 34–5

determining applicable stages 5–7

executive perspectives on 3–4, 136–7

impetus for change 18–19

integration of methods 2

and IT consultancy 24

longlists see longlists

make–buy decisions 20, 24

nature and characteristics of 11–13

objective of 238

position of selection method 2

pre-conditions of selection 1–2, 18–19

reasons for selecting off-the-shelf solutions 20–2

and requirements 56–8, 62, 65–6

and requirements document 72–3

and sophistication of modern software products 1

and supplier influence 34

and strategic decisions 17–18

senior management representative (response team) 123

sensitivity analysis (scoring process) 157

sequence of marking (RFI process) 112–13

Sequenced (requirement characteristic) 77

service provision 61

services costs 113

shipping versions 11, 128, 148

'shortlist of zero' 10, 87

Shrewd (requirement characteristic) 77

site visits (reference sites) 185

SLAs (service level agreements) 61, 75

small workshops 60–1, 62–3

'software space' 24

SoR (Statement of Requirements) 70–1

special interest groups 90

specialisation 10

Split (requirement outcome) 81

spoiling tactics 35

spreadsheets
   collating longlists 88
   demonstration analysis 178–9
   evaluation meeting schedule 127
   negotiation preparation 204–6
   reference sites 188
   RFI process 106
   scoping workshops 46
   scoring process 152, 157

staff (demonstration audience members) 164

stage outputs (scoring matrix) 137–40

staged decision-making 11–12

stakeholder engagement 5, 165, 237

stakeholder management 23, 89, 232

Standalone (requirement characteristic) 77

Standard (RFI coded response) 107, 110, 111

standard requirements 61

'standardised approach' 22

standing evaluation team 122

stop/go decisions 50–1

strategic decisions 17–18, 19

strategic feasibility 47–8

subject matter experts (response team) 123

subscription charging models 198

supplier criteria (scope decision level) 42–3

supplier relationships
   and critical partnerships 34–5
   and culture clash 31
   and demonstrations 164
   and documentation 33
   and effective behaviours 35–6
   and evaluation process 121
   executive perspective on 29
   and fairness/unfairness 35
   and implementation phase 222–3
   importance of project to supplier 32–3
   and knowledge workers 30
   and lead qualification 32
   and negotiation 192
   and negotiation 192, 199, 203–4, 213, 214
   and power positions 34
   providing information 30, 32–3
   strategic value of project 31, 32–3
   supplier constraints 29–30
   and supplier influence 34
   and supplier sales process 31–4
   and talent management 27–8, 30–6
   and unhappy losers 36

Supply Chain (requirements category) 73

support and maintenance agreement (negotiation process) 199

support/maintenance 21, 113

'tactical no-shows' 166

talent management 27–36

teamwork 10, 23–4

technical feasibility 48

technology policies 19

telephone interviews (reference sites) 185–6

Thematic (requirement characteristic) 77

threshold guidelines (scoring process) 154–5

time allowed (evaluation meetings) 125

time allowed (scoring meetings) 146

time management 80–1, 125–6, 149–50, 166

Timesheets (requirements category) 73

titling (definitions document) 141–2

ToR (terms of reference) document 52–3

tracking roles (evaluation team) 123

trade associations 90

transferring risk 28

'Trivial' requirements 82

'turnaround' spreadsheets 106

Twain, Mark 68, 217

unhappy losers 36

Unique (requirement characteristic) 77

unsubstantiated answers 111

unsupported statements (evaluation process) 130

Use Case 71

user community contribution 189–90

user licenses (negotiation process) 196–7

User-defined (RFI coded response) 107, 110, 111

users (scope decision level) 42–3

validating/agreeing/refining requirements 77–8

value-for-money bubble charts 115–16

'vapourware' 164, 213

venue selection 124, 146, 169, 210, 212

verbal information 33

video conferencing 122, 177

'vision-ware' 213

voting 81, 82–3

'weasel words' 204

weighting workshops 78–84, 148

work shadowing 60

'worst outcome' (negotiation preparation term) 205–6, 213

'wow factor' 56, 165

yardstick measuresment 6, 10, 12, 14, 69, 97, 155, 161, 171, 186